Alex Shoumatoff is a graduate of Harvard University
and a staff writer for the *New Yorker*. He is the author of
six previous books, including *The Rivers Amazon*,
Russian Blood and *The Mountain of Names*. He lives
outside New York City.

IN SOUTHERN LIGHT

TREKKING THROUGH ZAIRE AND THE AMAZON

Alex Shoumatoff

IN SOUTHERN LIGHT

A CORGI BOOK   0 552 13329 9

Originally published in Great Britain by
Hutchinson Ltd., an imprint of Century Hutchinson Ltd.

PRINTING HISTORY

Hutchinson edition published 1987
Corgi edition published 1988

Portions of this work originally appeared, in slightly different
form, in the *New Yorker*.

This book is set in 10/11 pt Ballardvale

Corgi Books are published by Transworld Publishers Ltd.,
61–63 Uxbridge Road, Ealing, London W5 5SA, in Australia by
Transworld Publishers (Australia) Pty. Ltd., 15–23 Helles
Avenue, Moorebank, NSW 2170, and in New Zealand by
Transworld Publishers (N.Z.) Ltd., Cnr. Moselle and Waipareira
Avenues, Henderson, Auckland.

Made and printed in Great Britain by
The Guernsey Press Co. Ltd., Guernsey, Channel Islands.

To Kanati, Gamaembi, and Baudouin,
com saudade

CONTENTS

INTRODUCTION

Some years ago a woman whose family had been entrenched for several generations in a comfortable enclave of the suburban Northeast asked me, with startling bluntness, 'Why do you keep going to these awful places?' I hope that this book will go some of the way toward answering her question. Both of the trips described in it were undertaken after two-year book-writing projects, in an effort to get back in shape and in touch with the natural world. They were taken to rain forests because I find them particularly fascinating. The trips are presented in reverse order: Benoit Quersin and I went up the Nhamundá in the summer of 1984, and the trip across Zaire, at the end of which we first met, took place three years earlier, in the spring.

The John Simon Guggenheim Memorial Foundation generously supported this project with a fellowship, while Benjamin T. Kernan, who also has the woods in his blood, gave me the use of his cabin in the Adirondacks. The lepidopterist John C. Downey helped me with the African butterflies but because of inexcusable oversight on my part was not acknowledged in the *New Yorker* excerpt. Thomas E. Lovejoy explained the oropendula-cowbird-wasp-botfly interaction. The huge debts I owe to Anna Roosevelt, Robert Carneiro, Richard Wrangham, and Robert Bailey will soon be evident.

Some names have been changed to protect privacy.
The absence of maps intentional.

9

PART ONE

IN THE REALM OF THE AMAZONS

The largest of the Amazon River's more than eleven hundred tributaries are awesome world-class rivers in themselves. Seventeen are more than a thousand miles long. The largest, the Rio Negro, discharges some sixty-seven thousand cubic feet of water per second—four times the volume of the Mississippi. Some have achieved sinister reputations. The Putumayo, which describes the border of Colombia and Peru, is infamous for the atrocities that its local Indians suffered during the rubber boom early in this century. The Roosevelt, or Rio Teodoro, as it is called on some maps—actually a sub-subtributary that flows into the Aripuaña—was unknown and uncharted until an expedition including Theodore Roosevelt descended it in 1913; one of the paddlers went mad and killed another, and Roosevelt's health was broken by the harrowing adventure.

The last decade has seen a lot of activity on some of the major affluents of the lower Amazon: the Tocantins, which comes in on the Amazon's right bank about a hundred miles above Belém, has been spanned by the gigantic Tucuruí dam, one of the world's largest generators of hydroelectricity. Up the Jari, a left-bank tributary, the American shipping magnate Daniel K. Ludwig bought up in 1967 a chunk of jungle roughly the size of Connecticut and planted pulp trees and dry rice, but the project was done in by an aroused anti-neocolonial Brazilian press, and Ludwig was ultimately forced to sell it, fourteen years later, to a consortium of Brazilian companies, at a loss of close to eight hundred million dollars. Up the Trombetas, which comes in from the north, farther upriver, one of the largest known deposits of bauxite, estimated at six hundred million tons, is being mined. Oceangoing freighters are a common if startling sight from its forested banks.

The next significant tributary on that side of the river is the Nhamundá, sometimes spelled Yamundá or Jamundá. It is comparatively small by Amazonian standards—about three hundred and seventy-five miles long—just about the length of the Hudson. It rises in an ancient crystalline massif near the Guyana border called the Serra Acaraí and, like the Rio Negro, is a blackwater river (unlike the Amazon itself, which is a white-water river, or the clear-water Tapajós, which comes in from the south, somewhat further down). Nothing of any scale or external significance is happening on the Nhamundá. It is virtually uninhabited. One can paddle for days without meeting a soul through the riotous primeval wilderness which it drains. The majority of scientists working in Amazonia I polled had never heard of the Nhamundá or didn't know where it was. It is one of the forgotten rivers of the Amazon system.

One reason for its neglect is that it doesn't empty straightforwardly into the Amazon's main channel but is broken up at its mouth by a labyrinth of islands and lakes. Some of its ducts lead to the Amazon, and at least one ends up in the Trombetas; during the nineteenth century geographers debated whose tributary, in fact, the Nhamundá was. Another reason is its comparative absence of exploitable resources. Some gold, calcite, bauxite, industrial-grade diamonds, and the usual commercial hardwoods have been found in the Nhamundá Valley, but none in any quantity. The three towns on the river's lower reaches—Terra Santa, Nhamundá, and Faro—can only be reached by boat; no airstrips or roads link them with the outside world. They are about equidistant—several days' journey—from the big centers of Amazonia, Manaus and Belém. Manaus and Belém are the capitals of the states of Amazonas and Pará, whose respective eastern and western borders are described by the Nhamundá. It is only natural that the politicians in these seething metropolises should pay little heed to the needs of three small, stagnant communities at the very edge of their jurisdictions.

Little scientific work has been conducted in the Nhamundá Valley, either. At the end of the last century a Brazilian botanist and a French explorer published accounts of what they had seen along the river, which remain of great value because almost nothing has changed since they passed through. In this century a handful of archaeologists and ethnologists have reconnoitred the lower Nhamundá; a botanical artist has twice gone up as far as the first rapids; and a missionary has lived among the Hixkaryana Indians, above the fourteenth sets of rapids, long enough to learn their language and to translate the Bible into it. The traffic has otherwise been entirely local.

The Nhamundá's one claim to fame is perhaps only a legend: The tribe that allegedly consisted of only women and children, for whom the Amazon River was named, is said to have lived on the lower Nhamundá. It is probably a good idea, before getting to the river itself, to review how the story of the women who lived without men came to be associated with the river, and the many versions of the story that have circulated.

The first Europeans to enter the Amazon Valley claimed to have been actually attacked by female warriors. The account of the engagement and the subsequent interview about the 'Amazons' with a male Indian ally captured during it are among the most vivid and celebrated passages in the annals of the Conquest. They appear in the chronicles of the Dominican friar Gaspar de Carvajal, who with the Spanish conquistador Francisco de Orellana and about fifty countrymen set out on December twenty-sixth, 1541, in a jerry-built brigantine down the Napo, an Ecuadorian tributary of the Amazon, having no conception of where they were going or what awaited them. The expedition was part of a massive assault by the recently appointed governor of

13

Quito, Gonzalo Pizarro (a brother of the more famous Hernando), on the unknown lands to the east—El Dorado and La Canela, the Land of Cinnamon. The expedition had run into trouble soon after crossing the mountains east of Quito and descending into the jungle: Most of the four thousand Indian bearers had perished, all two thousand of the hogs brought along for food had been eaten, weakness and despair had set in. Orellana was sent on ahead to find food and to return within twelve days. But as his party floated down the Napo no food was to be had. The men were reduced to eating, as Carvajal relates, 'the soles of their shoes cooked with certain herbs.' Several went mad after eating some unidentified roots. Unable to return because of the insuperable current of the Napo, or so Orellana later claimed, he kept on going.

After six months, fighting Indians and falling on their food stores all the way, the Spaniards passed on their left, still a thousand miles from the sea, the mouth of a large, dark river they called the Rio Negro. Two days later, on June seventh, 1542, they met some Indians who said (how the language barrier was penetrated Carvajal doesn't tell us) 'that they were subjects and tributaries of the Amazons and that the only service which they rendered them consisted in supplying them with plumes of parrots and macaws for the lining of the roofs of the buildings which constitute their places of worship.' As the expedition continued downstream, the villages became more numerous. On the twenty-fourth.

we came suddenly upon the excellent land and dominions of the Amazons. These said villages had been forewarned and knew of our coming, in consequence whereof their inhabitants came out on the water to meet us, in no friendly mood, and when they had come close to the Captain [Orellana], he would have liked to induce them to accept peace, and so he began to speak to them and call them, but they laughed, and mocked us and came close to us and told us to keep on going and [added] that down below they were waiting for us, and that there they were to seize us all and take us to the Amazons. The Captain, angered at the arrogance of the Indians, gave orders to shoot at them with crossbows and arquebuses, so that they might reflect and become aware that we had wherewith to assail them; and in this way damage was inflicted on them and they turned about towards the village to give the news of what they had

14

seen; as for us, we did not fail to proceed and to draw close to the villages, and before we were within half a league of putting in, there were along the edge of the water, at intervals, many squadrons of Indians.

The Spaniards debarked and 'a very serious and hazardous battle' ensued.

More than an hour was taken up by this fight, for the Indians did not lose spirit, rather it seemed as if it was being doubled in them, although they saw many of their own number killed, and they passed over their bodies, and they merely kept retreating and coming back again. I want it to be known what the reason was why these Indians defended themselves in this manner. It must be explained that they are the subjects of, and tributaries to, the Amazons, and, our coming having been made known to them, they went to them to ask help, and there came as many as ten or twelve of them, for we ourselves saw these women, who were there fighting in front of all the Indian men as women captains, and these latter fought so courageously that the Indian men did not dare to turn their backs, and anyone who did turn his back they killed with clubs right there before us, and this is the reason why the Indians kept up their defense for so long. These women are very white and tall, and have hair very long and braided and wound about the head, and they are very robust and go about naked, with their privy parts covered, and their bows and arrows in their hands, doing as much fighting as ten Indian men, and indeed there was one woman among these who shot an arrow a span deep into one of the brigantines [by then the Spaniards had built a second one], and the others less deep, so that our brigantines looked like porcupines.

It was only after seven or eight of the Amazons were killed that 'the Indians lost heart, and they were defeated and routed with considerable damage to their persons.'

A few days later Orellana was able to communicate 'by means of a list of words he had made' with the 'overlord' of his assailants, who was named Couynco and had been captured in the battle. He asked

what women those were who had come to help them and fight against us; the Indian said that they were certain women who resided in the interior of the country, a seven day journey from the shore, and that it was because this overlord Couynco was subject to them that they had come to watch over the shore. The

Captain asked him if these women were married: the Indian said they were not. The Captain asked him about how they lived: the Indian replied that, as he had already said, they were off in the interior of the land and that he had been there many times and had seen their customs and mode of living, for as their vassal he was in the habit of going there to carry the tribute whenever the overlord sent him. The Captain asked if these women were numerous: the Indian said that they were, and that he knew by name seventy villages, and named them before those of us who were there present, and he added that he had been in several of them. The Captain asked him if the houses in these villages were built of straw: the Indian said they were not, but out of stone and with regular doors, and that from one village to another went roads closed off on one side and on the other, with guards stationed at intervals along them so that no one could enter without paying duties. The Captain asked if these women bore children: the Indian answered that they did. The Captain asked him how, not being married and there being no man residing among them, they became pregnant: he said that these Indian women consorted with Indian men at times, and, when that desire came to them, they assembled a great horde of warriors and went off to make war on a very great overlord whose residence is not far from that of these women, and by force they brought them to their country and kept them with them for the time that suited their caprice, and after they found themselves pregnant they sent them back to their country without doing them any harm; and afterwards, when the time came for them to have children, if they give birth to male children, they killed them and sent them to their fathers, and, if female children, they raised them with great solemnity and instructed them in the arts of war. He said furthermore that among all these women there was one ruling mistress who subjected and held under her hand and jurisdiction all the rest, which mistress went by the name of Conori. He said that they had a very great wealth of gold and silver and that the eating utensils of all the mistresses of rank and distinction were nothing but gold or silver, while the other women, belonging to the plebeian class, used a service of wooden vessels, except what was brought in contact with fire, which was of clay. He said that in the capital and principal city in which the ruling mistress resided there were houses dedicated to the Sun, which they called 'caranain,' that inside, from half a man's height above the ground up, these buildings were lined with heavy

16

wooden ceilings covered with paint of various colours; and that in these buildings they had many gold and silver idols in the form of women, and many vessels of gold and silver for the service of the Sun; and these women were dressed in clothing of very fine wool, because in this land there are many sheep of the same sort of those of Peru; their dress consisted of blankets girdled about them from the breasts down, in some cases merely thrown over the shoulders, and in others clasped together in front, like a cloak, by means of a pair of cords; they wore their hair reaching down to the ground at their feet, and upon their heads were placed crowns of gold, as wide as two fingers, and their individual colors. He said in addition that in this land, as we understood him, there were camels that carried them on their backs, and he said there were other animals, which we did not succeed in understanding about, which were as big as horses and which had hair as long as the spread of the thumb and forefinger, measured from tip to tip, and cloven hoofs, and that people kept them tied up; and that of these there were few. He said that there were in this land two salt-water lakes, from which the women obtained salt. He related that they had a rule to the effect that when the sun went down no male Indian was to remain in all of these cities, but that any such must depart and go to his country; he said in addition that many Indian provinces bordering on them were held in subjection by them and made to pay tribute and to serve them, while others there were with which they carried on war, in particular with the one which we have mentioned, and that they brought the men there to have relations with them: these were said to be of very great stature and white and numerous, and he claimed that all that he had told here he had seen many times as a man who went back and forth every day; and all that this Indian told us and more besides had been told us six leagues from Quito, because concerning these women there were a great many reports, and in order to see them many Indian men came down the river one thousand four hundred leagues; and likewise the Indians farther up had told us that anyone who should take it into his head to go down to the country of these women was destined to go a boy and return an old man. The country, he said, was cold and there was very little firewood there, and it was very rich in all kinds of food: also he told many other things and said that every day he kept finding out more, because he was an Indian of much intelligence and very quick to comprehend; and so are all the rest in that land, as we have stated.

17

Scholars who have tried to reconstruct the voyage of the Spaniards from Carvajal's account have located the engagement with Couynco's tribe on the left bank of the Amazon, before the Trombetas comes in, most likely at the mouth of the Nhamundá. But how much of these two extraordinary passages is to be believed? Like El Dorado and the Fountain of Youth, the Land of the Amazons was a definite, if undiscovered, place on the still largely empty map of the New World. The women were out there somewhere, and every explorer versed in the classical myth of female warriors and in the medieval romances that retold or embellished it was on the lookout for them. Columbus, eager to find proof that he had arrived in the Orient and wondering if he had happened on the Island of the Female which Marco Polo had reported was in the Sea of China, wrote to his sponsors, Ferdinand and Isabella of Spain, on February fifteenth, 1493, that he had met on the island of Martinio—present-day Martinique—women who lived without men, wore copper armor, and took cannibals as lovers. (My source for this and the other sightings about to be mentioned is a recent book by the feminist Abby Wettan Kleinbaum, *The War Against the Amazons*, a diligent piece of scholarship peppered with digs at men, which traces the history of the idea of Amazon women in the West from Hippolyta to Wonder Woman.) Nine years later the Amerigo Vespucci expedition encountered anthropophagous women on an island in the 'West Indies'; two of its members disappeared, and a third was clubbed to death. Not long afterwards Hernando Cortes sent his cousin Francisco to the Pacific coast of northwest Mexico to look for California, the island 'on the right hand of the Indies,' according to García Ordóñez de Montalvo's enormously popular romance, *Amadis de Gaula*, where black women ruled by a queen named Caliphia 'live in the fashion of Amazons.' Francisco found no such women on that beautiful coast, but named it after their land. In 1543 a province of women who lived without men and were ruled by a queen named Gaboimilla was reported in the south of Chile, and in 1539, two years before the Pizarro expedition set out from Quito, rumours of a community of Amazons who reproduced by means of male slaves came out of what is now Colombia.

So it is reasonable to assume that when Orellana and his companions separated from Pizarro they, too, had Amazons

18

on their mind; and sure enough, scarcely two weeks into their voyage, while still on the Napo, they were told by an Indian named Aparia 'of the Amazons and of the wealth farther down the river.' One can't help wondering, especially in view of the language barrier and the immense cultural gulf that must have existed between the Spaniards and their informants, whether there wasn't a strong element of projection in this and the later reports about warrior women. The ability of even level-headed modern realists like ourselves to assimilate the alien and the incomprehensible is culturally circumscribed. Even trained anthropologists have been guilty of unconscious projection, of clothing the unsuspecting subjects of their research in theories brought with them into the field. It is unnecessary and probably unfair to conclude that Carvajal deliberately made up his reports. Looking back on his experiences as a conquistador in Mexico, Bernal Díaz del Castillo reflected in his memoirs, 'there is so much to think over that I do not know how to describe it, seeing things as we did that had never been heard of or seen before, not even dreamed of.' It would be surprising if the members of the Orellana expedition, passing through natural and human landscapes in which so little was familiar, didn't to some extent cling to preconceived notions of what was supposed to be there, however fantastic the notions themselves were; and if there was not a good deal of distortion of what they actually saw and were told in what they later said they saw and were told. To a large extent people are only capable of perceiving what they already have categories for; however outlandish, the Amazon-women category was one of the few things that Spaniards had to hold on to.

One also wonders if there wasn't more input from the Indian informants than simply having words put in their mouths; whether they didn't, on their part, to some extent tell the Spaniards what they wanted to hear. This has been a common problem for Westerners trying to get information not only in the Amazon but all over the non-Western world, where the local people for a variety of reasons often tell visitors that the object of their quest exists when it doesn't. Among the reasons are: politeness, reluctance to be the bearer of disappointing news or the source of unpleasantness, unwillingness to confess to ignorance about the subject, failure to understand the question, desire for

19

reward, desire to keep the visitor and his goods in the vicinity, desire to get rid of the troublesome visitor by sending him somewhere else, desire to protect oneself or something or somebody else, belief that the misinformation (obtained from somebody else) is correct, laziness (saying yes because the truth is too complicated to go into), indifference, different outlook on the subject, different outlook on what is true and real. The nineteenth-century naturalist Alfred Russel Wallace, who spent from 1848 to 1852 in Amazonia and later formulated the evolutionary principle of natural selection independently from Darwin, wrote, 'In my communications and inquiries among the Indians on various matters, I have always found the greatest caution necessary, to prevent one's arriving at wrong conclusions. They are always apt to affirm that which they see you wish to believe, and, when they do not at all comprehend your question, will unhesitatingly answer, "Yes." I have often in this manner obtained, as I thought, information, which persons better acquainted with the facts have assured me was quite erroneous.' Misinformation and imprecision, as we shall see, continue to be common problems in the Amazon.

Of the possible reasons for confirming the existence of the Amazons, the desire to get rid of the Spaniards and to save their own lives seems most likely. Even Indians who told the conquistadores what they wanted to hear were treated cruelly. Describing the aborted Pizarro expedition, the Chilean scholar José Toribio Medina writes, 'Among these mountains [east of Quito] they also found some Indians who were thorough savages and who lived in miserable dwellings; these Pizarro questioned on the subject of whether farther ahead there were valleys and plains, because his fixed idea was to find a road suitable for the horses; and, irritated when these Indians could not give him the kind of answer that he wanted, he delivered some of them over to be torn to pieces by the dogs, while others he caused to be burned alive.' News of the murders preceded the expedition. A few days later, Medina goes on, the Spaniards

caught sight of a certain number of Indians who were watching them on the other side of the river. The Spaniards then began to call out to them, telling them to have no fear and to come over, as indeed some fifteen or twenty of them did, bringing at their

20

head their chief whom Pizarro then presented with some trinkets highly pleasing to the savages, in order to get him to tell him whether he knew of any good country beyond, even though it might be far off. Being duly put on his guard by what he knew had happened to the other Indians, Felicola, as the chief was called, then told him, fully conscious that he was lying, that farther on there were great settlements and regions very rich, ruled over by powerful overlords; and by way of rewarding the chief for what he had related, Pizarro ordered him to be held a prisoner for such services as he might later furnish as a guide.

There are other possible explanations for the myth. It is possible that the overlord Couynco's description of the Amazons is a mangled third-hand account of real contact with the Inca or one of the other central Andean civilizations. Certain features of the description—the woolen clothing, the stone houses, the lack of firewood, the llamas, the sun worship, the cold, the gold—strongly suggest that a mountain people is being talked about. The sun figures in lowland South American mythology, but not as prominently as in the highland cultures, where sun worship was institutionalized; the Inca himself was considered to be of solar descent. Animals are on the whole more important than stellar bodies for forest mythmakers. Gold exists in the lower Amazon, mother lodes of it in places, but it doesn't seem as if the prehistoric Indians knew of these places, or had discovered the malleability and attractiveness of the metal and become metallurgists; although copper and bronze artifacts have been found in Peruvian and Bolivian Amazonia, and Sir Walter Raleigh picked up from an Indian in Guyana a description of how to make gold-copper alloy so detailed and complicated that it is considered authentic. Nor have stone houses been found in the lower Amazon, although petroglyphs, monuments, circles, and other man-made alignments of stone have, on both sides of the river. But no in-depth archaeological fieldwork has been done in the Nhamundá Valley. 'Who's dug? Who knows anything?' as the archaeologist Anna Roosevelt, who curates the Latin American collection at the Museum of the American Indian in New York City and is one of the few people who excavates in Amazonia, recently put it. What has been found in the region—fragments of very sophisticated pottery—has demonstrable affinities with what some of the

Andean cultures were producing at the same time. Some scholars believe that the New World Amazon legend originated from the cloistered communities of women that the Inca maintained. The women, called *akalakuna*, were sacred. They belonged to the emperor and the sun. They devoted themselves to weaving and were forbidden to have sexual relations, on pain of death to themselves and their lovers. Their fine cloth was economically important and was used for symbolic reciprocal gifts to neighbouring states. There were a lot of these nunlike women at Machu Picchu, to judge from the ratio of female to male skeletons found there—almost a hundred to one. At Jauja the *akalakuna* dressed up as warriors and fought the Spanish. The Inca art historian Thomas Cummins, to whom I am indebted for most of the preceding information, also pointed out that the Inca did get into the Amazon forest, where they built a city called Antisuyo. 'And to further complicate matters, structurally, in kinship terms, the Inca who lived in the mountains thought of those who lived in the forest as female.'

Another possibility is that the 'ten or twelve Amazons' who joined the fight against Orellana's men were in fact men. Wallace proposed this thesis in the course of a description of the Vaupés Indians of the upper Rio Negro:

The men . . . have the hair carefully parted and combed on each side, and tied in a queue behind. In the young men, it hangs in long locks down their necks, and, with the comb, which is invariably stuck in the top of the head, gives to them a most feminine appearance: this is increased by the large necklaces and bracelets of beads, and the careful extirpation of every symptom of beard. Taking these circumstances into consideration, I am strongly of opinion that the story of the Amazons has arisen from these feminine-looking warriors encountered by the early voyager. I am inclined to this opinion, from the effect they first produced on myself, when it was only by close examination I saw that they were men; and, were the front parts of their bodies and their breasts covered with shields, such as they always use, I am convinced any person seeing them for the first time would conclude they were women. We have only therefore to suppose that tribes having similar customs to those now living on the river Vaupés, inhabited the regions where the Amazons were reported to have been seen, and we have a rational explanation of what has so much puzzled all geographers.

Men of the Yagua tribe of the Upper Amazon, who wear shredded bark skirts, have also been suggested as prototypes for the Amazon women.

A final possibility, albeit remote, is, of course, that such a tribe of women without men did in fact live on the Lower Nhamundá.

News of a clash with Amazons in the unknown country east of Quito was greeted with skepticism in Europe by the more discriminating readers of Carvajal's account. Branding the whole thing 'full of lies,' the friar's countryman Francisco López de Gómara wrote in 1552:

Among the extravagant statements which he made was his claim that there were Amazons along this river with whom he and his companions had fought. That the women there should take up arms and fight is no novelty, for in Paria, which is not very far off, and in many other parts of the Indies, they used to do that; I do not believe either that any woman burns and cuts off her right breast [the women warriors who during heroic times are said to have fought the Greeks were named for this practice; the Greek *a-madzon* means 'without a breast'] in order to be able to shoot with the bow, because with it they shoot very well; or that they kill or exile their own sons; or that they live without husbands, being as they are very voluptuous. Others besides Orellana have proclaimed this same yarn about the Amazons ever since the Indies have been discovered, and never has such a thing been seen, and never will it be seen either, along this river.

Some accused Orellana of inventing the encounter to cover up for his desertion of Pizarro and his discovery of no gold and very little cinnamon. Two and a half centuries later, during which no further progress had been made in finding the women, the German scientific traveller Alexander von Humboldt, who spent from 1799 to 1803 in the Amazon and Orinoco basins, dismissed the stories about them as a 'romantic tradition ... The taste for the marvellous, the desire to adorn the description of the new continent with some traces of classical antiquity doubtless contributed ... to the first impressions of Orellana.'

But the vast majority of Carvajal's European audience wanted to believe in the women. Since 1512 the river he and his companion had descended had borne two names, given by explorers sailing along the coast of Pará, who had encountered its torrent of café-au-lait-colored water flooding the ocean many miles from shore: the Mar Dulce (the Freshwater Sea) and the Marañon (which one of its main source tributaries in Peru still bears). By 1552 these names had been superseded by two new ones: the Orellana River and the Amazons' River. The former never caught on; it was the latter leap of faith, or 'imposture,' as López de Gómara termed it, which took. Some say the Jesuit Alonso de Rajas first proposed the name. The name in Portuguese is O Rio Amazonas, the River Amazons. One still finds the 's' in English in the nineteenth century, in such works as Henry Walter Bates's *The Naturalist on the River Amazons*, but by then it was already falling into disuse.

The next Amazons to be heard about sounded almost like characters out of Spenser's *Faerie Queene*. A description of them was obtained by Sir Walter Raleigh in 1595 from a cacique, or chief, who claimed to have personally visited them 'not far from Guiana.' The women

> doe accompany with men but once in a yere, and for the time of one month, which I gather by their relation, to be in April: at that time all kings of the border assemble, and queenes of the Amazones; and after the queenes have chosen, the rest cast lots for their Valentines. This one moneth, they feast, dance, and drinke of their wines in abundance; and the Moone being done, they all depart to their owne provinces. If they conceive, and are delivered of a sonne, they returne him to the father; if of a daughter they nourish it, and retaine it: and as many as have daughters send unto the begetters a present; all being desirous of their owne sex and kinde: but that they cut off the right dug of the breast, I do not find to be true.

In 1620, as the Pilgrims were putting ashore at Plymouth Rock, a hundred and twenty less famous English and Irish colonists, led by one of Raleigh's captains, Roger North, sailed a hundred leagues up the Amazon with the intention of growing tobacco. The local Indians were amazingly hospitable—they helped clear the colonists' plantations, brought them food, told them about the Amazons—and all 'for a small reward and price, either of some Iron worke or glasse beades and such like contemtible things.' One of North's companions, 'a charming young Irishman' named Bernard O'Brien, as the historian John Hemming describes him, canoed hundreds of miles deeper into the valley and 'finally reached a land where he claimed, with perhaps a touch of blarney, to have contacted the Amazons.' Their queen was named Cuna Mucchu (the Inca for Great Lady and highly suggestive of Carvajal's Conori). O'Brien

sent a mirror, a holland shirt, and other merchandise as presents, offered to go and see her if she would send hostages, and promised to obey her orders. She sent three of her most esteemed women as hostages, and young O'Brien went to visit the Amazon queen. 'She asked if it was I who had sent the present and I said yes. She asked me what I wanted, and I said peace and permission to pass through her kingdom and to trade with her. She said she granted it to me, and gave me three of her women slaves in exchange for the merchandise. I dressed her in the holland shirt, with which she was very haughty. At the end of a week I took my leave, promising to return, and she and her vassals signified that they were sad at my departure.' The only information given by O'Brien about his week's visit was that he saw many women and no men, and that the women had 'their right breasts small like men's, artificially stunted in order to shoot arrows; but the left breasts are broad like other women's.'

The latter detail almost certainly confirms Hemming's view of the O'Brien account as blarney.

In 1639 a Portuguese expedition under the conquistador Pedro Teixeira repeated Orellana's descent of the Napo and the Amazon. The voyage took ten months. No female warriors were engaged or spotted this time, but the chronicler of the expedition, a Jesuit name Cristóbal de Acuña, picked up many stories about the Amazons and enthusiastically bought them all. 'The proofs of the existence of the Amazons on this river are so numerous, and so strong,' he reported, 'that it would be a want of a common faith not to give them credit . . . There is no saying more common than that these women inhabit a province on the river, and it is not credible that a lie could have spread through so many languages, and so many nations, without such an appearance of truth.' In the last village of the Tupinambá, who lived below the mouth of the Madeira (the next left-bank world-class tributary of the Amazon above the Tapajós), they were told not only of a tribe of pygmies and of men deep in the forest who threw off trackers because their feet pointed backwards, but of 'man-like women' who lived on 'lofty hills' high up the Cunuris River. 'Cunuris' sounds again like Carvajal's Conori, but the Tupinambá said that it was the name of the first tribe that lived up the river. Beyond the Cunuris were the Apantos, the Taguaus, and the Guacaras, the last of whom for a few days at a certain time of year were received by the women and invited to share their hammocks. Beyond the Guacaras were the women themselves, whose home was called Icamiaba, perhaps a corruption of *itacamiaba*, a word in the Tupi Indian language, then spoken by many Amazonian tribes, meaning literally 'a gift of stone in the forest,' and by association (as will be explained presently) 'the women without husbands.'

In 1734 the French scientist Charles Marie de La Condamine was sent to South America by his country's Académie des Sciences to measure an arc of a degree of latitude at the Equator as part of a project to determine the shape of the earth; the scientific community was divided over whether the earth was an oblate sphere or a prolate one. La Condamine's eight years on the continent were climaxed by a rather brisk descent of the Amazon, starting from the Peruvian Andes, during which it goes without saying he asked about the celebrated tribe of women. 'We questioned everywhere Indians of diverse nations,' he wrote in his *Relation Abrégée d'un Voyage Fait Dans l'Interieur de l'Amérique Mériodionale*, 'and we informed ourselves with great care if they had knowledge of the bellicose women Orellana claimed to have seen and combatted, and if it was true that they lived far from the commerce of men and received them but once a year, as Acuña reports. They all told us the women had withdrawn deep into the interior to the north.' While still on the Upper Amazon, he was told of an old Omagua Indian whose father had seen the women; he tried to find the man, but the man turned out to be dead. The man's son, however, a chief some seventy years old, was alive, and confirmed that his grandfather had met four of the women heading north; one had a child at her breast.

Another Indian, further downstream, offered to take La Condamine to the river Irijó, near the Amazon's mouth, which he claimed was inhabited by women who lived without men. But most of the stories La Condamine picked up centered on 'the mountains at the heart of Guyana, in a region not yet penetrated by the Portuguese of Pará or the French of Cayenne [French Guiana].' Observing the 'unhappy condition' of the Indian wives he kept meeting, he decided that the community had probably been started by a group of women who had run away. 'The vagabond lives of the women, who often follow their husbands to the wars, and are not much happier when at home with their families, might naturally put it into their minds, and at the same time afford them frequent opportunities, to escape from the hard yoke of their tyrants, by endeavouring to provide themselves a settlement, where they might live independently, and at least, not be reduced to the wretched condition of slaves, and beasts of burden,' La Condamine reasoned. He compared their defection to that of the 'maltreated or malcontent slaves' in the European colonies 'who went into the woods in bands or sometimes alone, when they found nobody to go with them and then passed several years and sometimes their whole lives in solitude.' (Some of these runaway slave or 'Maroon' communities, in Surinam, on Jamaica, and on the Middle Trombetas, still exist.) He also decided that the women no longer lived alone, that they had either been conquered by other Indians, or 'their daughters, being weary of their solitude, have at last forgotten the aversion their mothers had to mankind.'

On the twenty-eighth of August, 1742, the La Condamine party passed 'on the left hand the river Jamundas, which Father Acuña called Cunuris and maintained was where the Amazons lived.' This seems to be the first appearance in print of the river's present name. According to one source, La Condamine got it from some missionaries who lived up the river, among the Uaboi Indians (who had evidently replaced the tribes reported by Acuña a century earlier). Jamunda was their chief. La Condamine doesn't tell us where he heard the name, or whether it was already in general use. At any rate, it appears on maps from then on, and 'Cunuris' drops out of the picture.

Downstream and across the Amazon the remaining Tapajós Indians—those who had not fled deep into the forest, been enslaved, herded into missions, or killed by introduced diseases—showed him their most precious possessions, green stone amulets carved in the form of animals, which they said they had inherited from their fathers, who in turn had got them from none other than 'the Cougnantainsecouima,' their word for 'the women without husbands.' This twist to the Amazon-women legend was not new. Many of the chiefs' wives Raleigh had met in Guiana a

27

century and a half earlier had been wearing 'green stones' which 'they esteem as great jewels,' and which Raleigh understood had been acquired in trade from the Amazons. The stones that the Tapajós brought out were 'no different in colour or hardness from oriental jade,' La Condamine reported. 'One can't imagine by what artifice the ancient Americans could have cut and shaped them.'

The prestige of green stones at that time was, in fact, almost global. Tribal people in Asia and North and Middle America as well had long prized them as fetishes and ornaments. In some Amazonian tribes they were traded for women. In Europe they were called *pierres divins* and were sought after for the treatment of kidney stones, nephritic colitis, and epilepsy. (Another word for jade, in fact, is nephrite, from the Greek word for kidney.) The green stones of Amazonia are most commonly and characteristically carved into frogs. While their origin is still unknown, these amulets, which are known as *muiraquitãs*, have been found so far only in the Nhamundá-Trombetas-Tapajós region. They can be seen in museums. Private collectors have paid large sums for them. The largest and most beautiful *muiraquitã* I have seen was in the possession of an accountant and amateur anthropologist named Tonzinho Sonher, who lives across the Amazon from the mouth of the Nhamundá, in the city of Parintins. Sonher told me he had picked up the amulet when he was a child on the way to the cemetery to visit the family graves with his mother; it had just been exposed by a hard rain. He offered to sell it for three thousand dollars—a fortune in that part of the world. *Muiraquitãs* in private hands are sometimes hard to see because of a superstition that showing them brings bad luck. Not all of them are jade, and not all of them are frogs. They are probably the most prized archaeological object in Brazil, and are an important element of the story about the women without husbands which is told in the Amazon today. The story has many versions but is basically this: The women live on a sacred lake called the Mirror of the Moon. At a certain month's full moon, once a year, men from a neighbouring tribe come to the lake by canoe. When the visit has ended, the women present their lovers with the male offspring from the previous year's reunion, and with *muiraquitãs*, which they have obtained by diving into the lake from an aquatic spirit called the Mother of the

28

Muiraquitās. The stones bring the men good luck in hunting.

Within two centuries of contact, Amazon-women stories had become so widespread among the Indians that some of the more perceptive Europeans wondered if they weren't getting their own legend, modified by the fertile Amazonian imagination, told back to them. There has certainly been a lot of cultural exchange between Indians and Europeans in the Amazon. The belief in the vampire aspect of the wandering soul, for instance, is found in the Tapajōs Valley among both the Mundurucu Indians and the post-tribal river people, who are of mixed Portuguese, Indian, and African blood and are known as *caboclos*. The anthropologist Robert Murphy is of the opinion that the Mundurucu did not originally have the belief, and that its transmission to them was 'extremely complex. The Mundurucu may have received the concept from the whites [ie, the *caboclos*] and through the intermediary of another tribe.'

Alfred Russel Wallace, who in four years of Amazonian exploration was unable to find among 'the natives' any trace of the tradition of 'a nation of women without husbands,' wrote:

I can easily imagine it entirely to have arisen from the suggestion and inquiries of the Europeans themselves. When the story of the Amazons was first made known, it became of course a point with all future travellers to verify it, or if possible to get a glimpse of these warlike ladies. The Indians must no doubt have been overwhelmed with questions and suggestions about them, and they, thinking that the white men must know best, would transmit to their descendants and families the idea that such a nation did exist in some distant part of the country. Succeeding travellers, finding traces of the idea among the Indians, would take it as proof of the existence of the Amazons; instead of being merely the effect of a mistake at first, which had been unknowingly spread among them by preceding travellers, seeking to obtain some evidence on the subject.

The same idea had occurred to La Condamine a hundred and thirty years earlier. The enthusiasm with which travellers received tales about the women without husbands 'may have indirectly induced the Indians to adopt them into their customs,' he wrote. He marvelled how none of the Indians could have known the classical myth, yet it was found all over the northern part of the continent—in Peru, in Cayenne, in Venezuela, in Pará, and among tribes that had never seen Europeans. Surely, he decided, 'a report of such a nation had obtained footing among the Indians in the heart of meridional America before the Spaniards had penetrated there.'

The existence of a particular myth in a particular place, like any cultural artifact, can only be the result of one of the two processes—independent invention or diffusion— unless it results from a combination of the two, as when the original tale is embellished with elements introduced later from another culture's complementary tale. Similarly, the existence of the same myth in two places can only be explained in two ways: Either the people in each place were in contact, and one told its myth to the other or to a third party; or the same myth arose spontaneously and independently in each place. In the latter case, there are two basic explanations: Either comparable cultural and/or environmental circumstances gave rise to the same myth in each place (just as there are cases of parallel and convergent evolution among geographically isolated populations of animals and plants which have adapted to similar ecological conditions); or, as Carl Jung argued, the same 'collective unconscious' and spectrum of mental 'archetypes' and potential myth motifs are possessed by every culture and every person (much as the nineteenth-century German anthropologist Adolf Bastian advanced the theory of *Elementargedanken* or 'elementary ideas'). (A third possibility—retention from an earlier period when the two groups were one, or at least lived close together—is not applicable here.)

Let us look for a moment at the Amazons of classical Greek mythology. They are often given the epithet 'man-hating' (*anti-aneires*). 'Battle with them is considered a severe test of the hero's valour and . . . as warriors they are ranked with the monstrous Chimaera, the fierce Solymi, and picked men of Lycia,' the classicist Florence Mary Bennett tells us in a turn-of-the-century monograph called *Religious Cults of the Amazons*. The ninth labor of Hercules was to capture the girdle of their queen, Hippolyta. The Amazons removed their right breast, they were credited with being the first warriors to ride horses, and they were associated with pre-Hellenic horse and mother-goddess cults, with primitive fertility and war rites that involved sexual orgies and possibly the sacrifice of male victims. They may have been votaries or priestesses of the moon goddess Ma, and they may have possessed the powers of enchantment attributed to that heavenly body. They were considered beautiful, as surviving statues of them attest. They lived at the edges of the known world: in Scythia, near the Black Sea; in Libya, near the fabled kingdom of Atlantis. A population of Amazons at the foot of the Caucasus Mountains was visited once a year by men from a neighboring tribe. 'On an appointed day every spring,' the anthologist of Greek myths Robert Graves has written, 'parties of young Amazons and young Gargarensians meet at the summit of the mountain which separates their territories and, after performing a joint sacrifice, spend two months together, enjoying promiscuous intercourse under the cover of night. As soon as an Amazon finds herself pregnant, she returns home. Whatever girl-children are born become Amazons, and the boys are sent to the Gargarensians, who, because they have no means of ascertaining their paternity, distribute them by lot among their huts.' The Amazons attacked Athens and were defeated by Theseus, who married their queen Antiope. An annual festival called the Greater Eleusinian Mysteries was held around September to commemorate Theseus's defeat of the Amazons, and his overthrow of the matriarchal system.

The medieval romances about the Amazons focused primarily on their warlike and 'voluptuous' aspects, and the conquistadores' idea of the women was informed by these narratives. Always in the next valley, just beyond reach, the Amazons became a symbol of the Conquest. The hope of finding them, vanquishing them, and then taking them to bed, was the fantasy that kept the conquistadores going. 'The Amazon is a dream that men created to flatter themselves . . .' Kleinbaum argues perhaps a bit stridently. 'The conquest of an Amazon is an act of transcendence, a rejection of the ordinary, of death, of mediocrity—and a reach for immortality . . . Men told of battling Amazons to enhance their sense of their own worth and historical significance.'

Let us now look at the Amazonian myth. Like their Greek counterparts, the 'women without husbands' live at the edge of the known world, in faraway mountains at the

31

headwaters of cataract-infested rivers, along with forest ogres and other culture heroes. They get together with men from neighbouring tribes. They are associated with the moon, with water, and 'horizontality' according to the anthropologist Peter G. Roe, as opposed to the masculine erectness of plant life. They are seductively beautiful but not markedly bellicose—not, at any rate, superhuman adversaries a man must vanquish to prove himself. Nor do they remove their right breasts to enhance their skill as archers. These motifs, where they occur, are almost certainly European injections.

Two Amazon-women motifs seem to be indigenous to the Amazon basin. According to a myth that occurs sporadically among some tribes like the Vaupés and the Mundurucu, the women once possessed the sacred flutes, which Roe describes as symbols of phallic power and of the world of culture, as opposed to the world of nature. In some tribes of the Upper Xingu today, women who even look on the flutes are gang-raped. But at one time they sat around playing the flutes, and it was the men who had to carry the firewood and fetch the water, cook and submit to their sexual demands. This period of female supremacy ended, however, when the men tricked the women into surrendering the flutes.

In another myth, also quite widespread in the basin, the women have an animal lover—a cayman, a tapir, or a porpoise, perhaps. The men find out and kill the animal, and the bereaved women leave the men and go off to live by themselves in the forest, where they practice male infanticide. In some versions they kill the men before leaving.

Many societies have a story about the women once being dominant, and then something happened, the matriarchy is overthrown, and the women are repressed. The story is still found on the Middle Sepik River, in New Guinea. The Yahgan of Tierra del Fuego had it, too. The unlikelihood that these two societies were ever in direct contact, along with the fact that the story did not seem to exist in North or Middle America, the most likely diffusion route, suggests that we are dealing with an 'elementary idea.' Early anthropologists tended to accept the stories about an original matriarchy as historical fact. The Swiss ethnologist J. J. Bachofen wove an entire theory of cultural evolution around them. He hypothesized that the first human societies were promiscuous hordes controlled by the women, but after women introduced the institution of marriage as their 'mother-right,' the men became concerned about the paternity of their children and took over the descent system and, gradually, everything else. Few modern scholars take the stories about an original matriarchy literally any more, but there is still disagreement and a 'gender gap' about what they mean. Female scholars tend to interpret them differently than male scholars do; Anna Roosevelt, for instance, sees the myth as 'a rationalization of male-supremacist society,' while Robert Murphy takes a more Freudian view of it as 'a parable, a statement in mythic form about the current relations between men and women. Men issue forth from women and for several years thereafter are dependent on their milk. To become a man a man must overcome his dependence on his mother.' Among the particularly aggressively male-dominated Mehinaku of the upper Xingu River, the anthropologist Thomas Gregor reports 'mothers carry their infants about with them, sleep with them in the same hammock, and nurse them into the fifth year.'

Perhaps there is a more straightforward interpretation. Myths are attempts to explain how things got to be the way they are, and one way to do this—a common and effective storytelling device—is to say that things were not always so, that once, in fact, the opposite was true. The 'thing' in this case is a universal phenomenon, not only in the Amazon but in every known society: that the men are politically and economically dominant. No self-perpetuating matriarchy or exclusively female community has ever been authenticated. In the fall of 1983 the anthropologist Kim Hill found in the forest of Peruvian Amazonia two grown Indian women and their mother who had split off from their group and had been living by themselves for six or seven years. They had no agriculture and were poor archers, usually missing their quarry by a wide mark. They survived by miscellaneous foraging of tortoises and other wild food; and they were not a self-perpetuating community. The study of contemporary tribal people and the paleopathological analysis of female skeletons at archaeological sites suggest that women have been worked hard and have been more vulnerable to nutritional stress throughout history.

Perhaps the myth about the animal lover serves to explain other perceived phenomena or common experiences:

33

that not all women are acquiescent about their inferior status; that there are some women who emphatically do not like men and have no desire to be with them; that no matter how physically exploited a woman may be, nobody can make her like it; she retains her free will as well as (usually) the option of giving herself willingly to another lover and thus of subverting the attempt to be forcibly possessed. As the intrepid Victorian butterfly collector Margaret Fountaine, who spurned her well-bred British and continental suitors and ended by marrying a Syrian drago-man many years her junior, confessed to her diary, 'I love to be a woman and feel that power which a man can never possess, the power . . . to reject.'

The frog-formed amulets seem to be a later addition to the Amazon-women legend. Animal-shaped talismans of re-markably similar green jade have been found in Turkestan, and it was originally thought that the Mongolians who crossed the Bering Strait on a temporary land bridge during the last ice age and descended into the New World brought the actual stones with them. But that theory was dashed by the discovery in the Serra Tumucumaque, along the border of Brazil and Surinam, of the probable source of the jade for the Amazonian amulets. It is now thought that the Mongo-lians might have brought the idea of carving and esteeming the stones with them. Very similar frog-formed stones have been found in Mexico and in the Greater Antilles. There are some particularly nice ones from what is now the Domini-can Republic. 'In his important study of the frog motif in South American Indian art and the batrachian in American mythology generally, [the Swedish ethnologist Henry] Wassen has suggest several reasons why the aboriginal should have regarded these little animals with interest, and, seemingly, with awe,' the archaeologist Helen C. Palmatary has written: 'their great number in certain areas, the volume of their croaking and sometimes its quality, croak-ing as a harbinger of rain, and through rain the promise of fertility for the land. Some batrachian species served as an important food, others provided an important venom.' Permanently lubricated, triangular in form, and 'displayed,' with their legs parted and to the side, frogs are also quintessential symbols of female sexuality. The Mayans used the same word for frog and female genitals, and in Amazonian slang today the word *sapo* has the same double meaning. But the *muiraquitã* seems to be an androgynous figure, with both male and female attributes; its head is typically modified in an obviously phallic way—not something misanthropic women would be expected to have gone in for.

If, as all the evidence seems to indicate, the Amazons or the women without husbands never existed except in the various guises of a universal myth, one question remains: Why do so many of the stories say that the women lived on the Nhamundá? What could be up there? Could there be an undiscovered basis of truth to the stories. My curiosity about the myth and the river was originally piqued by the account, published in the fifties, of a man named Eduardo Prado, who claimed to have landed in a pontoon plane on the Lake of the Mirror of the Moon, 'at the foot of some hills lying parallel to the course of the Nhamundá,' and to have visited the women for several days. A close look at Prado's geographical and ethnographic information revealed that his account belonged to the 'blarney' tradition started by O'Brien, that it was nothing more than a pastiche of the stories that had been circulating about the Amazons since Carvajal, with convincing detail about the daily routine of Indian women throughout the Amazon thrown in. What emerged from checking into Prado's account was not only that the man was lying through his teeth, but that there was almost no information on the Nhamundá of any kind, although a populous and rather advanced culture seemed to have been occupying its lower reaches when the first Europeans blundered into the region. That a river the size of the Hudson should still be wild and unexplored seemed astonishing (actually dozens of rivers in the Amazon system remain in this category). Even if the women without husbands were no more 'real' than the bearded gnomes whose ninepin games were thought by the settlers of New Amsterdam to be responsible for the thunder in the lower Hudson Valley, a trip up the Nhamundá, I decided, couldn't fail to be of interest.

One afternoon not long after I had decided to go up the Nhamundá and see what was there, my good friend, the Belgian ethnomusicologist Benoit Quersin, looked me up in New York. He was between planes, on the way from a daughter's wedding in Albuquerque to Kinshasa, Zaire, where he heads the oral-traditions section of that country's

Musée National des Beaux Arts. I hadn't seen him in two years. Fifty-six now, a slender, deeply tanned man with short gray-blond hair, a large Gallic nose, and half-framed glasses hanging from a chain around his neck, he was cultivated but cool; a bass player who had once backed up Lena Horne, he had been touring Africa with a jazz band fifteen years earlier when an anthropologist in what was then the Belgian colony of Ruanda-Urundi had introduced him to tribal music and persuaded him of the need for it to be recorded. UNICEF had come through with funding for his anthology of Zairois tribal music, he told me, and he was well along on the project: He had got to and recorded most of the country's two hundred and eighty-some tribes. I told him about the trip I was planning to take that summer—my fourth to the Amazon—chasing a legend up a river called the Nhamundá. Then it occurred to me how nice it would be to have Quersin along. With his understanding of rain forests and their people, he would be the perfect companion. He wouldn't be put out by the inevitable foul-ups and delays, and his African perspective would be stimulating. I asked him if he would like to join me, and to my delight he said that he had always wanted to see the Amazon and had been waiting for an opportunity.

Quersin's only limitation, not knowing Portuguese, turned out to be no problem; he would get along fine with an entertaining repertoire of sound effects and gestures he had perfected in the field for communicating with people he couldn't converse with, and after two weeks he was already able to get basic things across in Portuguese. In Zaire we had spoken mostly French, but switching back and forth from Portuguese to French was too much work for me, so in Brazil we would use English. The Amazonians would treat Quersin with their characteristic deference and respect, addressing him as 'father' or 'doctor.' He bore a close enough facial and manneristic resemblance to the underwater filmmaker Jacques Cousteau, who had just finished making a special on the Amazon, that on several occasions he would be asked if he was a crew member of the *Calypso*.

Now that he was coming, why didn't he take care of the audio-visual end—of the tape recording and the picture taking—I suggested. I would do the negotiating and get us from place to place. He was delighted not to have to worry about logistics for the first time in years. We both had about

36

a month to spend. If we learned something new about the legendary women, *tant mieux*; if not, we would certainly make other discoveries.

On June thirtieth, Quersin flew over from Africa, I flew down from New York, and we met in Rio de Janeiro. We went to a money changer in the Centro and exchanged two thousand dollars for four bricks of crisp, newly minted five-hundred-cruzeiro notes—three million six hundred thousand cruzeiros in all. We saw some fine green jade *muiraquitãs* in the Museu Nacional, carved into frogs and other creatures (one seemed to represent a cicada). The pieces had been acquired long ago, and the only information about them was that they were from the Trombetas Valley. We flew to Brasília and spoke with anthropologists at the National Indian Foundation about the tribes of lower-middle Amazonia—the Mundurucu, the Satere-Maué, the Hixkaryana, the Wai Wai, and the Tirió. None of these tribes, to their knowledge, had the green amulets or an Amazon-women myth, or had ever had them (their information was inconclusive, however, as they admitted to never having asked about these things). The Hixkaryana, they said, who live on the upper Nhamundá, above the rapids, had been heavily missionized and had forgotten many of their legends. In their opinion, it wasn't worth chartering a bush plane in Manaus and flying to them, the quickest way to reach them. (The missionary-linguist Desmond Derbyshire, who spent twenty years among the Hixkaryana, later confirmed that the tribe lacks an Amazon-women myth and *muiraquitãs*). The Satere-Maué Indians, who live up the Andira River, across the Amazon from the mouth of the Nhamundá, were the most traditional Indians in the vicinity, and were accessible by boat; if anybody knew anything, they would. We were given permission to visit the tribe for a month (Brazil's roughly one hundred thousand tribal Indians are legally wards of the state, and permission to visit them must be obtained from the National Indian Foundation) and to ask them about the women and the stones.

From Brasília we flew to Manaus and caught another plane to Santarém, the largest city of lower-middle Amazonia, at the mouth of the Tapajós River. There we soon discovered that the duffelbag with ninety per cent of our gear, which we had checked through at Brasília, hadn't been put on the second plane. The despatcher assured us that the bag would come tomorrow, on the next plane from Manaus, or if not tomorrow, maybe the day after. We took a taxi into the city, with the driver, as Brazilian taxi drivers often do, blaming the potholes on the mayor.

Santarém, population a hundred and fifty thousand, looked a lot more modern since my last visit there, eight years earlier. A modern tourist complex called the Hotel Tropical had sprung up outside the city, but instead of going there we checked into a simple, cozy two-story wooden affair with slowly turning overhead fans called the Hotel Camino, overlooking the market and the Tapajós beyond, which at its confluence with the Amazon is as vast as an ocean.

At a restaurant on the quay we ordered *tambaqui*, which tasted something like swordfish, and struck up a conversation with a local lawyer who, apologizing for being pessimistic, predicted that we would never see our duffelbag again; with the Brazilian economy in dire shape, he said, a lot of luggage at airports had been disappearing. He told us about three local bush pilots, brothers named David, Delano, and Darlan Reichert, who were descended from Confederate emigrés to Santarém from Alabama in 1867.

By seven the next morning, Sunday, the square below was seething with life. Stalls brimmed with fruit; a Baptist with an accordion was singing hymns before a microphone. We bought machetes and checkered cotton hammocks, which are probably the most important pieces of gear for travelling in the Amazon. Quersin didn't see why he needed a hammock—they are an Indian invention, and nobody in Africa had one—but by the end of the trip he would be raving about its virtues. In the Amazon a hammock is like a portable cocoon that can be set up and settled into anywhere. It serves as a chair, a bed, and for Indians and *caboclos* alike, as a burial shroud.

I wanted to revisit a village called Alter do Chāo, an hour or so up the Tapajós, where I had spent a memorable afternoon in 1977, swimming and drinking cashew liqueur. The village had consisted of a square with a church and a few dirt streets lined with thatch huts. The river had been warm and clear blue, a few miles wide and lined with clean white sand. Below the village a large, limpid green lagoon sat at the foot of a lone hill clothed with grass and small contorted trees. The spot had been special for the Tapajós Indians, who had told La Condamine that most of their green stone frogs had come from the lagoon at Alter do Chão.

We asked four people in the square when the bus left for the village and got four different answers: nine-thirty, ten, ten-thirty, and eleven-thirty. It wasn't that they were giving us the runaround but that the punctuality our question presupposed was nonexistent. There was nothing to do but sit and wait. I wondered how we were going to learn about something that may or may not have existed centuries ago when we couldn't even find out when a bus left.

The bus eventually did come, and at about one o'clock it brought us to Alter do Chão, which had been discovered and developed into a weekend resort for the people of Santarém and was unrecognizable. Thatched huts were interspersed with stucco villas along many new streets, and thousands of people, most of them under twenty—the cooper-skinned, high-cheekboned, well-proportioned, but still rather small descendants of the Tapajós—were on the beaches. The next generation, Quersin predicted, would be inches taller. Coca-Cola, water skis, speedboats, jeeps with roll bars—all the standard American consumer items associated with summer fun—were in evidence. This was the year of Michael Jackson. He was the new myth, the new universal culture hero. Children were break-dancing and moon-walking on the beach to tape decks of his music. We met no one who knew the old legends of Alter do Chão; the only bit of information we gleaned was that somebody there was supposed to have a boat called the *Muiraquitã*. A regional salesman for blue jeans told us the market around Santarém was fantastic. The completion of the Transamazon Highway, followed by the discovery of gold, had brought progress to this side of the Amazon almost overnight, and nobody seemed to be looking back.

When we returned to Santarém in the evening we found that we were in luck: Our duffelbag had arrived, and there was still time to catch the boat across the river; so we hadn't been delayed, after all. The boat had two open storys with railings and was called the *Vitoria Regia III*, after the gigantic Amazonian water lily. We suspended our hammocks near those of dozens of other passengers and soon we were chugging through the warm insect-filled darkness. At about three in the morning we reached the city of Obidos.

Not many travellers came to this side of the river—the modernity that was making over the Santarém area was still perhaps fifteen years off—and the only lodgings in Obidos were private homes that took in guests; staying in one of them was like being taken into the family. Our homey little pension was called the Hotel Braj Bello. The adorably teasable ten-year-old daughter of the house made our beds and served our meals. Tinted photographs of her parents were in the dining room.

Later in the morning we walked around the city. It had started as a fort built by the Portuguese in 1697 on a bluff strategically overlooking the 'throat' of the Amazon, where the river narrows to just over a mile wide. The fort had been named for the local Indians, the Pauxis, who were perhaps the 'black-stained men' (their bodies evidently smeared with the juice of genipap berries) reported at the mouth of the Trombetas by Carvajal. The Pauxis had resisted the heavy-handed attempts of missionaries to bring them into the fold and had fled up the Trombetas, which comes into the Amazon eight miles above Obidos. Some of the Pauxis are believed to have joined the Uaboi, who were originally a Trombetas tribe but who by 1742, as we have seen, also on the run from missionaries, had moved into the lower Nhamundá Valley. The last Pauxis were heard from in 1914 in the forest northeast of Obidos, They are now presumed extinct.

As we were walking in a muddy lane by the harbour, thousands of Brazil-nut shells suddenly slid out of a second-story chute to our right and landed in a heap below. We went up some rickety stairs and looked in on the room from which they had been discharged. It was like a sweatshop from the century before. Four rows of women were sitting at lever-operated nut-crackers, cracking open the nuts one by one. Nobody was talking, which was unusual for a group of Brazilians. These were second-quality Brazil nuts, the foreman told us, destined for Belém to be made into soap. The women were paid by the kilo—fifteen cents—and they put in a six-day week. On Saturday evening the average sheller took home twenty-five thousand cruzeiros—about fourteen dollars.

Back outside we watched bundles of jute, an Asian fibre plant grown extensively in the Amazon's fertile floodplain, being loaded on a freighter from Liverpool. A man took us into a building belonging to an American company called Ricketts Industries and filled with frozen *dourada* and *piramutaba* catfish. The company has a restaurant in Shreveport, Louisiana, that specializes in catfish and hush-puppies.

But in spite of these international connections and American hits gushing from municipal loudspeakers at most corners, Obidos (population roughly thirty thousand) was still a quiet, traditional Amazon town. Its general layout was not significantly different from that of the next four towns we would visit, or from that of Santarém until quite recently, although the personalities of these communities, as we shall see, were as variable as those of individuals. In each place, the commerce was on the water, and the residences went up a hill behind. The architecture was mostly Portuguese colonial—green-, blue-, apricot-, or white-painted stucco houses, with white trim and red tile roofs. The adjectives 'clean' and 'cheerful', used by Henry Walter Bates to describe Santarém in the eighteen-fifties, were generally still apt. A few leading families were in control. The leading families of Obidos were Sephardic Jews, whose presence in Amazonia dates from the seventeenth century (the first wave of Jewish immigrants to New York City, in fact, came from east of the Amazon in 1720). The politics were paternalistic and nepotistic, and the local politicians macho and mustachioed. The population was young and mostly female, many of the men having gone to larger centers or elsewhere in search of work, and the dominant family type was accordingly, in the common Third World pattern, mother- or grandmother-headed. The range of physical types was quite limited. In each of the five towns, we would keep seeing the same (or so we thought) predominantly Portuguese old man, with the same wrinkled features, thin grey moustache, and wide-brimmed straw hat; and the same predominantly Indian young man, with the same front teeth missing, the same muscular build, and the same red shorts. In one town I finally asked one of the young Indian men if I hadn't seen him in Obidos a couple of days earlier. He said he hadn't been there in a year.

There were about half a dozen television sets in Obidos. The reception was terrible, but in the evening crowds gathered in the street wherever there was a home with a set

41

and watched through the front door. In a few years, if what was happening in the rest of Brazil was any indication, the numerous saints' days and other festivals that were celebrated as often as twice a week would probably lose out to soap operas from Rio. It turned out that we had arrived on the feast of Santa Ana, the patron saint of Obidos, and that night a statue of her, on a float with blinking light bulbs, was paraded through the square, followed by a generator carried on poles by four men, and then by a group of teenagers cupping lighted candles and wearing T-shirts that said 'The Adolescent Generation of the New City [i.e., district] of Geacino.'

There was a superabundance, in each of these communities, of small dogs that belonged to no one; at night several of them would start to bark, and soon every dog in town would join in. This could go on for hours. After the dogs had finally died down, still well before dawn, the roosters would start up. Fortunately, mosquitoes were not a problem in this part of the Amazon at this time of year except at sunset, when they would come out in force and bite fiercely for about twenty minutes.

Obidos had a marvellous ruin—a large colonial-style barracks on top of the hill, whose windows and roof were gone and whose walls were coated with black fungus. Several people told us that it had been built during the Second World War. On a wall in one of the rooms, however, parting vines that had shot up through the floor, we discovered a plaque with the date 1909. In a review of my book *The Rivers Amazon* the nature writer Frank S. Graham, Jr, wrote several years ago: 'The Amazon has little history to speak of. It was never the site of splendid cities or triumphant civilizations. Powerful nations across the sea showed little interest in carving it into spheres of influence. Time there has not risen to the level of history.' The problem is not, as I see it, that the valley has no history, but that the memory of it is so short. To most of the citizens of Obidos, 1909 and the Second World War were all the same. Because of the people's temperament, and because of the speed with which things decay, the past is quickly forgotten in the humid tropics. Archaeologists are beginning to discover that there were, in fact, good-sized and probably quite splendid settlements in the Amazon, perhaps even deserving to be called cities.

We called on the Franciscan monks who have a mission in a Tirió Indian village near Surinam. A young Tirió woman—perhaps fifteen—was nursing a child in the cloistered courtyard of their parish house, looking among huge banana leaves as beautiful and innocent as a subject of Gauguin. 'The tribes which live in the hills of the watershed [between the Amazon and the Guianas] today such as the Wai Wai and the Tirió are somewhat taller, paler, and more classically handsome than other Indians,' John Hemming writes. Perhaps the Amazons of Carvajal were men or women of this stock.

The woman's name was Deacui (this is a phonetic approximation of the way it sounded to me, and as in my rendering of Indian words to come, there may be considerable distortion). Deacui didn't speak Portuguese, but we talked with a *mulata* schoolteacher in the parish-house library who told us that the Tirió didn't have an Amazon-women legend that she knew of (this was confirmed the next morning by Deacui's husband, who did speak Portuguese), but that 'near the Tirió,' on the Brazil-Venezuela border, she had heard that there was supposed to be a tribe of tall, fair, blond, blue-eyed Indians who were 'the remnants of the Amazons.' She had recently assigned her students to canvass the community for stories about the women. A seventeen-year-old girl in the class had interviewed a fisherman who had told her that once when he had been fishing along a creek, he had felt the tail of a horse graze his cheek from behind. He fell to the ground and hid his face because he knew it was the Amazons, and he didn't want to look and be enchanted. 'To us, the Amazons are horsewomen, female *cavaleiros*' the schoolteacher explained. Similarly, in French, the word *amazone* means horsewoman. To ride sidesaddle is *monter en amazone*. The fisherman's women seemed also to have become like sirens or mermaids, about whom there are many stories in the Amazon and, Quersin pointed out, in the Zaire basin as well, where the most frequently sighted mermaid is known as Mami Wata, pidgin English for Mother of the Water. Her tail is detachable, so that she can come on land and seduce men.

We talked with one of the monks, Brother Angelico, who was seventy-three and spoke Portuguese with a heavy German accent and had the kind face and the flowing white beard of Saint Nicholas. He told us that he had lived for twenty years with the Tirió and had never heard about this fair-skinned tribe, but that fair skin was esteemed by them. 'Their chief, Yunure, says he is white, but he is Indian. The darkest of his four wives once told me, when she was expecting her first child, that if the baby came out dark she would kill it.'

Among the Tirió, he went on, there were about seventy Kaxuiana Indians who had originally lived on a tributary of the middle Trombetas called the Rio Cachorrinho ('little dog' in Portuguese—perhaps an attempt to approximate the tribe's name) and had been befriended by his compatriot, a missionary and ethnologist named Protasio Frikel. Brother Angelico showed us a paper Frikel had written about the Kaxuiana, which told how many of them had died of diseases caught from neighboring Brazil-nut gatherers and descendants of fugitive slaves. By 1968 only seventy-one were left. Many were suffering from tuberculosis, venereal disease, and 'eczematous sores' all over their bodies. There weren't enough marriage possibilities in the new generation, so sixty-four of them went to live with the Tirió. The other seven, I read with interest, went up the Nhamundá. I wondered if they were still there.

An old woman told us about a jade frog *muiraquitá* her father had owned, whose greenness, she claimed, 'became more alive in the afternoon,' but he had given it long ago to the great Amazonist Ladislau Neto (who wrote a book about the valley called *Immature Land* and died a leper); and a young woman showed us four '*muiraquitás*' that she had found in her back yard. One was an antique gaudily enamelled green glass bead—probably a trade bead used in early dealings with Indians. The other three were black stone beads with meandering white lines in them, possibly made by Indians themselves. The meaning of *muiraquitá* had evidently expanded to include anything worn about the neck—not just a stone frog—made or thought to have been made by Indians and to bring good luck; most of the *muiraquitás* we would see or hear about were in fact beads or rings for the finger or the ear dug up in Indian burial grounds.

A third woman told us that the best place to find *muiraquitás* was Faro, at the mouth of the Nhamundá. She said that she had once gone there and within an hour fifty people had come to the plaza with pieces of *muiraquitãs* to sell her. They were in pieces because, as she understood it, the chief of the tribe that had made them would give one to a couple on the eve of their marriage, and after the wedding night the husband was supposed to strike it; if it shattered, this was taken as a sign that the marriage had been consummated. Above Faro there was a lake called the Mirror of the Moon. She had not been there, but the water, she understood, was limpid, and that was where the *muiraquitãs* came from and where the Amazons had lived. The women would come down to the Amazon, visit men from other tribes, and come back pregnant. The male children would be sacrificed and thrown into the lake or would be turned over to the men. The women lopped off their right breast. 'Good news,' I told Quersin. 'The actual lake where the women are supposed to have lived still exists.' This had been unclear from my reading.

Our next destination was a place called the Costa de Paru, where the Brazilian botanist, explorer, and Indian pacifier João Barbosa Rodriguez claimed to have pinpointed the attack on Orellana and his men. Born in 1842, Barbosa Rodriguez was an exuberant figure in Amazonian scholarship. He published more than a hundred works, mostly on the classification of palms, a subject about which he was regarded as an expert during his lifetime but on which he is now considered to have been 'out to lunch,' as one modern botanist has put it. (The same, unfortunately, is also true of the Greek he was fond of dropping.) He founded in Manaus the first herbarium of Amazonian flora (the building that housed the collection is now a high school, and the specimens themselves have mysteriously disappeared) and later became the director of the Jardim Botanico in Rio de Janeiro. He wrote about lingua geral, the language that was in general use among the tribes along the main river; about the fables, superstitions, fossil reptiles, and antiquities of the valley; about his expeditions up the Urubu, Jatapu, Capim, Trombetas, and Yamundá (as he spelled it) rivers. But his most extraordinary work was undoubtedly *The Muiraquitã: A Study of the Asiatic Origin of the Civilization of the Amazon in Prehistoric Times*, published in 1889, an almost phantasmagorical exercise in the cultural diffusionism then in vogue, in which he argued that the original 'race' of the Amazon, the 'inappropriately-named Amazons,' was more advanced than the Incas and was indeed the mother of all the South American cultures, in view of the fact that it had brought with it all the way from Asia *muiraquitãs* made of the green jade found only in Turkestan and obtained by women who had dived for it into the rivers of Khotan during the full moon. These migrating Mongolians had left in their path, on the way to Amazonia, versions of the amulet like the *chalchihuitl*, a green stone placed in the mouth of dead chiefs in southern Mexico. With the discovery of jade in Brazil, however, Barbosa Rodriguez's laboriously constructed theory crumbled. His collection of *muiraquitãs*, said to have been unrivalled, is also sadly lost. One of his most perfect jade frogs, 'which I had the honour to offer to her highness Senhora Dona Isabel,' the queen of Brazil, he tells us, he found in 1888 on an island eighteen miles above the mouth of the Trombetas, where he decided (without sharing his reasoning) the attack on Orellana and his men must have taken place. He named the site the Costa de Paru. He also found evidence of extensive human occupation there—'an infinity' of pottery fragments—and he argued that these 'Amazons' must have been the ancestors of the Vaupés Indians, whom he had visited on the Rio Negro several years earlier, because the Vaupés still made stone *muiraquitãs* (cylindrical quartz ones, though) and had told him that they had originally lived on the Amazon itself, along a lake inhabited by the Mother of the Muiraquitãs, who one day took the form of an animal and was accidentally killed by one of their hunters, which caused there to be a 'revolution of the waters,' and the Vaupés had to move. Particularly devastating floods, he argued, struck the Amazon once or twice a century. His discovery that there had been one a little after 1580 fitted neatly into his theory and explained 'what to this day is unexplained'—the disappearance of the Amazons.

While I had reservations about the interpretations of Barbosa Rodriguez, the Costa de Paru was one of the few concrete sites we had, and it behoved us to see what, if anything, was there. Early on our second morning in Obidos we went down to the harbour and learned from some men lounging around the gaily painted boats that there indeed was a place called the Costa de Paru, on an island several hours above the mouth of the Trombetas, as Barbosa

Rodriguez had said. Islands in the Amazon are among the most evanescent of landforms. New ones are continually forming and old ones are being washed away. Most of them are teardrop-shaped, with their blunt end facing current and slowly being eaten way, while at the same time suspended particles of sediment precipitate into the quiet eddy below them, so that what they lose on one end they gain on the other, and they are in effect slowly creeping downstream. These 'lenticular' islands give the Amazon its characteristic 'braided' or 'gangliform' drainage pattern, as the geomorphologist Hilgard O'Reilly Sternberg has explained. But the large, soggy island whose southern, Amazon-fronting, shore is known as the 'Coast of Paru,' is the result of different circumstances. It is the results of sediments suspended in the Amazon being slowed down by the outpouring Trombetas and the Nhamundá. As islands in the Amazon go, it is relatively stable, even though for several months of the year, during the rainy season, it is largely under water.

By noon we had found a boat to take us to the Costa de Paru: the B/M *Ytaura*. It was a cattle boat very sturdily built of *itaúba*, or stonewood, with a capacity for maybe a dozen cattle, a good deal larger that what we needed—we could have taken along a band—but nothing else in Obidos had been available. In design it was a typical Amazonian *motor*—as this type of craft is called—flat-roofed, open-sided in front, manned by a crew of two: the *motorista*, who sat at the wheel at the bow and communicated by tugs of a bell cord with the *mecânico* in the engine room, who dickered with the thirty-horsepower diesel engine and stood its din with the help of *cachaça*, the raw white Brazilian rum.

Almost immediately, as we chugged beneath particolored purple and pink clay cliffs riddled with swallow holes, it started to rain. Two black-bellied tree ducks in tight formation sped over a vast floating mat of water hyacinth in which the lemon wings of jaçanas hunting for snails and other food flashed delicately here and there. The numerous kapok trees along the bank were hung like Christmas trees with bulbous red pods, a few of which had split open, releasing a local blizzard of drifting seeds borne on tufts of floss. This floss is exported as stuffing for mattresses and life jackets.

Although it was going down from its high-water mark a month earlier, the river was still up, and much of its floodplain, or *várzea*, as it is called, was still under water. At this time of year the only way the people who lived in the *várzea* could get around was by canoe. Most of them raised cattle, and their main business now was to paddle around and gather grass to bring to the *marombas*, the elevated corrals built up on pilings in which the animals were penned. With the fish scattered in every direction, this was a stressful time of year. The little settlement of Nucleo Sagrado Coração de Jesus Costa de Paru, which we reached after several hours, was still flooded except for a small strand on which a group of muddy youths were playing a game like capture the flag and having the time of their life. We walked along an immense floating bole of the amazingly buoyant and water-resistant *maçaranduba* wood to the elevated frame house of a man named Antonio Gomez, who brought chairs and coffee to the porch. There were almost a hundred people here, he told us, and they were all kin. The oldest was his Uncle Amerigo, a man of about seventy with a lot of gold in his teeth who soon joined us. 'My grandfather told me that when he came here as a boy, there were Indians living here'—Maués, from across the river, he guessed. And Antonio said that in October, when the water was down, the children would pick up all sorts of *vestigias*, especially along the big lake in the interior of the island—stupid little things in the shape of fish and other animals made of clay. I asked if he had any to show us, and a boy brought a fish made not of clay but of stone—a faithful enough representation that the assembled company recognized it as a *cará* (the popular name for the various members of a common family of predatory fish). 'But this was made long before your grandfather's time,' I said to Amerigo. Two holes had been drilled through it, possibly so that it could be strung and worn around the neck. It would have made a handsome gorget, but the boy's only interest in it was as a skipping stone, for which it was also admirably suited. Antonio gave it to me as a memento, and I reciprocated with a postcard showing, in triptych, the World Trade Center, the Statue of Liberty, and the Empire State Building. Back in New York I took the fish to Anna Roosevelt, who said that the two holes had no use but were an enigmatic motif that cropped up quite frequently on prehistoric artifacts from that part of the valley. 'Why two holes?' she asked, turning the fish in her hands. 'It must mean something special. Perhaps the holes are for attachment. But to what?'

We spent a pleasant hour on Gomez's porch but learned nothing that either supported or sank Barbosa Rodriguez's theory; whatever evidence there may or may not have been was either under water now or had washed away in the century since his visit. If the Amazons had lived here, it was news to Gomez and his kin. This was pretty clearly a blind alley. We got on the boat and chugged back to the mouth of the Trombetas, where we were caught in a fantastic storm whose gale-force winds and high waves forced us to tie to a flooded tree for an hour. Then we went up the Trombetas about twenty miles, and were dropped off at the city of Oriximiná in time for a late supper.

Founded in 1877, Oriximiná was much younger than Obidos. It had been modelled after, had until recently been dependent on and now had surpassed Obidos. Most Amazonian municipalities are solely supported by federal funding, but Oriximiná has tremendous deposits of bauxite in its 110,000 square kilometres, most of which are unexplored wilderness extending up to Surinam and the Guianas; it is the fourth-largest municipality in Brazil. A multinational company has leased the mining rights, making possible all sorts of improvements. 'In 1975 there wasn't a single school outside the city limits. Now we have two hundred and fifty teachers spread out all over the area,' the mayor, Raimundo Oliveira, told me the next morning. He was sitting at the reception desk in front of his office making telephone calls and hearing out one by one a group of humble petitioners waiting in the hall; one was a woman who wanted money to buy medicine for her child. Another local man told us that the municipality enjoys the status of a national security area, which, he explained with typical Brazilian wit, is only given to places that have a lot of minerals, or where the opposition party has been winning consistently.

Not only did Oriximiná have a promising future, it was a lovely town. Fresh breezes of the Trombetas made the heat and the humidity unnoticeable. It is a clear-water river, and as a huge freighter called the *Maritime Dignity* headed up it to take on bauxite another fifty miles or so above Oriximiná, the water sparkled. When the waitress at the Hotel Equatorial—which was more of a night club and restaurant—unshuttered the tall windows of our room (we seemed to be the first guests in some time), they gave on a courtyard and a pantiled villa behind—as sedate a scene as any provincial village in the south of France. The merchants of Oriximiná seemed to be thriving. A number of them had recently come from polluted and crime-ridden centres like Belém. Oriximiná was between Santarém and Obidos in evolutionary terms; it was in the first phase of *décollage*, or takeoff, to use a term usually applied to developing countries.

Eighty per cent of the people who live along the Trombetas from Oriximiná to the first rapids, the mayor told us, are native-born *crioulos*, descended from escaped slaves. Above the rapids, about a thousand Wai Wai Indians live on the Mapuera, the main right-bank tributary of the Trombetas, and up to the north-flowing Essequibo, in another drainage system over the Guyana border. At the Oriximiná headquarters of the Catholic missionaries for the Wai Wai, we met a twenty-year-old member of the tribe named Rocinaldo who spoke a little Portuguese. Eager to be of help, he kept saying yes to my questions until he finally understood them, then he said that the Wai Wai don't have an Amazon-women legend or *muiraquitás*, but women of the tribe wear yellow necklaces called *eletanos*, which bring luck.

We heard about some other Indians from a man named Argemio Wandereley Deniz, a member of one of Oriximiná's big landowning families. In 1957 a friend of his named Virgilio Almeida had been looking for Brazil nut trees in the forest about a hundred miles to the northeast when he had run into ten Indian women who were *bem claras*, light-skinned, Deniz assured us. Each woman was carrying a howler monkey in her arms. Almeida had not seen them since, although he had seen traces of them, and twice he had led Seventh-Day Adventist missionaries from Santarém to the place. The *adventistas* had left presents; and when they returned, the presents had been destroyed. Sensing my skepticism, Deniz took us to his father, Antonio José, who was sitting in his dark-panelled office on the quay going over his books. The old man told the story somewhat differently: The women were probably following their men on a hunting party. With them was an old man who aimed an arrow at Almeida, and Almeida backed off. The father was pretty sure they were an itinerant band of Rocouyenne (also known as Wayana, about a hundred and fifty of whom have in fact been reported in that area). Later in the day we talked to Vergilio's son Paulo, who told us that last year three *adventistas* had gone back and made contact with them; everybody had stood around trying to understand each other. There were a little over a hundred and fifty Indians in the group. He didn't know what tribe they were, but they weren't light-skinned, and the men wore lip discs. The *adventistas* were planning to return later in the year to spend a few months with them. Visiting them was unfortunately out of the question for us. They were two weeks off overland and by canoe. Almeida, the only person in Oriximiná who knew the way to them, was in the forest; he was expected 'any day.' We knew how vague that was.

Although Oriximiná was 'poised on the platform' of progress, as the mayor put it, there was still a lot of irrationality in the society. At the tiny branch of the Federal University of Fluminense in town, we met a young dental intern from Rio who had been studying the local superstitions in his spare time. The fear of the *bôto*, the freshwater dolphin of Amazonia, was particularly strong, he told us, as it is through the animal's range in the river system, among both *caboclos* and Indians. The *bôto* is held to be like a male mermaid who comes ashore and seduces women, or penetrates them in the water. In Oriximiná this belief was used to explain awkward pregnancies. It was so unquestioned that women registering the birth of a child sometimes gave the *bôto* as the father. Even the physical education teacher, the intern went on, who had been to Belém and had completed higher education, was not willing to renounce her fear of the *bôto*. A woman who had slept with a *bôto*, it was generally believed, never slept with a man again. There was a stall in the market where dolphin perfume and amulets made from dolphins' genitals were sold to men who weren't having success with the opposite sex. The female counterpart of the *bôto* was the *mati-taperê*, the striped cuckoo, who at night became a woman dressed in black, seduced men, and sometimes conveniently transmitted venereal disease. There was also a collection of phantasms known as *visages* (a local corruption of *visagems*, Brazilian slang for 'spooks'), and near some falls upriver were a circle and a triangle of stones, which it was said, if disturbed, spontaneously moved back in place.

51

On the other side of the Trombetas there is a big lake called the Lago de Sapucuá, whose shores were thickly populated in late prehistoric times. Several frog *muiraqitãs* and many intriguing potsherds have been found there. The mayor's family was from the lake, and he was happy to put us in touch with the owner of a boat and to find us a guide from another Sapucuá family that seemed to work for him. As a parting gift he presented me with the bizarre ancient-looking ceramic object on the reception desk, which I had been admiring. In all I collected twenty-one such pieces, mostly animal figurines, from local people who attached no value to them (and in fact, though prehistoric, they have almost no monetary value, as no market has been established for them) and simply gave them to me as a gesture of friendship, like the postcards I handed out. They called them *caretas*, faces; archaeologists refer to them as *adornos*. I wrapped them in tissue and packed them carefully in a rusty rectangular kerosene can, and later back in New York I showed them to Anna Roosevelt, who dated all but perhaps one from somewhere between AD 500 and 1500. The styles of the pieces vary tremendously, from powerfully realistic to conventionalized beyond recognition; they are a 'multicomponent assemblage,' as Roosevelt described them. But they all belong to the 'incised-and-punctate horizon' of prehistoric South and Middle American pottery. A ceramic tradition is a series of styles that develop in one place and prevail there for a long time; a horizon is shorter-lived and spreads over a wide area. A horizon extends through space, while a tradition extends through time. Incised-and-punctate simply refers to the main ways the clay has been worked: by cutting and poking. This horizon is associated with chiefdoms, with people at an intermediate cultural stage, between the high civilization of the Andes, and the tropical-forest culture of Amazonia's remaining Indians. Animals were among their favourite subjects. The ceramic heads or faces of frogs, birds, bats, jaguars, monkeys, caymans, river turtles, small squirrel-like animals called agoutis, and other animals were typically attached to their dishes, jugs, bottles, and other vessels as handles or lugs, as wings, tabs, and nubbins. Some of these *adornos* are faithfully representational, others are stylized in the extreme, like miniature gargoyles. The incised-and-punctate horizon spreads over northern Amazonia, Venezuela, and Colombia, and into the Greater Antilles. A number of archaeologists believe that it originated in the Orinoco Valley. Within the horizon there is a lot of regional variation. The vessels that the Tapajós people, across the Amazon, were making just before contact were so lavishly and fancifully encrusted with *adornos* that the effect is almost rococo. In the lower Trombetas and Nhamundá valleys, and particularly along the shores of Lake Sapucuá, the people went in for minute punctation, and their *adornos* are stippled with numerous pits and short gashes. Counterintuitively, as the civilization of the chiefdoms became higher, the *adornos* became cruder and more sloppily made, because they were more mass-produced. There was obvious degeneration of the style.

The object on the mayor's reception desk consisted of four protuberances, each with a round hole at the end, that were suggestive, to me, at least, of bulging frog eyes, with an incised appliqué band between them. It seemed to be something that lived in the water, or perhaps it depicted the concept of things that lived in the water in general rather than a specific organism. 'What do you think? A highly conventionalized batrachian motif?' I asked Roosevelt. But the handsome, silver-haired woman was more interested in the gritty black texture of the clay. 'Sponge-spicule tempered,' she declared. 'A little freshwater sponge that is partial to black water was burned and crushed and mixed in the pottery as temper.'

The Lago de Sapucuá is thirty kilometres by six to eight —the largest expanse of open water in the soggy maze of lakes, islands, and interconnecting channels between the Trombetas and the Nhamundá, and one of the largest lakes in the state of Pará. A plausible derivation I heard in Oriximiná breaks down the toponym into *sapo* (frog) and *qua* (the sound of a frog croaking). By six the next morning we had set off for a tour of the *terras pretas*, the choice dwelling sites along the lake, capped with a foot or so of rich black soil, which are now inhabited by scattered families of *caboclos*, but until about the sixteenth century had been substantial settlements of Uaboi or Conduri people, about whom very little is known. Similar black-earth districts, the former dwelling places of the Tapajós people, are found along the right bank of the Amazon. Chemical analysis of *terra preta* samples has recently confirmed that the earth is in fact 'anthropogenic': its blackness is due to carbon staining from the ashes of centuries of fires, binding to the soil particles. Bits of pottery, particularly *caretas* usually litter the black-earth sites. There is even a ditty in the Trombetas-Nhamundá area, to the effect that wherever there are *terras pretas* you will find *caretas*.

Several theories have been proposed to account for the almost always fragmentary state of the pottery at these sites. Perhaps the Indians smashed their own wares ceremonially, perhaps at the climax of bacchanalian fertility rites. Among the present-day Caribs it is usual when a woman dies for whatever pottery she owned to be destroyed. The early missionaries are known to have destroyed a lot of the Indians' artifacts, particularly those that were associated with their beliefs. The early *caboclo* settlers may have wanted to obliterate the evidence of this extinct, intimidatingly alien and sophisticated civilization, whose dwelling places they were reoccupying (I can't see them going to the trouble, though); or perhaps they broke the pottery unintentionally in the course of digging up with their hoes the deep-rooted tubers of their manioc bushes. Another explanation, which an educated *caboclo* gave me, was that 'our ancestors the Indians broke everything when they were leaving.' But none of these theories is really necessary. 'Refuse pottery is always fragmentary,' Roosevelt argues. 'These *adornos* weren't firmly attached, and most of them probably just snapped off.'

It was an active hour for birds, and as we entered a channel known as the Paraná de Sapucuá, which is fed by the lake but is also one of the largest and straightest ducts of the Nhamundá, we saw silhouetted against the sky formations of ibises and large parrots and, on the highest branch of a dead tree, a pair of vigilant orange-billed toucans; and for a moment we were caught in a blizzard of monstrous green dragonflies. The boat was a lot smaller than our last one had been, and its crew was two withdrawn young brothers, Orlando and Francisco, with whom conversation during the next two days was minimal; our guide was an old fisherman named Antonio Gado. At the entrance to the lake we chugged up to the first *terra preta*, a settlement called Aimy, with about thirty inhabitants, most of them named Sousa. The smell of wood smoke, mixed with the fragrant

54

black resin of the *breu* tree, which a man was heating up to caulk his canoe with, was in the air. The history here was as obscure as it had been at previous stops. Nobody remembered a jade frog *muiraquitâ* that a woman from Aimy named Katita Arara had sold in the twenties to the great Brazilian anthropologist Curt Nimuendajú (who was later poisoned by some rubber gatherers because he had sided with some Indians in a land war). One old woman, though, had known Katita Arara, who was long gone; she was amazed when I produced the name (which I had found in Henry Wassen's fifty-year-old paper on the frog motif among South American Indians). She told us that according to her mother the Indians who had lived here stole children. I asked about the *bôto*. 'A woman who has been with the *bôto* slowly grows pale and dies,' she told us, 'unless she is treated by a spiritist with the help of certain leaves. The *bôto* can do the same thing to a man. He can come in your dreams.' A woman who lived nearby had had a baby who was 'spotted like a calf' and was considered to be a child of the *bôto*; so the porpoise, it seemed, was also used to explain illness and birth defects. The *mati-taperê*, she told us, came during the flood, 'whistling a seductive tune'; nobody at Aimy had actually seen her. The old woman gave me a *careta* which Roosevelt tentatively identified from the bump, or caruncle, on its maxilla, as the head of a king vulture. It was broken off at the neck, part of something bigger.

At Cabeceira de Ascensão, the next *terra preta*, an old man carrying a gun and a basket and skunked on *cachaça*—he had evidently had no luck hunting and had got drunk—embraced me, asked me to forgive him for his weakness, and then came out with what seemed to be a *caboclo* saw: 'The things that are no good for you are good for you.' The next site was of particular interest because it was called Cunuri—the name that keeps cropping up in connection with the Amazon women. Conori was Carvajal's queen, Cunuris was the first recorded name of the Nhamundá and the name of the first tribe that lived up the river in the seventeenth century. According to the Jesuit Mauricio de Heriarte, who arrived in this part of Amazonia in the sixteen-sixties, one of the tribes up the Trombetas was called the 'Conduris'; and a map drawn in 1691 by a

Bohemian missionary Father Samuel Fritz locates the 'Cunurizes' Indians at the site of present-day Obidos, which suggests that the Cunurizes had some connection with or maybe were even the same as the Pauxi. Another Jesuit, João Felipe Betendorf, briefly mentions in his *Cronica*, published in 1698, that one of his colleagues, Father Manoel de Souza, 'armed himself with all the sacraments' and went into a village of the 'barbarous Cunurizes,' and after persuading them to let him put up a few crosses, 'far from medical attention,' he died. The Cunurizes held his corpse in such reverence that they built a house for it. The only other thing Betendorf says about the Cunurizes is that they were 'continually diverted'.

In this century Nimuendajú classified as Conduri not only the prehistoric inhabitants of the Trombetas and Nhamundá valleys but people who lived on the other side of the Amazon, west of Santarém, where he found the same sort of stippled, amusingly grotesque *adornos*. The Conduri sometimes lived on low flat-topped mountains, but most of them settled along lakeshores. Another Brazilian ethnologist, João Barbosa Faria, classified the prehistoric people of the Trombetas-Nhamundá region as the Uaboi and called their ceramic style 'the style of the lakes.' He was referring to more or less the same people.

The meaning of the name variously transliterated as Conori, Cunuris, and Conduri can only be guessed at, as the language of these people was never recorded. But the sounds are suggestive. Taylor's Portuguese-English dictionary gives the primary meaning of *cunha* as 'an Indian or half-breed girl.' Cuña Muchu is (according to Hemming) Quechua for 'Great Lady.' 'Conduri' has a typically Quechua ending and is close to the Quechua word for condor; and à propos of the connection between the Amazon women and frogs, one can't help noticing how similar the Indian name of the Amazonian tree frog *Hyla venulosa*—*cunuauaru*—is. The croaking of this frog, which figures in many Indian myths, is furthermore supposed to sound like *cunha cunha*.

The Serra de Cunuri, which had been visible in the distant northwest from Oriximiná, rises to a little over three hundred feet. We asked a local *caboclo* to take us to the top. He led us through scrubby pasture, shooing emaciated zebu cattle, which kicked up the black dust of *terra preta* as they trotted off. The *terra preta* here was vast. It went back more than a mile from the lakeshore and stopped just below the summit of the *serra*, where it gave way to the infertile red upland soil typical of roughly ninety-eight per cent of the Amazon Valley. Concurrently with this transition, the going got rough. The final rise became steep, and the vegetation became impenetrable grass towering over our heads. After fifty feet of flailing with machetes in the nostril-searing midday heat, we decided to take our guide's word that there was nothing up there. Nothing was going to be learned here, in any case, without digging, and that required time, training in modern stratigraphic archaeology, and permits, none of which we had. Very little up-to-date archaeology, in fact very little methodical excavation of any kind, has been done in the Amazon. No Conduri site has been systematically dug. The best study of Conduri pottery, published by Peter Paul Hilbert in 1955 (in it Hilbert identifies eleven separate distinguishing features), was based on 'surface finds,' like the *caretas* we had been given. Our *caretas* would be worthless for many types of analysis, because we only knew the rough locale where they had allegedly been found. A methodical dig here, for instance—this *terra preta* was a prime candidate—might reveal when the incised-and-punctate horizon had arrived and how the Conduri had developed their idiosyncratic version of it. The presence of trade beads in the same layer as *caretas* would establish that the Conduri had retained their style after contact, like the Shipibo of the Upper Amazon, who to this day continue to make pottery in their prehistoric 'polychrome' horizon. If bones were found, the Conduri could be compared genetically, through their crania and teeth, with other groups, and this would yield data on migration. Their bone chemistry could be analyzed, as Roosevelt has done with prehistoric skeletons from the Middle Orinoco, to find out whether corn or manioc had been the Conduri's staple, and how much meat and fish, as opposed to plant food, they had eaten. 'Only when you plant corn can you be an agriculturist fully,' Roosevelt explained. 'Manioc is not sufficient as a dietary protein. It has to be supplemented with hunting and fishing, and this has a dispersing effect on social organization.

'A large cemetery would probably reveal whether the Conduri had been stratified,' she continued. 'One would

57

look for differences in how the bodies had been buried and for "differential access to resources"—whether some had eaten better than others, which would be evident from differences in body size and in the condition of the teeth; teeth present a complete health record to those who know what to look for.' A large cemetery with only well-nourished, elaborately buried female skeletons would of course be the jackpot.

By studying what is known about comparable cultures, it is possible to make educated guesses at what the Conduri were like. They probably had a lot in common with their neighbours and contemporaries the Tapajós, with whom they seem to have been in close contact; Conduri pottery is common at Santarém *terras pretas*. The Tapajós, we know from the descriptions of seventeenth- and eighteenth-century missionaries, lived in villages of up to five hundred families. They were heavily into trading. They worshipped painted idols, the sun, and the moon. The eighteenth-century missionary João Daniel once watched a group of Tapajós rush out of one of their big wattle-and-daub houses and greet the new moon with upraised hands, as if asking for its blessings. Corn was the staple, and a portion of the harvest was taken to the house of the corn goddess Aura (or the Devil, as the missionaries refer to her) to be made into wine, which was stored in great jars and drunk at weekly festivals in a jungle clearing where drums and trumpets were played mournfully and everybody danced into frenzy. The dried bodies of important ancestors were hoisted up to roof beams and left suspended there for years, and on certain occasions their ashes were drunk. There was a definite noble class. Polygny was practiced by the men who could afford more than one wife. Descent was reckoned matrilineally, and a woman chosen from the high nobility was consulted as an oracle—the hereditary elite was starting to acquire a religious aura. (It is easy to see how a similarly matrilineal society across the river might have been misconstrued as a 'republic of Amazons' by Europeans with no understanding of tribal kinship. But there is a big difference between matriliny, which is still for the benefit of men, and matriarchy.) And as ancestors and individuals were venerated, human figures became more prominent in the art of the Tapajós. Plump female images surrounded by many children, touching their tummies or pubic areas; male images clutching their erect phalluses, emphasized sex and fertility and reflected the populationist ethic of an expanding chiefdom.

The Tapajós had slaves before they were themselves enslaved. They tipped their arrows with curare and were thus able to forestall their own downfall until the slavers had finished preying on less well-defended tribes. By the end of the eighteenth century they had died out in the pattern common throughout the valley—from European diseases and absorption as much as from enslavement—and the last Tapajós took sanctuary in the inaccessible depths of the forest above the rapids of the river that bears their name, where they regressed to the hunting-and-gathering way of life and eventually resurfaced as or merged with the Mundurucu. The fate of the Conduri seems to have been similar, except that their extinction took place some decades later. If they can be equated with the Uaboi, they fled up the Nhamundá and became the Hixkaryana; after 1850 nothing is heard about them.

The best description of the Indians who were living on the Trombetas in the seventeenth century, including the Conduri, is from the Jesuit Heriarte. Neither sex wore clothing. They grew more manioc and less corn than the Tapajós did, and they penned the huge river turtles that came to nest by the millions on the sandy banks of the Trombetas when the river was down. Manatees would have been abundant in the morass between the Trombetas and the Nhamundá, and their meat would have been important. The local clay was good for making pottery, and the beautiful wares they made (we don't know whether still in the incised-and-punctate horizon) were esteemed by the Portuguese and used for trade to other tribes. The Trombetas had been so named by the Portuguese 'because of the great number of trumpets used by the natives in their ceremonies and drinking festivals,' the archaeologist Helen C. Palmatary tells us.

The incised-and-punctate horizon spread over the whole circumcaribbean area, which during the last centuries before contact was broken up into numerous warring chiefdoms. A chiefdom, in Herbert Spencer's typology of pre-industrial political organization, is a 'compound' society; it is a group of villages that are no longer independent but have come under the leadership of a paramount chief. The anthropologist Robert L Carneiro has written that 'supercommunity aggregation'—the step from autonomous villages to chiefdoms—'took two million years to achieve. But . . . once village autonomy was transcended, only two or three millennia were required for the rise of great empires and the flourishing of complex civilizations.' The earliest chiefdoms, in Mesopotamia, only go back to about 5500 BC. By no later than 1000 BC the Greeks were surrounded by warlike chiefdoms including the ones that inspired the classic Amazon-women myth. The evolution of chiefdoms in the Amazon Valley was a comparatively late development—perhaps no earlier than the first centuries of the Christian era, Carneiro told me recently. The first humans in the valley had only arrived roughly ten thousand years earlier, and their cultural level seems to have been primitive. The chiefdoms in the Amazon were mainly distributed along the *várzea*. As the prehistoric population grew, competition for the narrow band of fertile land became increasingly fierce. Villages were conquered by other villages and were either gutted or allowed to stand at a price— subordination—and this, Carneiro maintains, is how chiefdoms arose. The population of the valley at contact may have exceeded six million people, some of whom, like the Tapajós and to some extent the Conduri, lived in large sedentary chiefdoms on or near the floodplain of the Amazon or its tributaries. Some of these chiefdoms were on the verge of becoming states; they were 'maximal chiefdoms,' in Carneiro's term. The Omagua chiefdom extended ninety leagues, according to Cristóbal de Acuña, and on the Mojos plain of Bolivian Amazonia there were a hundred thousand square miles of raised fields and causeways. No one knows what heights the Conduri may have reached in the centuries before contact. The abundance and the sophistication of their pottery suggest that they got to be stratified, or at least specialized. It seems likely that some of them were excused from food production and allowed to devote themselves to turning out wacky *caretas*. They don't seem to have gotten into serious earthmoving or construction—mound building and the like—yet. But this *terra preta* was vast. It could have accommodated at least three thousand and maybe as many as ten thousand people. A settlement of ten thousand people is regarded as a city. This must have been one of their main centres, but you would never know that now.

On the way back down we passed through an acre or so swarm of gigantic black grasshoppers. They were longer than my first finger, with green stripes on their abdominal segments and a red accent on either side of their heads—another species for the long list of Amazonian hyperboles. We watched as several dozen of them soundlessly chewed up, leaf by leaf, a plant they had landed on.

Farther along the lake's north shore an old man offered to sell his spread, which included a rubber grove. 'I've been here for thirty years,' he called back as with a spry, teetering bowlegged gait he led us among the diagonally scored *Hevea* trees. 'I want to move from here. I'm getting old.' 'Where to?' I asked. 'Near the cemetery.' Back in his outdoor kitchen, he gave us three different kinds of citrus, the last of which burned the inside of my mouth; then in response to a question about the *bôto*, he launched into a story. 'When I was single I was turning a *tracajá* [the second-largest species of river turtle] on the beach. I looked up and saw a man heading into the nearby swamp. My dogs went after him and dragged him down into the water, and he turned into a *bôto* and swam away.' The eyes and mouths of his grandchildren, who had crowded around the table, were wide open. 'When the *bôto* turns into a man,' he went on, 'the first thing he does is stuns the woman so she can't move. Then he does what he wants. When the woman revives, she turns yellow. Takes her blood, the *bôto* does. If you don't kill him while he's on land, as a man, the woman dies. His children are born crazy, writhing, screaming, with a hole on top of their head just like his blowhole.'

Quersin, who had been taking hundreds of pictures of *caboclo* life, marvelled at its isolation. Most of the *caboclos* along the lake lived in small extended-family groups, often miles from the nearest neighbor, or in larger settlements of several related families—not quite a village, but a *povoado-zinho*, 'a little place that has been peopled.' Rural Africans are much more gregarious. It was puzzling that such prime habitat, fertile, full of fish and game, should be so thinly populated.

At dusk we pulled up to the dock of a friend of Antonio Gado's named João Bente and asked if we could spend the night. Bente's hut was out on a point at the mouth of Angels' Creek. It was lonely and idyllic, like the lone-hut-in-the-jungle Amazon scenes that are standard décor in bars and restaurants throughout Brazil. As we got out, the mosquitoes launched a massive attack, and we underwent several minutes of hell, with heatless flames. They were probably Anopheles mosquitoes, which can transmit malaria by passing on the blood of previously bitten people with the disease. We were taking weekly pills prophylactically against the two main types of malaria, *Plasmodium vivax* and *P falciparum*, but there didn't seem to be much malaria around at the moment. Bente had been drinking and was at first belligerent, but this gradually turned, with his wife's entreaties, into aggressive hospitality. It ended with us sleeping at his insistence in their bedroom, while they slung their hammocks in the hall. He was forty-four, and the thumb and first two fingers of his right hand were gnarled and paralyzed. A long time ago he had been bitten by a bushmaster. 'I was working for this citizen across the river,' he told us. 'Taking care of his cattle. It was February. We came back late that night. We had been dancing Carnaval. My wife had just had a baby, so I had to sleep outside in the kitchen. Our little dog curled up under my hammock. In the middle of the night I was awakened by its cries. I reached down to see what the matter was—and it was then that I was bitten. For twenty-four hours I was in a coma. I had a hundred and twenty injections, one a day.' A hundred and twenty was unquestionably stretching it.

That night, Friday the thirteenth, the moon was full, and the lake and the smooth gray *terra preta* of the clearing were flooded with its light. A limpkin kept calling its Brazilian name, *carão*, tirelessly, over and over, all night long, but there was a curious absence of frogs.

In the morning we chugged along to a place called Mafada, where a white *cabocla* with auburn hair and light brown eyes—she looked Irish—unearthed near her pigpen with a few scrapes of a hoe the weathered *careta* of a bird, to show how easy they were to find. We made our way over to the Lago de Pirarucuá, a smaller lake to the southwest, crossed it, and entered a blackwater channel that was not much wider than the boat but went on for several hours. It was lined with flooded *jauari* palms whose segmented trunks bristled with black needles. Several times one had fallen in the way, and we had to stop as Orlando hacked out a passage; or grass had fouled the propeller, and Francisco would have to dive under the boat and take it off. The brothers' teamwork—with Orlando yanking the bell cord and Francisco accelerating, reversing, or cutting the engine in response—was smooth and tight. At one point the channel opened into a pool, and we came upon an osprey who had just caught a large fish and had risen with it in its claws high above the pool. Suddenly it went into a steep dive, with its wings folded at sharp angles, and buzzed its mate, who was sitting on a dead branch. Its mate rose up and they both flew off together. Late in the morning we reached the town of Terra Santa, on a beautiful blackwater lake in what was clearly the Nhamundá delta.

There had been an outbreak of yellow fever a few months earlier in one of Terra Santa's outlying communities. Six of the thirteen confirmed cases had been fatal, and a rash of psychosomatic cases—people with colds thinking they had come down with it—had followed. The Amazonian health agency SUCAM had vaccinated the population and sprayed houses to kill the Aëdes mosquitoes that transmit the virus. Several years earlier, SUCAM had stopped spraying because it thought that yellow fever, which took thousands of lives in the Amazon during the last century, had been eradicated; but this year the virus had reappeared in several remote communities here and across the river. A specialist had come from France to investigate the outbreak in Terra Santa. He had stayed at the Loureiros' house, which was in fact the only lodgings in town, and he had been the last foreign visitor, we were told by a short dark woman named Joselia Loureiro who showed us to a room where we could hang our hammocks. Joselia's father, a demolitions man, was working for the bauxite mines up the Trombetas, and she was running the household. Besides taking in guests— her dream was to open a real hotel in a couple of years— Joselia sold clothing, shoes, and other articles in the front room. By evening we had got to know each other well enough for me to ask her why, at thirty-four, she had never married. 'Better single than badly accompanied,' she said. 'The men here have no means. A man would ruin in a year the business it has taken me five to build up.' As in Zaire, where the women's *petit commerce* is the real economic life of the country, the women of Amazonia are often more practical and hard-working than the men, and it is often they who keep the family together. The lineage that mattered in Joselia's pedigree went through her mother and her mother's mother to her great-grandparents, who had eloped to Terra Santa from a town farther up the Amazon Valley because both of their parents had been against the marriage; successive generations of daughters had established the family here. With many women functioning without men—raising families, running businesses, and never marrying—it struck me how much modern Amazonian society itself functions like a society of Amazons.

When Joselia heard that we wanted to go up the Nhamundá, she decided to help us; she knew it would be hard to find a boat and provisions in Faro or Nhamundá, the towns still fifteen miles to the west, above the point where the Nhamundá begins to break up into many channels. Our plan was to go up the river at least as far as the first rapids—about two hundred miles. Joselia introduced us to a man named Emir Dantona who had spent a month the year before exploring the Nhamundá and its tributaries for gold and diamonds. Dantona had taken an outboard instead of a *motor*, and he said that with three hundred litres of gas we could get to the first rapids and back. An outboard, he went on, had many advantages: You could make side trips up creeks and into oxbow lakes, and travel at twice the speed.

Joselia arranged for us to rent at a nominal daily fee the municipal outboard, which was aluminum, seated six, and had ADMINISTRATION OF TEODORO LOBATO stencilled on the side. Her younger brother João, a currently unemployed gold prospector, was interested in going along. 'Fantastico,' I said. But João had never been up the Nhamundá, so we would have to find somebody in Faro or Nhamundá who knew the river. Dantona recommended his guide, a man in Faro named Preginho.

We would need to carry drums of gas. While João went to arrange them, Joselia took us to a friend who sold dry goods and supplied us with eight kilos of rice, four of ground and roasted manioc *farinha*, two of salt, six of sugar, three hundred oranges, a dozen limes, six bottles of Armadillo brand *cachaça*, two cans of cooking oil, ten cans of meat-and-bean *feijoada*, three hundred grams of seasoning, a dozen tins of sardines, two packets of coffee, six of tobacco, some thick monofilament line, a dozen double-O fishhooks, and two wide-brimmed straw hats. Another man lent us a map of the Nhamundá which he had drawn. It was

64

much more detailed than our more reliable map, based on high-altitude infrared photographs. It named the major bends, creeks, and settlements and was helpful for about the first hundred miles, then it became increasingly sketchy.

After we had got our supplies, Dantona invited us to a bar. The pharmacist's son, he was mainly of Italian descent and was several heads taller than most Terra Santans. He was thirty and had gone to high school in Belém, then travelled all over Brazil. About a year ago his mother had fallen ill and he had returned to Terra Santa to take care of her. Earlier in the year he had founded a weekly newspaper called *Solidarity*, which was now in its sixteenth edition. The padre let him run it off on his mimeograph machine. Its circulation was two hundred and fifteen. 'The population of Terra Santa is about seventy-five hundred, living in about a thousand houses, not to mention hundreds of street dogs. They just shot thirty dogs yesterday,' he told us. 'We have five dancing clubs and a hundred and twenty-five *festas* during the year, sometimes three a week. In January there is the feast of St Sebastian for two weeks, then in February and March pre-Carnaval and Carnaval. May is the month of flowers. June has the June festival. July is the feast of St Isabel, the patron saint of Terra Santa. Each outlying community and creek mouth has its saint.

'There are two cars, four horse carts, four boatbuilders, two soccer fields, one grandstand, six football teams, one youth club, one mothers' club, and only about twenty people you can carry on a conversation with in Terra Santa. The culture here is twenty-thirty years ago. Everybody is in the same class. There is no discrimination as there is, say, in Oriximiná. People with better income send their children to Belém, Manaus, or Parintis [the nearest big city, out the delta and across the Amazon, about four hours by boat] for high school, and they don't usually come back, so there isn't much influx of new ideas. Everybody is a known entity. The television reception is unpredictable, so the main entertainment for grownups is gossip, and for children a soccer ball and a fishing line. Sex starts at twelve.'

The year before, Telepara, the state telecommunications franchise, had installed a telephone in Terra Santa, and it was now possible to call anywhere in Brazil or, by satellite, in the world. When he heard this Quersin went to see if he

65

could reach his wife, who lives in a village in Vaucluse, France. It was her birthday.

Dantona told us that he had been to the Lake of the Mirror of the Moon. It wasn't far above Faro, on the right bank, and under a mountain. 'It isn't very big,' he went on, 'just a few hundred yards across. The day I saw it there was no ventilation, and the water was dead calm, full of leaves, and pretty dirty. As I understand it, it was called the Lake of the Mirror of the Moon because the Indians used to make up their faces in it before ceremonies.'

Dantona took us to see a woman who had several dozen *caretas*, which she said we were welcome to. When the lake went down, she would walk along the shore and find some more. We chose nine. They were all rim sherds—lugs or nubbins in the form of birds, a cayman with open jaws, what looked like a pig with a stylized snout. Roosevelt later pointed out the difference between the head of a bird of prey, whose style was so definite, almost institutional, that it had to be early—perhaps AD 500—and the much more sloppily made possible pig, whose head was perforated with crude parallel gouges—a far more recent piece, from when the horizon was decadent. My favourite piece was an 'everted rim composite,' as Roosevelt called it, made up of a froglike puckered mouth and bulging left eye and, instead of a right eye, two eyes on either side of a reduced human face—a neutral mask, neither smiling nor frowning, that had been pasted on. I asked if there were any more *caretas* in Terra Santa. Nobody could think of any, but Dantona had an idea. He went away and in a few minutes the municipal music ('Bridge Over Troubled Waters') stopped and his voice came over the loudspeakers inviting anyone with *caretas* to bring them in twenty minutes to the Ara Bar to be analyzed. Only one person came, a shy teen-aged boy with a statue of a frog, which he had glued to a wooden stand, then he had decorated the edges of the stand with zigzag lines of blue ball point-pen ink and written 'Souvenir of Terra Santa' on it in Portuguese. He said that he had found the statue in the street and washed it off. Dantona held it up. 'The artist who made this must have been genial,' he said. Sitting with its hands on its knees, the frog was two and a half inches high. Both it and its seat were riddled with punctations. It wore a crown and above the crown there was a hole that went all the way down to the statue's base and another hole at its navel. Thomas Cummins, to whom I described the piece over the telephone, said it sounded like a *paccha*, a fecundity statue, often in the form of a frog, used by various Peruvian water cults, which spouted at the navel water poured into the top of the head. This was not a rim sherd, but a complete statue, perhaps some kind of idol—a frog king, perhaps. Roosevelt pointed out that there was no way to tell what sex it was.

The boy just gave me the statue. He wouldn't even let me buy him a Coke.

The town of Faro started as a mission for the Uaboi Indians, who as we have seen had fled from the missionaries in the Trombetas Valley, and in 1742, when La Condamine passed through, were led by a chief named Jamundas, for whom the Frenchman renamed the river. By 1749, if not earlier, other missionaries—Capuchins of the Order of Piety—had caught up with the Uaboi and had collected them, along with the local Cunuris, Chereues, Paracoiana, and Paracuata, into a compound called St John the Baptist of the Lighthouse, which in time was simplified to Lighthouse (Faro). The colony functioned smoothly for the rest of the century. Its agricultural projects prospered, and it went from a religious to a secular community with two classes—the nobility and the people. But in 1798, new 'draconian regulations,' enforced by frequent use of a pillory, were imposed; and three years later the Uaboi bolted en masse upriver. Small groups of Uaboi occasionally came down to Faro for certain festivals until 1840, but after that nothing more is heard of them. A century later the missionary-ethnologist Protasio Frikel asked some Hixkaryana, whom he was visiting on the Upper Nhamundá, if they knew what had become of the Uaboi; they laughed and answered, 'That is who we are.' A short list of Uaboi words compiled before they withdrew from colonial Brazil is 'basically identical''with present-day Hixkaryana, according to Desmond Derbyshire, who attributes the differences to 'weaknesses in elicitation and transcription techniques.'

From 1837–38 Faro was occupied by rebels called *cabanas* who had seceded from Brazil and declared Pará a sovereign state. It was a bloody conflict. Forty-five thousand people were killed in Belém. The nobility and the landowners in and around Faro buried their valuables and fled upriver. This disturbance had a further dispersing effect on the local Indians.

The Faro that Barbosa Rodriguez found in 1878 was so depressed and demoralized that he was moved to compare it in Latin with the '*campus ubi Troya fuit.*' From a distance, as he came up the river in a long dugout manned by ten *caboclos*, Faro presented 'a most agreeable aspect.' Its setting, with a view across miles of water to hilly country on the other side, was spectacular, but when he got out and walked the town's three parallel streets, he found twenty-one of the seventy-five houses he counted (all but twelve of which were crudely made thatched huts) in ruins and many others abandoned. The walls of the church were crumbling, and the municipal chambers were in such a precarious state that the local administrators had been holding their meetings in a private home. There were only five commercial establishments, two run by outsiders. The inhabitants— about a hundred in town and three thousand four hundred and forty-six scattered over the municipality—were 'disanimated'; they lived by fishing and raising cattle and couldn't be interested in growing anything. Coffee was a luxury item.

Barbosa Rodriguez was unable to find anybody on the lower Nhamundá who remembered the 'women without husbands' or was even familiar with the term for them in lingua geral—*icamiabas*—and he succeeded in picking up only one story about them—from a ninety-year-old woman in Faro named Felicia, the daughter of a Paracoiana with a Chereue, who told him that the women without husbands got their *muiraquitãs*, which they gave to the men who fathered their children, from the Lago Jacyuaruá, the Lake of the Mirror of the Moon; the *muiraquitãs* were alive, Felicia said, swimming around in the form of various animals. When a woman saw a *muiraquitã* that she wanted, she would cut herself and let her blood drip into the water over the creature, which would stun it, and as she brought it up into the air it would turn to stone.

In the century between Rodriguez's visit and now, Faro continued to stagnate in its beautiful setting. At one point the urban population seems to have fallen to twelve. During the thirties a family of Germans named Rossy, who had emigrated to São Paulo in the previous generation, came up to Faro and began to harvest the woods of the Nhamundá

Valley, especially *pau-rosa*, or rosewood, a tree in the laurel family whose essential oil is an expensive raw material of some perfumes. The Rossys employed many people at their sawmill, and the town became dependent on them. But by 1970 the *pau-rosa* was gone, and Mario Rossy, one of the sons, moved the sawmill across the Amazon to Parintins, and Faro went into decline again. In the early seventies a comprehensive survey of the Amazon Valley by the Brazilian Projeto RADAM described Faro, rather optimistically, as 'a stagnant town making a comeback.'

The next morning João, Quersin, and I set out for Faro in the municipal outboard. A series of grass-choked channels led from the labyrinthine delta of the Nhamundá into the river's lower section, which seemed like a vast lake and is in fact known as the Lago de Faro. Like most of the lower Amazon's tributaries, the Nhamundá is a 'drowned river' for some distance from its mouth. As sea level rose on the order of three hundred feet at the end of the last Ice Age, around ten thousand years ago, the Nhamundá's water backed up and flooded its valley, as if its mouth had been dammed to create an artificial reservoir.

As we came up the Lago de Faro we saw two canoes under sail. The sails were square and red and they were rigged on one or two masts. One man paddled at the bow while another, at the stern, held his paddle as a rudder. The Lago de Faro is one of the last places in the Amazon where these craft, which are known as *igarités*, haven't been displaced by boats with engines. Continuous strong breezes and poverty have delayed their disappearance here. On the left bank beyond the canoes, as austere in its monumental surroundings as an alpine village, was Faro.

Knowing that the mayor of Faro was away, Joselia had written a letter to the vice-mayor, Roduval Machado, identifying us as 'researchers' and asking him to put us up on the second floor of the municipal building, as there were no lodgings in the town. Machado, a languid young man with a pencil mustache, turned out to be one of half a dozen men standing at the dock. The municipal building, a couple of feet away, was actually a residence of some vintage which the municipality was renting until the new municipal building, under construction next door—the main undertaking of the administration of Teodoro Lobato—was ready. The floor of the room to which Machado took us was

69

littered with bat droppings which had fallen through a large hole in the ceiling. 'We don't get many foreigners,' Machado told us as the custodian swept them up. 'Six years ago, I think, two Germans came looking for a tree that flowers blue in October.'

When he learned what we were after, Machado said, 'I am in doubt about the Amazons.' As he understood it, the women had made up their faces in the Lake of the Mirror of the Moon, and according to an account he had read by a Frenchman who claimed to have been captured by them and held as their sexual slave (earlier in this century, as he recalled), they had gone in for headshrinking. 'Old man Rossy had a plantation on top of the mountain overlooking the lake,' he went on, 'and he drained the lake to see if there were any *muiraquitâs* in it. I don't know if he found any. There is supposed to have been another, smaller lake on top of the mountain, but I walked the length of it one time and didn't find a thing. There is also a story about a spring there that gushes out of a stone and never dries and has brilliant golden fish in it. I didn't find that, either.'

I asked Machado what the population of Faro was and he said he didn't know offhand; he'd have to look it up. I asked if he could do that, and he said the problem was he didn't know where the vital statistics were kept. 'Where are the vital statistics?' he asked one of the men with him, sounding a little put out. 'I think the padre has them,' the man said. A boy was despatched to the church. Fifteen minutes later the boy returned with a message from the padre: 'What makes you think I have them?' Eventually the vital statistics were turned up—at the hospital—and they revealed a 1981 total of 4,635, 2,234 of whom were 'urban'—hardly any more people than Faro had had a century ago. The place had stood still economically, too; we saw no sign of a 'comeback.' The fifty registered business establishments were mostly bars; the pharmacy was the sorriest-looking one I had seen in Brazil. Bates's adjectives 'clean' and 'cheerful' were not applicable here. 'Faro is isolated,' Machado explained. 'It has poor communication with the rest of the world. The few people with means here invest their money elsewhere. The municipality itself is broke; what little money comes from Brasília has to be shared with the four other good-sized communities in its jurisdiction, including Terra Santa; we are the "poor father," and there are no aluminum revenues,

70

such as Oriximiná has, either. The Indian influence here is predominant. A lot of people have no initiative, and for those with initiative there is nothing to do.' Dantona had said there was a lot of drunkenness, stealing, and prostitution in Faro, and that people here weren't above asking for handouts, which never happened in Terra Santa.

João who had gone to find Dantona's guide, the man named Preginho, returned with him. Preginho was a short carpenter (preginho means 'little nail'); he said he was busy and unable to go with us but had taken the liberty of asking his brother, who had said he could and would meet us in the morning. Preginho seemed trustworthy (unlike, say, Machado), so it seemed safe to assume that we would be in good hands with his brother. This settled, we went back down the lake for several miles to the town of Nhamundá to top off the fuel supply (this being our 'last chance for gas') and to see a man named Nogueira, who lived in a floating store permanently moored at the Nhamundá dock and who was said to own a frog muiraquitã. Nhamundá is on the Amazonas side of the river and is about the same size as Faro. It seemed in better shape; Machado had explained that Amazonas has forty municipalities to Parás eighty-six, so it can do more for them.

Nogueira's merchandise took up two storys of a large motor and spilled over into an adjacent barge (a third story was living quarters for him and his family). There were sacks of rice, beans, and farinha; dried and salted slabs of enormous primitive fish called pirarucu; rope, shoes, hats, fresh eggs, hoses, candy; a pharmacy in one cabin with all kinds of colourfully packaged medicine, some no longer considered safe in the countries that had developed and introduced them; lots of mestiço children and grandchildren running around; a bar, a restaurant; a dozen full-time employees; another half-dozen men snoozing on railings with straw or leather hats pulled down over their eyes; two guitarists playing chorinhos, an extravagantly romantic, highly syncopated type of Brazilian music. Life on Nogueira's boat seemed like a continuous party. I bought a kilo of onions, the first greens we had seen since Oriximiná, and Quersin bought a black rubber slingshot to drive the pigeons from his roof when he got back to Zaire. We found Nogueira, a blithe-spirited man in the white uniform of a pharmacist, and the young mayor of Nhamundá, a sullen sometime bush pilot, sitting in sun-deck chairs at the prow. He told us that he lived on a boat 'for philosophical reasons' and that his *muiraquitã* was frog-formed and smoky grey. 'It came into my hands in 1964. I traded for it.' He couldn't show it to us, he said, because it was in a safe in Belém.

Back in Faro we met a shoemaker who hadn't made a pair of shoes in several years and seemed to personify the indolence of the place. 'I have no leather or tanning equipment,' he complained, 'because I have no customers.' Seeing our onions, he asked for some. I told him we needed the onions for our trip, but that João was going to have to make another trip to Nhamundá to make some last-minute purchases from Nogueira—some suntan oil, a dozen shotgun shells, four more cans of outboard motor oil—and he could pick some up for him, but either this was too complicated for the shoemaker, or he didn't have the money, and he desisted.

In the morning we met Preginho's brother waiting at the dock with a shotgun and a ditty bag. He introduced himself as Edson Carvalho, but in fact, as we would discover, to everybody up the river he was known by his Indian name, Songa. He was Satere-Maué on his mother's side and he had grown up on the other side of the Amazon in one of the tribe's villages up the Andira River. He and Preginho were not real brothers; they had been brought up in the same family, but they had no blood in common, and they looked nothing like each other. Songa was thirty-three, quiet, handsome, of medium height, strong-looking, and no more Indian in appearance than the average *caboclo*. Other than these qualities, he communicated nothing about himself. In the eight days we were together, I came no closer to understanding what motivated him, what he thought about us, or about anything.

With a fourth person in the boat now, it rode very low, and even as João turned the accelerator handle down to full throttle and held it there, it went very slowly through the water. We ascended the lake at a diagonal and started to go up along the Amazonas side. After ten miles or so we had to stop and transfer gas from one of the large plastic drums to the smaller metal can that fed the engine. We stepped out into warm black water that was so inviting Quersin and I sank into it. Our submerged limbs were amber, and the acidity of the water stung our eyes. Its color came, like tea, from having been steeped in dead leaves, and it had passed through sand instead of more soluble sediments that would have discolored it. The shore here was clean white sand in which a low, dry type of forest known as *campina*, bristling with branches and festooned with air plants—orchids, bromeliads, ferns—managed to grow. A cashew tree planted fifteen years earlier, when the *serra* above was being explored for bauxite, had already acquired the massive girth that a white oak in New England, say, has only after a century or two. Songa told us that a man had been murdered on the *serra* and thrown into one of the test holes. I asked what for. Money, he said. Nearby a hidden bird—one of the six brilliantly coloured species of trogon—kept calling; the sound usurped the silence as completely as the pulsing shrieks of a police car.

After skirting for several hours a series of low, flat-topped, east-west-trending *serras* that broke off at the water's edge and were spattered with violet-blossomed Tabebuia trees, we approached the Serra do Espelho, the Mountain of the Mirror, the seat of the women-without-husbands myth for at least the last hundred years. It was no higher and no more conspicuous than the earlier *serras* of the series; from afar it gave no indication how it had attracted this reputation. On the bank below the mountain a man named Chico de Brita was standing before his hut. Songa shouted to him that we had come to see the lake and would stop to see him on the way back, and we entered a channel that came into the river just below his hut.

After about a hundred yards the channel widened into a pool that doglegged to the right. The pool was maybe two hundred yards in diameter, and as Dantona had said, it was still, murky, and full of leaves. So this was it. I wouldn't have even called it a lake; to me it was a pond (a *lago* in Portuguese can be a pond as well as a lake). The French explorer Henri Coudreau, who went up the Nhamundá in 1899 with his wife Olga, described it, with understandable exasperation, as a *mauvais petit lac*. 'If the Amazons discovered or invented by Señor Orellana and cultivated by so many lovers of the marvellous ever manufactured the sacred stone [i.e., the *muiraquitã*] and invoked the moon from the borders of this *mauvais petit lac*,' he wrote in his journal, 'it must be well recognized that time has completely effaced all trace of their passage.'

Coudreau asked the local people if they remembered Barbosa Rodriguez, who had visited the lake twenty years earlier and had found no trace of the women or the stones either. They had no memory of him, and they themselves had never seen a *muiraquitã* and had only heard of the amulet from 'people who came from the city.' In the early fifties the archaeologist Peter Paul Hilbert climbed the Serra do Espelho and reported that it was a hundred and twenty-four metres high and was capped by a small shallow expanse of *terra preta*, suggesting a settlement of only a few huts—a seasonal farming community, perhaps, occupied during planting and harvest time. For some reason he did not investigate the shores of the lake. We discovered more *terra preta*, covered by half-dead bacaba palm and hard-wood forest, on the north shore. It was not extensive, as it ran up almost immediately against the flank of the *serra*, which was too steep for settlement—hardly enough for a 'republic of Amazons.' The opposite shore of the lake was being farmed by Chico de Brito, whom, as there was nothing more to be learned without digging, we went to talk to.

Chico de Brito was a sun-beaten, grizzled man of about fifty. He had been living at Espelho for twenty years. His wife and seven of their progeny, in two generations, were with him now. A metal sign next to the door of their hut said MALARIA NOTIFICATION STATION. One of his sons, De Brito explained, had been instructed how to draw blood; the samples went to Parintins for analysis. But the results and the medication would take weeks to arrive, he admitted, by which time the patient might have already died. 'Sometimes malaria appears, but it is difficult,' he said. A severe outbreak just across the river in the eighteenth century had forced the inhabitants of the original Faro mission of the Uaboi to move down to its present site.

De Brito showed us thirty-two scars on his legs and proceeded to describe how he had got them. 'I was cutting a vine to weave a basket for carrying manioc a hundred yards downstream. My son and I had already killed two collared peccary. I said let's go hunt the big white-lipped ones. So we did. I saw one, fired at it, and it ran off wounded. Suddenly we were surrounded by a herd of them clacking their tusks in anger. There were four hundred of them—a city of them. I dropped my gun and scrambled up a tree. My son jumped into another one. But my tree was small and rotten. It snapped and sent me into the middle of them. The pigs went crazy. I'm lucky to be alive.

'When I got here, Fran Rossy was already dead. He's buried up on the *serra*, where his house was. He wouldn't let anybody up there. They say he had a shortwave radio. During the war two Germans visited him and left him a boat.' We had heard in Obidos that a U-boat had gone up the Jari, a left-bank tributary of the Amazon closer to its mouth, and that one of the crew had died of fever and was buried under a cross with his name and serial number on a *serra* overlooking the river. The discreet Nazi presence is another unwritten chapter in the history of the valley.

De Brito took us over to the edge of his yard, where we could see a green pool, maybe fifty yards across, through the trees. 'Is this the spring with the golden fish?' I asked. De Brito said it was, but that he had never seen any of them himself. 'But Rossy found a lot of *muiraquitãs* in there,' he claimed, contradicting what Machado had told us. I asked De Brito if he had ever found any *muiraquitãs* himself, and he said no. What about *caretas*? He went into his hut and brought out seven he had picked up on the bank the previous October.

It was a remarkable collection: a flanged 'ledge rim' of a large vessel, with the stylized face of a person or a monkey—Conduri at its most sophisticated. The large head of a fish, broken off at the neck and as lifelike as a death mask; part of a bottle or a closed vessel, Roosevelt later guessed. Songa identified it as one of the tastiest catfish, the *jandia*. The weathered but still recognizable head of a howler monkey, with remnants of paint. A floridly punctate rim sherd adorned with what looked like a smirking, comically contorted pair of lips. A snapped-off lug that was in itself a frank, dignified bust of a monkey. A conventionalized bird lug, just like one already in a Conduri collection in Philadelphia. We could sense again from these pieces a profound understanding of animals. I wondered if the Conduri had the concept of an animal alter ego, as many of the remaining Amazonian tribes do, and as the Tapajós did; in some Tapajós statues the animal crouches on the person's shoulder.

The seventh piece was a complete departure in both style and subject: the head of a woman with elaborately tressed hair. No ordinary woman would have sported such coils;

she must have been very important. Her mouth and eyes (overarched with lightly incised brows) were simple slits. She seemed to be part of a freestanding statue, perhaps an idol, and she looked, more than any native New World artwork I was familiar with, almost—*mirabile dictu*—Grecian. One of the earliest theories about the female warriors who were being reported in the Amazon Valley was that the women were in fact an emigré remnant of the original Scythian Amazons—a theory that seems preposterously improbable, although prehistoric Brazil and the classical world may in fact have been in contact. In 1982 amphoras of the type carried on Roman ships in the second century were found on an ancient shipwreck in Guanabara Bay, near Rio de Janeiro.

Back in New York, I showed the piece to Richard Keresey, the classical art expert at Sotheby Parke Bernet, the art auctioneers, to get his opinion on whether it was in fact Grecian or made under Grecian influence. I didn't tell him until afterwards where it was from. He took it in his hand and after some deliberation said, 'I've never seen anything quite like it. I don't see anything Greek about it at all. If it is Greek it has to be pre-Hellenic and very primitive. The color and the condition and the musty smell all suggest that it is ancient, but the only way you could tell for sure would be to send it to Oxford, England, for thermo-luminescent dating, and that doesn't always work. I wonder if it isn't Oriental. The first thing it reminds me of is of the pre-Buddhist Hamiwa sculpture of Japan.' He summoned a woman in the Oriental Art section, who said that it couldn't possibly be Hamiwa and returned the ball to Keresey's court by suggesting that it was Cycladic, an early Bronze Age civilization on the Cyclades Islands in the Aegean. Keresey heard her, but he was thinking about the hair. 'The hair is very curious,' he went on. 'Look at the almost childlike way the coils of clay have been applied. Maybe it isn't hair at all. Look at how the whole heap of coils is under skull level, almost as if it were trying to show the contents of the brain.' He thought some more, and then said, 'Maybe it's tribal. It reminds me a little of some North American Indian art from the nineteenth and twentieth centuries.' The idea grew on him, until at last he declared, 'I would go for primitive, within the last two hundred years. Without putting it down, it's most unsophisticated.'

Keresey's brains hypothesis is discredited by the fact that the coils spill over the back of the woman's neck like hair; to Roosevelt and all but one other of the twenty or so people who have seen the piece, they looked like hair. But where would an Indian have got the idea for such a classical-looking coiffure? Very little is known about prehistoric Amazonian hairstyles, but the coiffure of Inca women is known to have been elaborately tressed and emblematic of the woman's rank and stage of life, and the Inca are known to have made elaborately coiffed fertility statues and ancestor fetishes out of gold and other metals. The hair of present-day Quechua women (who are the descendants of the Inca) is elaborately and emblematically tressed (and in Zaire a woman's hairstyle identifies her tribe) but with the hair parted in the middle and braided in interwoven pigtails; both Inca and Quechua female coiffures are nothing like the Medusan look of these coils. I showed the piece to Robert Carniero, who thought it looked post-contact. 'Because it is an undatable surface find, you can't be sure it wasn't made under Western influence,' he explained. Roosevelt also felt that it was 'quite European' and pointed out that 'in Aztec areas many figurines that look Greek or Roman were made by natives after contact.'

But the question remained: Where did the Indian artist get the idea for the coils? Certainly not from the hair of any Europeans he might have come in contact with; but maybe from a book the Europeans showed him, or maybe, as the art critic Calvin Tomkins, whom I also consulted, ingeniously suggested, from engravings on their muskets, armor, or scabbards.

Another curious point is that Carvajal, it will be recalled, described the women who attacked him and his fellow expeditionaries as having 'hair very long and braided and wound about the head.' Could the artist have been feeding back the Carvajal account or the classical Amazon myth? With typical *caboclo* generosity, De Brito handed us his whole collection, asking for nothing in return. João gave his wife two of the cans of *feijoada*.

To me the woman's head looked like an Amazon, and it revived my interest in the myth, which had suffered after seeing the lake. What had there been here? I wondered as we pulled away from De Brito's dock. The surface of the pond had been absolutely still. On a moonlit night it would

77

have made a perfect mirror, offering a rare opportunity for people in the centuries before the arrival of silvered glass from Europe to examine themselves. In a way, the nondescriptness of the lake argued in its favor: If the legend had been arbitrarily assigned to this place, wouldn't a more picturesque one have been chosen?

We decided not to climb the serra. It was thickly over-grown, and De Brito assured us that we would find nothing. Instead we crossed the river and examined the original site of Faro. It is known as Tauaquera, lingua geral for burial ground. Many bead and ring muiraquitás had been looted from the graves of the Uaboi here. It was still a cemetery for the local caboclos. In a clearing along the forested bank about a hundred weathered gray wooden crosses, all from this century, some radically tilting, had been planted. Small waves of black water quickly lapped the black-earth shore.

That night we reached the Boca do Nhamundá, the 'mouth' of the river, where the drowned lower section, the so-called Lago de Faro, gave way to the extravagant mean-dering typical of a lowland river, with oxbow lakes being thrown off at nearly every change of direction. Another lone family, who were friends of Songa, had settled at the Boca do Nhamundá. Their homestead was called Castanhal, 'the place where there are Brazil nuts.' We reached its dock just as the light was failing and unloaded the boat in choppy, milky water, with Songa urging us to hurry because stingrays would be moving into the shallows for the night. A well-preserved muscular man of about forty-five named Casimiro Gomez, with the copper skin and hairlessness of an Indian, came down the bank and helped pile our things under a large thatched roof on poles—a structure known as a barracão, which he had built for the annual festival of the place's patron saint, São Miguel. The festival began on September twenty-eighth and lasted a night and a day.

Casimiro's family consisted of four people: his mother Rosa, his half-sister Sabena, and Sabena's son Adenildo, whom Rosa had given to Casimiro to raise, as Casimiro's wife had died without giving him any children. Rosa, an energetic and strong-willed woman in her sixties, was the head of the family. Sabena was a handsome woman of about twenty-five, with the innocence of a ten-year-old; she was in fact mildly retarded. She had had six children, each by a different man. Two had died, and Rosa had given the other three to their fathers or to other families up and down the river. One of the fathers was Chico De Brito. Sabena looked pregnant again.

The Gomez family had cleared five hundred meters along the river and fifteen hundred back, and was growing manioc, two kinds of banana, soursop, guava, cherimoya, inga—no oranges, though; the orange we gave Adenildo was the first he had ever tasted—and no greens except for some onions whose tops were sprouting from a kerosene can. Rosa had an herb garden in which she picked not only seasoning for fish, but lemon grass for colds, mint for cough, and mocha coffee for asthma. Certain wild fruits—sorva, maçaranduba, pixuna—were gathered in season; and in December and January the Brazil nut trees whose towering crowns loomed in the forest behind dropped their ripe nuts, heavy wood globes the size of volley-balls that contained one to two dozen of the seeds which are the Brazil nuts of commerce. The sale of the nuts provided the family with virtually its only cash. 'Money is hard here,' Casimiro told us. 'I tried lumbering It was heavy work and got me nowhere. The regatões exploit you. You end up always owing.' (The regatões were the river traders who came up in motors with kerosene, cloth, shotgun shells, batteries, and other modern items mostly obtained from Nogueira, and went back down with the caboclos' plant and animal produce.)

Aside from the eggs of their chickens, all their animal protein was wild. Three kinds of turtle skulls and a string of manatee collarbones were hanging from ridgepoles in the cooking area. 'A manatee only lasts a week,' Casimiro told us. 'Everybody comes to eat it.' Each morning at three to four o'clock, depending on where he was going to fish, Casimiro set out in his canoe. The best fishing was an hour away.

The life at Castanhal had an austerity that we had not yet seen. The people along Lake Sapucuá had been better off, João explained, because they could get to Oriximiná in one day and sell their goods there without being ripped off by regatões. Songa had canoed from Castanhal to Faro in one day, but the wind on the Lago de Faro was bad, he said, and it was easy to flip. So the Gomezes had to be almost completely self-sufficient, almost completely off the cash economy. The Gomezes were one step removed from tribal Indians, and had many of the same adaptations—like the tipiti Casimiro was in the process of weaving from Mauritia palm fronds, which looked like a giant Chinese thumbscrew and operated on the same principle; it was for squeezing the poisonous prussic acid from manioc. The basketry tube would be suspended from a roof beam and crammed with soaked, grated manioc, and a weight would be attached to the bottom, causing liquid containing the acid to ooze out.

The Gomezes were comparable to a family of settlers in the Kentucky wilderness circa 1780. The nearest neighbor was ten miles upriver. Casimiro had run a wire from a small transistor radio twenty feet up a pole and was pulling in sacred music from Manaus loud and strong. Quersin asked him why the families on the Nhamundá lived so far apart. 'Each has his own work,' he explained.

Songa mixed us some excellent *caipirinhas*—the Brazilian national drink, made of *cachaça*, sugar, and lemon, with the taste and the punch of a margarita—and as we lay back in our hammocks and listened to Casimiro we reflected that people everywhere are probably equally blind to what they have. 'If it was up to me, I'd leave this place,' he was saying. 'But my mother doesn't want to go. She thinks the city is bad.'

'What stupidity,' João said passionately under his breath.

The full moon rose over the Lago de Faro and flooded its ghostly, sparkling surface. We talked about the rest of the river. Neither Casimiro nor Songa had been above the first rapids, but Casimiro told us that it was two days by canoe to Caçaua, the main village of the Hixkaryana, and from there 'only three days' on foot to Guyana. The Hixkaryana went up to Guyana all the time, he said. If this was true, we could conceivably trek right up over the border.

Casimiro picked up the faint purr of a motor coming up the lake, listened intently for a moment, and then said, 'José.' So few boats came up this far that the sounds of their engines were recognizable to the local people from miles away. José was another of Songa's brothers. He had some business upriver. We didn't see his spotlight; he was navigating by moonlight. Casimiro stood on the bank and blinked his flashlight downriver for several minutes. By the time José arrived, Quersin and I had turned in. I was vaguely aware of a succession of sounds in the night: first, people talking in animated Portuguese; then, hundreds of *cunauaru* tree frogs croaking in long staccato volleys; and at about three o'clock half a dozen male howler monkeys roaring from maybe a mile away, perhaps warning each other to keep back, or defending a fruit tree. The roaring sounded like cold wind rushing through a mountain pass. It is one of the loudest sounds made by any animal.

We got off by six-thirty, and having left the extra gas and the heavy baggage for José to bring up later in the morning, we were finally able to zip along with the bow out of the water, which boosted João's morale considerably. He was worried about our weight and the gas and was already anxious to return to Terra Santa; he was going to work for his brother-in-law, who had bush planes and supplied prospectors from Itaituba, up to the Tapajós.

At the settlement of a man named Luis Moura we looked into the possibility of switching our boat for a dugout he had; but the dugout was much longer and at least as heavy, and it wouldn't have solved our weight problem. Moura's compound was a wallow of pigs, dogs, chickens, and people. A frowsy young barefoot woman in a ragged dress stood in the door of his elevated frame house. Moura was the most successful entrepreneur above Faro. He farmed, ranched, lumbered. He paid wages, and he took the produce of *caboclos* down to Nogueira and sold them modern goods at exorbitant prices. We had met him coming down yesterday, towing a barge full of cattle and a canoe with a low arching basketry roof at the stern. He was giving four old people a lift to Faro so they could pick up their retirement cheques.

At midmorning we arrived at a settlement on the left bank called Jacamim. The *jacamim* is the grey-winged trumpeter, and one of these birds, which belong to a small family grouped between crakes and rails and are subtly colorful (the colors all being on the blue end of the spectrum), was strutting around. Trumpeters tame easily and are said to be good at catching snakes. Several *caboclo* families lived here, and some Indians were camped here temporarily, helping the head of the community, a man named Almerindo, convert his recently harvested manioc into *farinha*. This was being done in a well-organized operation under the supervision of Almerindo. In one corner of a *barracão* set up specially for the purpose, a black woman and an Indian man were nimbly nicking the coarse brown skins off the tubers

81

with machetes. The peeled white tubers were then soaked, then fed into a gas-powered machine that grated them into pulp. The pulp was then stuffed into a tipiti, and the prussic acid was expressed. Then the pulp was sifted by hand through a sieve. The big nuggets were baked into cakes that looked and tasted like unleavened bread and were called *beiju*, or they were made into a porridge known as *mingau*. The fine bits were placed in shallow metal pans four feet in diameter and roasted into golden *farinha*. Almerindo was hoping to get forty sacks of *farinha* out of this harvest and to sell them for about seven dollars apiece to the passenger boat that stopped at Nhamundá once a week on its way to Manaus. He was a man of about fifty. His wife was considerably younger and was nursing a week-old baby with a bottle. The baby was Sabina's, by Songa. Sabina hadn't been pregnant, she just given birth, and Rosa had given the baby to Almerindo. Songa seemed strangely uninterested in it, for the father. Almerindo's wife offered us some meat of a recently killed tapir, which was like beef but denser.

These were the 'nomadic' Indians Dantona had told us about. He didn't know what tribe they were—maybe Tirió. I wondered if they could be the seven Kaxuiana Prostasio Frikel reported as having moved to the Nhamundá in 1968. Their chief, known to the *caboclos* at Jacamim simply as Antonio Indio, wasn't around at the moment but would be back in a few hours, we were told. Antonio's wife, Francisca or Temso, was the dignified woman of about sixty sifting manioc pulp; their daughter Maria, a.k.a. Jaruui, was bagging the *farinha*. I asked the young Indian man peeling tubers if he was a Kaxuiana from the Rio Cachorrinho and he said in Portuguese that he was. His name was Kanati. He was twenty-two, with high cheekbones and a bent nose like a hawk's beak and hair sprouting sparsely on his chin and from the sides of his mouth and shooting out straight to page-boy length under a cap of the sort of gray plaid worsted that business suits are made of, with the visor unbuttoned. Rolling himself a cigarette, he told us, 'I left the Cachorrinho when I was five years old with my father and my brother and we went to live with the Wai Wai in Guyana, in the village of Kanaxeu, on the Essequibo River. Eight years ago I came here to the Nhamundá, where Maria's parents were living. I made love to her, and I've been here ever since.' Maria was his age, tall, light-skinned, with long straight black hair and a large, beautiful face, strikingly different from *caboclo* women and from Kanati himself. The Kaxuiana, who had all been absorbed by the Tirió except for the ones here on the Nhamundá, had themselves been a mixed group. They had come originally from the 'high *serras* to the West,' which Frikel guessed were the Andes, and had later been joined, in a bloody process of fusion, by two waves of an Amazonian tribe named Warikena. Maria was Warikena, while Kanati said he was half Tikiano, another tribe of the Upper Trombetas, he told us, about which I have been able to find out nothing. There is considerable phenotypic variation from tribe to tribe in the Amazon basin.

Francisca sang a mournful, monotonous song, an 'old dance' of the Kaxuiana called *kokodi*, into Quersin's Sony TC5-370 stereo cassette recorder; and Maria sang two hymns in Wai Wai. I asked Kanati how long it took to trek from Caçaua to Guyana. He said two or three weeks, if you kept moving. He had once spent three months doing it with some Wai Wai. So that was out. He said that he would go with us to Cafezal, the place upriver where the Kaxuiana lived—there were four couples now, three with children—and talk to his brother-in-law Bernardinho, who had a canoe and was a *cachoerista*, expert at shooting white water.

José came up the bend but would not dock at Almerindo's; they were feuding over something, or *politicando*, as Kanati put it. We decided to save gas by hitching our boat to José's *motor* and riding with him to the Lago de Jacytara, as far as he was going. There seemed no point to wait for Antonio; these Kaxuiana were so acculturated that if they had ever had a women-without-husbands myth they had probably forgotten it. To offset the new weight of Kanati, we advanced him the sack of oranges, which he left with Maria. The Lago de Jacytara came soon, and after we were under our own power again Kanati squatted at the bow and, propping his elbows on his knees, stayed there without moving or talking for the next hour or so.

The river was like a smooth black corridor gently insinuating itself between monotonous walls of green that rose to a fairly uniform height of about thirty-five feet. The terrain was mostly flat and choked with vegetation, and there was a lot of standing water, not only frequent large lakes opening to the right or left at most major bends, but often the trees on either side would be in water, forming a type of inundated forest peculiar to black-water rivers and relatively poor in species, known as *igapó*. Often the lower branches of the trees came right down to the water and were smothered by a purple-flowering creeper in the pea family that was all over the place, so it wasn't immediately apparent that for much of the Nhamundá's length for much of the year there was nowhere to get out, let alone to build. No wonder it was so deserted. The only artifacts we saw that afternoon were two makeshift huts that lumberjacks had thrown up in front of Lago Duarto. Sometimes the descending river, as it made one of its gradual swings to the right, would collide with a rib of terra firma, and a high slumped bank of red clay, 'created by the weight of the water that throws itself here,' as Kanati put it nicely, would be exposed. On the highest ground there would often be a tree or two rising to a hundred feet and littered with flowers whose showy white bracts surrounding a dense mauve influorescence sounded to several botanists I described it to like the giant cashew, *Anacardium spruceanum*, popularly known in Brazil as the *caju-açu*. Songa gave me three different names for it on three occasions. all of which were wrong. He didn't know many of the trees; neither did Kanati by name; and João knew almost none. It was comforting to be able to put a name on some conspicuous element of the forbiddingly complex vegetation that closed in from every quarter—to know that yon long spike up there studded with red florets was the arboreal orchid *Aechmea huebneri*; or that this exquisitely slender palm shooting up twenty feet higher than its neighbors before producing a sparse, wispy crown, was the *açai*, whose fruit could be made into a refreshing drink. Another tree that stood out because of its height, its smooth tan bark, its candelabra-like branches, and the frequent gaps in the foliage of its crown, was called mulattowood.

There would be occasional glimpses of a bird: a heron hopping up to a higher branch in precise anticipation of the flight path of a butterfly, which flew right between its mandibles, so that they didn't even open noticeably ('What expertise!' Quersin exclaimed with admiration); a flock of orioles known as yellow-rumped caciques making their leisurely way from tree to tree.

As Kanati and I talked, I realized that he had already had an unusually full life. At fourteen he had been drafted into the People's Army of Guyana and had served for three months as a policeman; then, because he hated beating up people, he had taken off for Surinam to visit the other Kaxuniana, including his father, who were living with the Tirió, on Xaparwini Creek. From there he had made his way to Paramaribo, the capital, where he had some Tikiano relatives, and he had been befriended by a missionary who had taken him in a plane out to some island in the Atlantic; he couldn't remember the name. He had been exposed to seven languages; he had down Kaxuiana, Wai Wai, and Hixkaryana, which are quite similar; he knew some Tirió, which is quite different; most of his English, learned from a Protestant missionary at Caxineu, he had forgotten; he had a smattering of lingua geral; and now he was talking Portuguese, in which, when he had first come down to the Nhamundá, he had taken a crash course with the padre in Faro for several months. He knew the world Quersin and I were from better than Songa or João. 'New York is near America?' he asked. 'I will go there.'

Late in the afternoon we stopped at the last *caboclo* homestead on the river, at the entrance to Lake Mucurão. The left bank here was high and steep and, we discovered, blanketed with *terra preta*. The homestead was called Vista Alegre, Gladdening View. An old woman, Maria Batista de Jesus, had been living there for eighteen years. She told us that she had found *caretas* of turtles, caymans, and vultures, and she gave us one—a nubbin so stylized that it was impossible to tell whether it was zoomorphic or not, with a meandering pattern of squares and angles incised on the bit of rim that had broken off which, Roosevelt said, was more sophisticated than the rest of my collection, and possibly represented a new regional variant of Conduri. This was virgin archaeological territory. The highest previously reported (by Hilbert) *terra preta* up the Nhamundá was Tauaqueira. The de Jesus family was way out there. The nearest human, apart from Maria Batista's husband, who was off fishing, was two days downriver. Her grandsons were down roasting coffee beans for Moura. (Songa would tell us afterward that another grandson, when he had been a six-year-old boy, had disappeared one day here, and nobody had ever found out what happened to him.) Maria Batista let us have a few dozen of the lemons that strewed the floor of her grove, and then we left, in a hurry to reach before dark a place called Banho, Bath, where there was an abandoned hut and *barracão*; the owner had gone to Belém, Songa told us. Banho was sited precisely at the center point of a left-hand bend. As you looked up and then down the river, the two halves of the bend's perfectly bisected arc seemed like mirror images. Songa and João took the boat into a little cove upstream and threw out lines baited with tapir meat. Kanati got a fire going and started to cook rice, onions, *farinha*, and sardines. Stuffed in the roof's thatched ceiling were the snout of a peccary, with the short tusks, sharp on the inside edge, still in their sockets, and the head of a turtle known locally as the *cabeçudo* (and to science as *Podocnemis dumeriliana*), which Kanati claimed was big enough to feed a whole family. He said that river turtles came up to nest as far as the rapids. As the sky darkened, the fishermen returned with two white piranhas—a disappointing catch— and nighthawks made nervous forays over the river, gliding, flapping, snapping up insects, emitting little nasal sounds; then night fell. Quersin produced another marvel of Japanese microtechnology—a Sony ICF-7600A nine-band shortwave radio, and tuned in Washington, Paris, Jerusalem—the big time—and a Spanish-speaking country, we couldn't make out which, where something that sounded like '*la flexibilizacion del estado d'urgencia*' had just gone into effect. After a while Quersin turned it off, and we lay in our hammocks listening to the tremulous fluting of a tinamou.

The next morning Kanati had English names for us: Quersin was Father, I was Chief. We went over the lakes and creeks and bluffs we would be going by: Inferno, Casimira, Piriquita, Barãozinha, Barão Grande, Jauari. 'From here on up there is nobody except Indians and the watchman of the *companhia*,' Songa told us. The *companhia* was a calcite mine that had been discontinued in the early seventies. We crossed from bank to bank, keeping to the inside of each bend, sometimes skirting a tree that, craning out from shore toward the light as the water ate at its roots, had finally toppled, bringing its attendant vines down with it and stretching them taut as cables. Kanati noticed a movement in a tree. We came under and watched a howler monkey watching us as it moved slowly along a branch. Its coat was burnt orange—a red howler. Kanati wanted to shoot it but Songa had left his shotgun and our shells on his brother's boat. We were not sorry that there was nothing to kill the monkey with, but we were puzzled by Songa's action. No responsible guide would have forgotten his gun, as Songa claimed to have. He obviously couldn't be counted on. Several days later, when we parted company with him in Faro, he said he was going right back up the river to hunt ducks; maybe he had already decided to do this. Later I asked Kanati privately why Songa had left his gun and Kanati said, 'Because he's no good. Everybody knows that.' He was taking good care of the boat, though, cleaning the spark plugs when the engine wouldn't fire, siphoning gas by mouth from one tank to another, a horrible job. But I looked at him closely and noticed for the first time a deadness to his eyes that was frightening; and thinking back on his indifference to his newborn child the day before, I was glad Kanati was along.

For the whole day we were virtual prisoners of the river, stopping only to refill, while Kanati held on to a branch so that we wouldn't drift downriver. The smoothness was deceptive; the water was moving right along. We went maybe a hundred miles. The river remained about seventy-five feet wide. It reminded Quersin of the Ubangi, except that the Ubangi was a clear-water river. He had found ancient dwelling sites up the Ubangi that looked like *terras pretas*, with beautifully decorated potsherds that nobody made any more, and he had recorded a fantastic bird song, of which he gave a tour-de-force imitation. 'In fifteen years of going all over Zaire, I never heard it again and nobody has identified it,' he said. 'It must have been the Charlie Parker of that species.'

We spent much of the afternoon in our own thoughts and projects, Quersin sitting beside me with his straw hat and two pairs of glasses—reading and sun—perched on his nose, filling page after page of a notebook with swift, meticulous, minuscule writing; then reviewing the book of useful French-Portuguese phrases he had picked up in Rio, getting a chuckle from the *en bateau* section, given our present situation: 'Can you show me the way to my cabin? The sea is rough. I don't feel well.' Kanati, at the bow, was lip-reading and feasting his eyes on the advertisements in a sumptuous glossy magazine I had brought from New York.

Some of the pictures were of things he was unfamiliar with. He asked what an American Express Gold Card and a nuclear submarine were, and I tried to explain. I finished Jim Harrison's latest novel, about a resourceful, self-abusive engineer who, driven crazy by a plant some Indians give him for his grand mal seizures, jumps off a huge dam he is building in the Amazon and survives. Then, having exhausted the light reading, I started Lévi-Strauss's *The Savage Mind*.

A succession of lakes and creeks passed without event: Fusil, Veado, Fusinho da Anta, Chave, Bemtivi, Remanço Grande, Arreia, Torre Macaco, Gaviãozinho, Gavião Grande, until at last we came to Pitinga, the largest of the Upper Nhamundá's tributaries, about the width of a street, entering from the right. Dantona said he had followed it for two days until he was stopped by a waterfall; he said there was a *serra* with savanna, in the distance. Two dolphins, the first we had seen on the Nhamundá , were feeding at Pitinga's mouth. They were the larger pink species, *Inia geoffrensis*. We got out at a small clearing on the bank and watched them racing up and down in a feeding frenzy or perhaps alarmed at our presence, surfacing to blow every few moments with a sucking, snorting sound. Kanati said that this was a good place for fish, and he wanted to catch some, but Songa had for some reason forgotten to save some of last night's piranha for bait—an elementary rule of river travel. We were now down to seventy-five litres, and it was clear that there wasn't going to be enough gas to get us to the first rapids and back. I was feeling dumb and duped. Why had Dantona said that three hundred litres were enough? Why hadn't Songa been able to tell us that we couldn't make it? Because, he said, he had never gone up the river in an outboard; he only knew the distance in diesel fuel. 'This guy doesn't know what's happening.' Quersin muttered disgustedly. 'You see now, this river is long. I told you,' Kanati said. 'Maybe there's some gas at the *companhia*,' Songa said.

Soon after we had set out again, a large green iguana charged to the end of a sandbar and stood its ground magnificently as we drew near. A pair of macaws (either the scarlet or the red-and-green species; against the sky it was impossible to tell) flew over, scooping the air with strong, shallow wingbeats, trailing long straight tails, one a little ahead of the other. A green kingfisher, the mid-sized edition (between the similarly marked Amazon and pygmy kingfishers) took off rattling around a bend. We went along a stretch of terra firma bank on the Amazonas side where there had been a fire a while ago. New green vines were already working up the charred black trunks and their dead vine cabling. The flames had not reached the bushy green crowns of the tallest trees, emergents like the gigantic *sumauma* or silk-cotton tree. 'We set fire to this last year,' Kanati said. I asked why. 'Just for fun.' He was getting excited about our visit to Cafezal; he promised that he would order a tapir to be killed in our honor and would sing some beautiful songs into Father's tape recorder. 'When I left, in March, there were four chickens. I wonder if they're still there.'

There were half a dozen small prefabricated buildings at the *companhia*, an airstrip, and a huge gouge in the bank, where barges could be run up and loaded. The mine had shut down eight years earlier, but there was a chance that it might resume operation, the assistant watchman, who lived in one of the buildings with his wife and four children, told us. He said he had only ten litres of gas, but that we were welcome to them. There was a radio in another of the buildings, but it was *esculhambado* (a great Portuguese word here meaning roughly 'flooey'), and he didn't know how to make it work, and the watchman, besides, who had taken his sick wife to Parintins and wouldn't be back till the end of the month, had taken the key to the shack with him.

'No help here,' I said to Quersin, who was standing in the warm mud beside the boat, getting temporary relief for the chafed, raw skin between his toes.

When we pulled into Cafezal about an hour later, the whole community came running down the bank and gave us an excited greeting of falsetto *oooeees*. Potiu or Bernardinho was the son of the chief Antonio; he was in charge of Cafezal in Antonio's absence and, at twenty-seven, the senior male of his generation; the chieftainship was patrilineal, as was clan membership. Kanati, who was younger and a relative newcomer and did not have a canoe, deferred to Bernardinho. Bernardinho was married to Kanati's fifteen-year-old sister Alaxuca or Regina, about whom Kanati had not told us. Regina already had three children. Then there was Bernardinho's twenty-six-year-old sister Karauki or Maria, a half-sister of Kanati's wife Maria; they were daughters of Antonio by different women. She was married to her quiet paternal first cousin, Moritiuro or João. They had five children, and João had a younger brother Sebastião, who was down in Faro. The compound was not noticeably different from a *caboclo* settlement, except that the huts were sided with slats of split saplings. Dogs, cats, chickens, and *jacamims* were similarly in residence. But the compound was somehow earthier and cozier, and the presence of the Indians themselves was somehow energizing, perhaps because they were more alive to their surroundings. I asked Bernardinho how he spent his time, and he said, 'Here we never stop. We make *farinha*, we sell lumber to the *companhia*. We take people on trips when they come.' The last people who had come had been a party of German missionaries three years before. They had wanted to go up to Caçaua but had also underestimated their gas. Bernardinho had taken them up in his canoe, but this had been in October, when the water was low. Bernardinho said they grew a lot of Cayenne bananas, a long, especially rich and filling variety. The fishing was poor locally, so they did a lot of hunting. The edges of the clearing were littered with the bones of past meals, including the strikingly human-looking but smaller skull of a bowler monkey. Bernardinho asked for some batteries for his flashlight so that he and João could shoot something for dinner, and as he went off with his shotgun Regina slapped him lustily on the back and said, '*Mata*. Kill.' Soon we heard two pops in the darkness and the hunters returned, each with a paca, a large brown rodent with nocturnal habits and four rows of white spots running the length of its body. 'The paca comes at night to the bank to eat a little flower,' Bernardinho explained, 'and there we wait for him.' Quersin took a flash photograph of Bernardinho and João holding up the animals surrounded by everybody, then the pacas were turned over to Regina and Maria to prepare for supper. We contributed some onions, which fascinated Bernardinho, who had never seen an onion before. He asked if they grew above the ground or below it. Pacas are life-term monogamists, and these two had apparently been a mated pair. The female had been pregnant; the foetus was removed and later given to the dogs. Bernardinho said that he usually hunted with bow and arrows, because shotgun shells were so expensive;

Moura sold them for more than a dollar apiece. Cash was hard to come by. He showed me a stack of spears in a corner of Antonio's room. The FUNAI agent who lived with the Hixkaryana had given Antonio the model for them, and he came to buy them once a year. The spears were each carved from a single piece of wood and their points were smeared with red paste from urucú berries. They had nothing to do with traditional Kaxuiana craftsmanship and no value either as weapons or art. They were probably destined for one of FUNAI's indigenous art shops in the airports and bus stations of São Paulo, Rio, or Brasília. In the same room there was a ceremonial club with a vulture's head, masterfully carved by Antonio—'We used to kill people with this fifty years ago,' Kanati said—and a cotton weft-warp openwork hammock intricately woven by Francisca thirty years ago and still strong. Bernardinho said that it had taken his mother a month to make. (All these time spans should be taken as very approximate.) The knowledge of how to make these works of art had apparently not been passed on to his generation nor, apparently, had the ability to tell any of the Kaxuiana myths. The language had—Regina, for instance, spoke very little Portuguese—and some plant lore had apparently been retained. There was a little arrowroot growing in a kerosene can which Bernardinho said was for bathing the dogs in so that they would hunt well. It looked as if the next generation would be absorbed into the *caboclo* population and would become more or less like Songa. They were a population that had fallen below replacement level. Being Indian had no prestige in the world below the rapids, but this small group still had tribal solidarity, perhaps heightened by knowing that they were the last of their kind.

We tried the pacas, which had been grilled over the fire and were superb; it was obvious why the rodents have become rare over much of their wide range, from Mexico to Paraguay. Kanati belted out wretchedly off-key a Wai Wai hymn he had learned in Guyana, for which he gave an English translation: 'No smoke, no drink rum, go to heaven with Jesus.' Tens of thousands of feet above us the blinking red and green lights of a jet plane, headed north, slowly crossed the star-studded heavens. 'Where is it going.' Bernardinho asked. 'Maybe to Caracas, or even the USA,' I said. 'It goes by six times every morning,' he said. Kanati warned not to leave any bare toes dangling out of our hammocks because there were vampire bats around that liked to suck them.

Just after sun-up Bernardinho, Kanati, (Kaxuiana) João, João's oldest boy, Quersin, and I loaded our gear and set out in two canoes for the rapids. We had paid Songa and Terra Santa João and had left some of the food with them. If the rapids were passable we would go up them and seventeen others, each of which had a name, to Caçaua, and from there we would either proceed with Kanati and maybe some Hixkaryana to the Wai Wai on the Mapuera, who could take us down to Oriximiná in about a week, or fly out in the next plane. If we didn't come back to Cafezal tonight Songa and João were to wait a few days, as we would try to send back some gas with Bernardinho. Bernardinho said he couldn't tell if we could make it up the rapids until he took a look at them.

Travelling by canoe—I was in the first one, between Bernardinho and João's son—we were much more aware of the life of the river. The teeming sounds within the trees were no longer drowned out. We moved more slowly and closer to the bank, often right under overhanging branches. All sorts of details that we had been missing now presented themselves to our senses: the sound of the river straining against a snag; lots of little brown bats suddenly flying up together from a tree trunk, to which, perfectly camouflaged, they had been clinging; a tiny hummingbird nest with tiny eggs that Bernardinho said were tasty raw; the scent of white mimosa flowers; the citrine smell of ants living symbiotically in the hollow stems of a taxi tree, paying their rent by being ready to bite anything that brushed against the tree (Bernardinho said their bite was very painful, but still not as painful as that of wasps. 'If we get attacked by wasps, jump in the river, that's the only way to survive,' he said); a large butterfly, probably an acraea, mimicking a sunlit leaf, with wings divided in horizontal zones of brown, yellow, and brown; scores of water striders, known as 'mothers-of-the-water,' slipping off a branch and sprinkling the water; a black-collared swallow skimming the mirror surface of the river for a distance of maybe fifty yards, then pulling out in a graceful climb; a loud crash back in the woods that Bernardinho said could only be a tapir; dark toucans with white bibs (one of three possible species) gorging themselves on açaí palm berries; a carib grackle, a red-crested cotinga, a black-fronted nunbird rustling, darting among branches; a morning-glory vine (Ipomoea?) blossoming in lavender trumpets; a dozen or so gray socks—a 'village,' as Bernardinho called it—of cacique nests hanging down together; three blue-and-yellow macaws coming over, calling raucously; a king vulture soaring way overhead, with white underwing coverts held out motionless; a small, apparently languid anaconda, about five feet long, stretched out along a branch ahead, in fact ready to drop on anything that came under. Bernardinho flicked some water at it with his paddle and it thrashed off the branch and dropped into the river in one blurred motion.

We stopped at an abandoned camp of some Brazil-nut gatherers and ate two kinds of guavas from trees there until the others came up. Dozen of butterflies—swallowtails, pierids, Melpomenes, and Eratos—were frolicking and feeding in the sunny clearing overgrown with flowering herbs. Lunch was boiled paca with onions and *farinha*. Eating was taking on new importance, perhaps because after a week or so of ingesting almost exclusively natural foods, my system was getting cleaned out and my sense of taste and smell were coming back; or because much of what we were eating was new; or because almost everywhere we looked, something seemed to be eating or being eaten.

At about one o'clock we began to hear a loud, dull roar upriver. The water became choppy, opaque, foamy, and full of eddies, and the air became moist with spray. Turning a final left-hand bend we were confronted by a smooth, solid sheet of water about a hundred yards across, with a drop of ten feet or so—a kind of mini-Niagara, with a quarter-mile of white-water riffles behind it. This was the *cachoeira porteira*, the gateway cataract. There was no need to confer with Bernardinho. It was impossible, even in an outboard. The expedition had run up against a literal wall of water.

We paddled over to a large *motor* that had been run into the flooded bushes below the falls and was being painted by a young Hixkaryana man. The *motor* belonged to FUNAI; when the river was lower, goods were ferried between it and Caçaua by outboard. The Hixkaryana took care of the boat and was maybe also responsible for guarding the Nhamundá/Mapuera Indigenous Area, which began at the rapids; at the moment the rapids made that job unnecessary. He said he had nothing, neither diesel fuel for his boat nor gasoline for ours. This was a rather bold lie, as he was sitting on a full drum of diesel fuel, which I pointed out. He then said he wasn't authorized to use any fuel or give any out or to take the *motor* anywhere and didn't even know how to run the engine. I asked if it was possible to walk up along the river and Kanati said that it was 'too ugly.' 'We are sad,' he said. 'You will come back in August with a *motor* and an outboard and we will go to Guyana. Songa is no good. He ruined your trip. He knew but he didn't want to tell you.' Quersin was exasperated. 'The lack of reliable information here is . . . no better than Africa,' he said. To me, the confusion about the gas and the rapids somehow recapitulated the confusion about the Amazons; both were part of the same general confusion.

There was nothing to do but to accommodate to the situation. Quersin and I recalled that we had never intended to go beyond the rapids in the first place. Kanati remembered that the padre was coming up to Jacamim from Faro on the twenty-seventh to officially marry him and Maria, so it was just as well that he got back; and Bernardinho said that one of his teeth was acting up and he would go down with us to Nhamundá to get it taken care of.

Soon below the rapids Kanati saw a sloth up in a tree. He climbed up to where he could reach the sloth with a machete and started to flail away; then he yanked the bloody animal down, tearing its long black claws from branches they were frantically fastening to; and he threw it into the canoe. I objected that it was still alive, and Kanati, after getting in, held its small, flat head with little ears, over the side. A sickening death rattle come from under the water. Kanati seemed completely unfazed by the murder he had just committed. I could see how the sloth's fur parted at and flowed out from its belly, instead of at the spine, in the usual mammalian pattern; this was because sloths spend almost all their lives upside down, eating leaves, digesting (a month-long process, as the masticated cellulose passes through the many compartments of their stomachs), moving with great caution from branch to branch, as they are quite helpless on the ground; even mating and giving birth upside down. They have only two predators: the few people who eat them, and harpy eagles. This one's fur was tinged green with algae, which is eaten by the larvae of the equally specialized sloth moth. Adult sloth moths have severely reduced wings, as they remain on sloths and flying is unnecessary. That night, back at Cafezal, the sloth was cut up and boiled by Regina and passed around. Terra Santa João refused to touch it, I tasted two pieces. The first was bland and tolerable, the second was just awful—a great plus in sloths' chances for survival as more people inevitably penetrate their world.

The next morning, Friday the twentieth, a small convoy descended from Cafezal. It was made up of the outboard (whose motor was running at the slowest possible speed, to get the most from the gas, just fast enough to overcome the current and make it possible to steer), with the same five people who had come up in it, and, in tow, a dugout with Bernardinho and his family. The plan was to go down together until the gas ran out—there were now about sixty litres left—then Kanati, Quersin, and I would take off in the canoe and try to catch Almerindo before he went down to Nhamundá with his *farinha*, on Sunday morning. If we missed Almerindo we would just keep going, and the others would have to wait for Almerindo and make their own arrangements with him. João wasn't very pleased with this plan, but as he had to stay with the boat there was no alternative. Songa, passive as ever, said, 'Whatever happens is the same to me.'

On the way down a little fish skipped about six times over the water in an effort to shake off a basslike cichlid known as a *tucunaré* (itself tasty); a hawk swooped down on a huge (rice?) rat about thirty feet up in a tree, and crashed through branches with it in its claws, struggling to carry it off and get airborne. Kanati spotted a howler monkey in a tree, quickly untied the dugout, stepped in, picked up and loaded Bernardinho's shotgun; Bernardinho meanwhile back-paddled, then nosed the canoe right under the tree; the rest of us continued, and after they were out of sight, there were three booms in succession, punctuated by piercing whistles from a small bird known as the screaming pia. 'It seems that whenever food presents itself it is killed and consumed immediately,' I wrote in my notebook. 'There is no procrastination and no evidence of a sense of conservation (as in Kanati's torching of the forest "for fun"). Even Indians, it seems, are not conservationists unless they have to be.'

At a plantation of Bernardinho's he and Kanati went in and cut two enormous hands of green plantains and Barba-

95

dian bananas. We stopped for lunch at Pitinga. Bernardinho threw in a line and in less than a minute pulled out four white piranhas; a fifth sheared the monofilament line clean above the hook. Songa and Kanati skinned, gutted, and spitted the monkey (it was also a red howler, but its coat was darker, a more fuscous brown, than that of the one we had seen several days earlier), and we ate it, too. I was beginning to feel uncomfortable about eating all these wild mammals, which I would have much preferred to have just watched, but the monkey was a great improvement over the sloth.

The gas lasted until midafternoon. People and goods transferred crafts, and Quersin, Kanati, and I started off in the dugout just as it started to rain—an intense local shower precipitated from a lone congested cumulus. I looked back at Regina, who was nursing her baby, delivered at Cafezal by her mother-in-law, under our plastic sheet; with her slanted eyes and full, wide mouth framed by chopped bangs of straight black hair, she was a beautiful Madonna.

We were somewhere in the middle of the hundred-mile stretch between Pitinga and Banho where nobody lived and there was very little dry ground for even a temporary shelter. Kanati said that we would just have to keep paddling through the night, but Queresin and I valued our sleep, and we kept looking for somewhere to put in. About half an hour before dark we finally saw a little rise in the forest and got out. Kanati said, 'Wait here,' and went into the forest with my machete. We could hear him running around and cutting materials for a lean-to—poles, vines, palm fronds. Two of the poles he planted firmly in the ground about six feet apart. Then he placed a third pole horizontally against them, about six feet up, and lashed it with vine. At the two junctures of the upright poles with the crosspole, he then laid two more poles and lashed them together at a slight incline to a tree about six feet away. Then he laid seven saplings across this triangular frame and lashed them down. Then he covered the frame with fronds, whose leaflets were sparse and thin and not the best roofing, but there were none of the right kinds of palm around; we added a plastic sheet for extra protection, which was a good idea, as a heavy rain started to fall at about two in the morning and we stayed dry in our hammocks below. The whole affair took Kanati no more than half an hour to put up from scratch. Quersin was impressed. 'It would have taken two Zairois an hour just to gather the material,' he said. Kanati said that the structure was called a *rabu de jaca*, which means a cayman's tail (*jaca* being abbrievated slang for *jacaré*). On page 830 of Volume 3 of the Smithsonian Institution's monumental *Handbook of the South American Indians*, in a section on the villages and houses of the Guyana tribes, I later found the basic design of Kanati's lean-to illustrated after a drawing made in 1924 by the anthroplolgist Walter Edmund Roth, who said that it was called a *banab*. It was completely different from the lean-tos that the Cayapo Indians make roughly six hundred miles to the south, which have a Quonset-like frame of bent saplings covered with wild banana leaves.

We made a fire, heated up and ate some more of the monkey, and then lay in our hammocks watching the cool green abdomens of enormous fireflies streak through the darkness and listening to the dense, pulsing rhythm of frog and insect choruses, which blended together almost like a band, with the frogs on bass. It sounded not unlike a Brazilian samba. I have often wondered whether the night sounds of the jungle helped inspire this infectious type of music; to my knowledge the connection has never been investigated. Quersin recorded the concert with his multi-directional external microphone, and six months later a cassette labelled 'Nhamundá/*nuit*' came in the mail, with a note from him that said, 'Binary/ternary, like all forest music.'

The next morning I took a walk in the woods and picked some tucuma palm nuts, whose thin layer of orange meat tasted vaguely like coconut, but not as sweet. Kanati said he only ate them when he could find nothing else. We passed a curassow humming from the shore the sound of its Portuguese name, *mutum*, the sound of a machete swooping through the air, cluing in not only potential mates but also predators to its whereabouts. We passed a stand of twelve-foot-tall plumed reeds locally known as arrows and used for the long, light shafts favored by the Amazon tribes. Further down a group of nests of crested oropendolas—larger black-and-yellow relatives of the caciques seen a few days back—hung from the branch tips of a tree. The nests were the same sort of gray woven-grass socks, but longer. Near them was a cylindrical affair resembling a quart-sized aluminum thermos, but whiter: the paper nest of some wasps. Because they keep other flying insects out to the area and thus protect the young oropendolas from being parasitized by botflies, oropendolas like to build their nests near wasps. Oropendolas without wasps nearby have been discovered to be more apt to let cowbirds lay eggs in their nests, because young cowbirds snap instinctively at all flying insects and thus perform the same function for the comparatively helpless young oropendolas as wasps do, but at the price of having to be fed. Because oropendolas can live better with cowbirds than with botflies, the oropendola-cowbird interaction is one of the few cases in which there is actually some advantage to being parasitized. The advantage to the wasps may be proximity to a chemical odor secreted by oropendolas which repels the insects that prey on wasp nests.

We spent the night on a channel off the river, in *barracão* belonging to a family that had gone down to work for Moura several months earlier. It was as well kept a compound as Castanhal had been. The dirt floor had been neatly swept, and a stack of firewood, an ax, and a bar of *breu* had been left in the kitchen area. A scrawny cherry tomato plant was growing on the edge of the clearing but not doing well, and onions, whose bulbs Bernardinho had never seen, were thriving in a trough. We ate and turned in to get an early start for Jacamim. A spider monkey maybe five hundred feet away started to call. Kanati reproduced the timbre and the spacing of the calls with a series of short whistles, which the monkey answered. He made me a proposition: what if he went back to America and worked for me, then came back in a couple of years for his family? I would love it, I said, but how were we going to get him into the country? He had lost his Guyanan identity papers when his canoe overturned in one of the rapids below Caçaua, and in Brazil he was, as an Indian, a ward of the State, for whom going abroad would require special permission. Then there would be the Immigration and Naturalization Service to contend with; he was in precisely the age, nationality, and income categories for which visas of any kind are almost impossible to obtain. 'You wouldn't like it there anyway,' Quersin said, closing his hands around his throat and pantomiming suffocation.

The next morning we saw a day-flying *Urania* moth, black with swallowtails and opalescent green wingbars, a common but always arresting sight in Amazonia. We stopped for coffee at a three-man, one-woman lumber operation that had been going since October. They were cutting stonewood, dragging the boles out of the forest, and hewing from them thick red planks, some of them thirty feet long, dugouts (a two-to-four-day job, depending on the length), or heavy paddles (which could be knocked out in two hours). The women kept the camp. Her *chachalaca* chick kept her company while the men were in the forest, she said. They had pretty much cleaned out the stonewood here and were breaking camp in twenty days, a magnificently built man named Paulo told us. Paulo was an Arara Indian on his mother's side. The Arara are a small tribe (numbering about two hundred in 1972) of the lower Xingu River, across the Amazon and downstream. They were rudely introduced to the modern world by the construction of the Transamazon Highway near them. At first they were hostile, killing three geologists in 1976 and a settler a year later; now they are in transition. Paulo spoke lingua geral and explained that his father was *cararua*, a term meaning other people, not Indian. As we prepared to move on he asked in a tone of regretful surprise something that sounded like *Kawati maceçeru*, which Kanati said meant 'You are already leaving?' and Kanati shouted back to him after we had pulled away, '*Kubaxe*,' which he said meant 'Make love' (i.e., to his wife).

Now we were in lake country. Kanati knew little *allées* in the inundated forest that led to the lakes and were known as *furos*, literally 'holes,' but perhaps best translated as 'cuts.' We took a few and cut straight across the lakes back to the main channel avoiding miles of circuitous loop. The entrance to the *furo* to the Lago de Jacytara proved elusive. At last Kanati thought he had found it, and gliding into a dark *igapó* forest, we proceeded mainly by pushing off with our paddles from trunks, many of which were buttressed to help them stay up in the still black water. The *furo* seemed not to have been used in some time. Vines had grown across it and it was clotted with debris. About a hundred yards in a troop of squirrel monkeys passed about thirty feet overhead, too intent on spanning the fifteen feet or so between trees to notice us. Gingerly, one at a time, they would walk out to the edge of a branch and then hurl themselves into the air. Small, light, they were spectacular leapers. About fifty of them passed, some with babies clinging to their backs. They did not all take off from the same branch, but followed several converging routes, like a stream with several interwoven channels. Half a dozen larger capuchin monkeys came with the last of them; it was a mixed troop, the hyperactive squirrels stirring up insects for the capuchins, who had more powerful jaws to open up fruits for the squirrels. Sometimes nunbirds follow in the wake of squirrel monkeys for the same reason, but we didn't see any.

Shortly after this we got hopelessly lost and eventually found ourselves right back at the entrance of the *furo*; giving up, we continued down the main channel. A stout-bodied butterfly with sapphire-and-black checkered wings joined us for a while, flying off only when I spooked it with my zoom lens. It looked like a metalmark, possibly *Lasaia agesilas agesilas* (Latreille).

We stopped at a *caboclo* settlement, where Kanati traded the remainder of our rubbing alcohol for a charred side of spider-monkey ribs, and moved on again. I asked Kanati when we were going to get to Jacamim; it was nine o'clock, and we were an hour overdue. 'It's not very far,' he said, and then he added, 'and it's not very near.' I leaned out over the water and threw my weight into each stroke, and we started to move. At nine-thirty we heard the sound of a *motor* below us. That would be Almerindo heading off for Nhamundá. We had missed him. When we finally pulled into Jacamim, two hours later, Antonio Indio, the chief of the Kaxuiana and Kanati's father-in-law, hailed us from shore with what seemed to be the greeting here on the Nhamundá: 'Where are the fish?'

Antonio Indio's real name was Kauka. He was the tallest of his family, about six feet, and he looked about sixty, with sparse white stubble on his chin, and his skin was still tight around his well-developed torso. 'I am from the time when they didn't count years of age,' he told me as we sat down together in the *barracão*. He had on a gray Nehru cap and projected calm, humility, simplicity, dignity, and wisdom. I asked how it was that he had come to live at Cafezal. 'In 1968, Father Protasio came in a boat to our village on the Cachorrinho River and took away ten of us at a time. The whole tribe went up the Paru do Oeste to live with the Tirió, near Surinam. We were the last seven to leave—my wife Francisca and my wife Augusta, who is dead now, and our four children: Bernardinho, João, and both Marias. Father

Protasio told us to wait. He would be back. But we didn't wait. A *cariwa* [Kaxuiana for non-Indian, cf. *cararua* above] gave me a gun and told me to go hunting. But it wasn't good for my wives to be left alone. When I came back they said the *cariwa* had been bothering them. So we all went up the Mapuera to hunt tapirs. We thought we'd be back in two or three weeks. But we have never returned.

'We canoed up *cachoeiras* and then followed paths we had never seen before, and after fifteen days we came to Caçaua; there were no Wai Wai on the Mapuera yet and the only Indians up there were the Hixkaryana. We stayed two years at Caçaua, then Nonato (the chief of FUNAI's post there) told us to go down to the *cachoeira porteira* and be watchmen. He said to work with the *regatão*, moving supplies up to Caçaua and not to let anybody pass. We did this for a while, but we weren't getting any money for it, so we decided to go off on our own and moved down to where we are now.'

I asked him if he knew any stories about the women without husbands and he said, after a long silence, 'I can't remember.'

Three hours after our arrival the outboard, with Songa, Bernardinho, and João paddling full steam, arrived. They were way ahead of schedule, having not stopped either night, but taken turns sleeping in the boat. João, eager to get back to Terra Santa, had pushed everybody, and he was devastated to hear that we were stuck at Jacamim until at least Tuesday, when Almerindo was due back. In fact, we were not: A few hours later Bernardinho and Kanati canoed down to Moura's and got him to come up that night and tow us down to Nhamundá. The next evening Quersin and I caught the weekly boat to Parintins, where we ran into some Satere-Maué Indians. I asked one of them if he knew anything about the women without husbands. He didn't speak much Portuguese and thought I was asking about single women in general, and he said, 'There are many women who live without men. They want men but can't arrange them. There are other women who don't want men, and many women who live with men but don't have children. It is the same with men.' We ended up not visiting the Satere-Maué because they didn't seem to have the myth, and because we had by then found a tribe that did— the Kaxuiana.

Late in the afternoon Kauka and I sat together in the *barracão* and we talked some more. Angled sunlight flooded the clearing. The women and girls had gathered on a log at the edge of the lagoon and were singing softly while combing each other's hair. Several dozen tiny *pium* mosquitoes, whose bite leaves a small blood blister that itches terribly, were trying to feed at my ankles, but a few drops of Muskol kept them away. Some of the children were swimming. Almerindo's wife warned them to stay close to shore. The day before, Almerindo had shot a big anaconda from the dock, but not fatally (that was two anacondas in four days—a lot). Kauka had brought with him another of Francisca's intricately woven cotton hammocks, called a *makira*, and a rectangular pubic covering, or *tanga*, made of red, blue, and white beads woven in a crenellated pattern. They were beautiful work. I thought he wanted to sell them and asked how much, but he only wanted to show them to me and said, 'Nobody will ever make these things again. My daughters don't know how to, and you can't get the right cotton or the right beads any more.'

I was ready to conclude that the Amazon-women myth, if it had ever existed, was extinct among the Kaxuiana, and trying to find out if Kauka knew any other myths, I asked him if the Kaxuiana had any stories about how the moon had got there. But he had been thinking about my earlier question, about the women without husbands, and he had remembered a story about them, or decided to tell it; and looking out across the river, he began to speak in a melodious storytelling voice. (To make the following more coherent, some of the repetitions and some apparent inconsistencies have been deleted, and some sentences have been rearranged so that they flow more smoothly into one another, with every care being taken not to change the meaning.) 'My father used to say that the old people said the Amazon women lived on the *serra*,' he began. 'There were five women: Tiaruui, Amacoco, Carawiki, Coyatinu, and [the last took a while for him to recall] Woru. One day while their husbands were sleeping—they had been having a *festa* and dancing all night—the women left. They clutched hot peppers to their breasts and started to dance in a circle. Slowly they started to leave the ground. Higher they rose. When the men awoke they were flying. They threw down the peppers. They pelted the men's eyes with a rain of peppers so that the men couldn't shoot them with their bows. The women went to live on the *serra*.' What *serra*? I asked. 'The big *serra* at the end of the Cachorrinho,' he said. 'All these rivers end in *serras*.

'One of the women had a child,' he went on, 'whom she left behind, under a basket. The men turned over the basket and found the child. One man—the shaman—took the child and cut it into pieces. As when a hunter gives pieces of meat to many people, the father gave the pieces of his child to his companions. Each man took two pieces. The father let the shaman keep the child's ear and vagina. They all hid the pieces in their rooms.

'Eight days passed. The father says today we will see our women. Let's go. Each man went into his room'—here Kauka sketched with his finger in the dirt the layout of their compound: It was a series of adjoining rooms—'and he discovered that each of the pieces of the child had grown into a fully formed woman. But the shaman went into his room and he found that the ear had become a bat and the vagina a little bird.

'The shaman cried. "Give me one of the women," he said. But no one would. He went walking along the riverbank with his bow and arrow, asking. He saw one of the birds that sings *tikwa*'—Kauka imitated its call in falsetto—'I don't know its name. The shaman became the bird, and left. The women who were from the flesh of the child had children at their breasts, but the children had not been made by men. The children were called *imroyana*. They were the founders of the Kaxuiana.'

And what about the wives who had gone to live on the *serra*? 'The man in the house on the *serra*, the owner of the *serra*, saw these women and asked how it was that they had got here,' Kauka said. 'He tried to find out what happened. The women said nothing happened. We just flew up here. And they flew again to make him believe. The women lived there for many years, and they had children, but the children were not made by men. If the child was a boy, they gave it to other Indians.' (How interesting, I thought: As in some of the other women-without-husbands myths, and like the women who had grown up from pieces of the child, these women were able to reproduce on their own, by parthenogenesis. I wondered if the Kaxuiana had made the connection between sex and reproduction. The

103

Cayapo, whom I visited in 1976, seemed not to have. According to one informant, they believed that pregnancy resulted from eating a certain plant that grew on the forest floor and looked like a penis.)

'A thousand men went to see the women of the serra,' Kauka continued. 'They were taken there by the owner of the serra. First they went up the river, then overland. It took three months walking. The husbands were with them, too. They found their wives but the women didn't want to come back.

'Finally they got to the big serra. The owner said, "Here I live. On top of the serra. Let's go up." After two hours of climbing they arrived. They heard noise and conversation. The owner said, "Here the women live. Let's go see them. Don't be scared. They will offer us supper and something to drink."

'They came to a big house. It was about this time of day. Everybody sat down. The women arrived. They were beautiful, wearing tangas. The owner of the serra said to the women, "If you have something to eat and drink you can bring it." Each woman lay down on her bed with her breast pointing in the air and lifted her tanga and said, "Supper is ready." The men started to get on top of the women, but they just squatted over them, they were not supposed to make love to them. One man, squatting over the most beautiful of the women, could not control himself. He wanted her and put his wood into her. The other women killed him on top of her. Didn't I tell you they don't like men?

'For this, because the women don't like men, the men went away. They went away and none of the women wanted to go back with them. The owner of the serra arranged a plane called tereimane for the men to go away.' (The 'ancient times' of Amazonian myths are full of such anachronisms because, as Thomas Gregor has put it, they are 'frozen.' As in dreams, logic and temporality are irrelevant. I asked Kauka about the plane existing so long ago, and he said, 'They made it themselves. It was small. This plane made no noise. It was like a vulture gliding in the air.') 'The men got to Belém and with the women who had grown up from pieces of the child founded the Kaxuiana. Belém then was a malocca [a large communal house, containing a whole village] called Xurutahumu. From there they went to

Kurumukuri, which is now Santarém, and to Pauwiti, which is now Oriximiná. And from there they spread out everywhere. Thus all Indians were founded. Each tribe has its own language and its own story of who they first were. But the first Indians were those who came down from the *serra*.'

I asked Kauka if the words Conori, Cunuris, or Conduri meant anything. He said, 'The Conori were a tribe around here. It was also the name of my father, who was the chief of the Kaxuiana before me. His name was José Sarubi Conori, and he called me Conori.' How extraordinary: the name of Carvajal's queen of the Amazons, and later of a tribe up the Nhamundá and of the river itself, was also the hereditary epithet of the Kaxuiana chief.

As he began talking his daughter Maria, Kanati's wife, and Regina had come to the edge of the *barracão*, and they had been standing there, nursing their babies in the gathering darkness and listening. It was obvious that they believed every word. 'They sing Kaxuiana songs to their children, but they don't tell the stories.' Kauka said. 'Only I know this story. Nobody else can tell it any more. How the Kaxuiana were founded and spread.'

When Quersin understood that the myth, at least, was still alive, and that these were the descendants of the men who had been left behind by the Amazon women, his eyes widened, and he said, 'So you see, we had to miss Almerindo's boat.'

PART TWO

ACROSS ZAIRE

The plane got into Kinshasa at three in the morning. I let the most honest-looking of the taxi drivers who surrounded me outside the arrivals gate show me into his battered yellow Renault. 'Where to?' he asked in French. 'The Inter?' 'What is the Inter?' I asked 'The Inter-Continental Hotel,' he said. I said that sounded fine. We settled on a fare of fifteen dollars, the driver jump-started his car with the help of a push from his colleagues, and we headed into town. When we got to the Inter, he helped carry my baggage to the front desk, and I handed him the money. He said it wasn't enough, that I had agreed to pay him fifty. An argument for which I was in no mood, having been on planes and in airport waiting rooms for the last two days, followed. The man at the desk was unsympathetic; his cheapest room worked out to a hundred and twenty dollars a day. I finally got the taxi driver to take twenty dollars by telling him that was all the money I had, and signed the register incredulously.

Though hardly in the hundred-and-twenty-dollars-a-day category, the Inter succeeded remarkably well in providing the comforts Westerners require. Air conditioning kept the modern tower generally twenty degrees cooler than outside. The outdoor buffet was lavish. A meal there cost the same amount as the waiter who served it made in a month. The Inter was part of a chain; in the lobby, where Texans with Stetsons, Senegalese with flowing caftans, and other intercontinental types were often lounging around, there were posters of other Inter-Continental Hotels in Rio, Nairobi, and Abidjan. Mobutu Sese Seko, Zaire's President for life, owned a good part of the hotel, and his informants were said to include most of the staff. The telephones were unpredictable. Sometimes it took half an hour to make a local call, sometimes you got right through. A *matabish* (equivalent to the Latin American *mordida* and the Asian *baksheesh*) to the man at the switchboard was said to improve service dramatically. The walls of the bar were decorated with bland, characterless wooden masks—airport art, nothing like the extraordinary carvings that still come out of the interior. To the left, as I entered at the cocktail hour that evening, a little Egyptian man with slicked-down hair and a polka-dot cravat was playing a listless approximation of the theme to *The Sting* on a piano. I joined a freelance writer from Los Angeles and a Dutchman who developed new markets for a large drug company, who were sitting on neighboring stools and trying to have a conversation. 'Maybe the big powers should rape Zaire as quickly and thoroughly as possible,' the American told me.'Then leave it alone once and for all. Or maybe they should pull out now and let it crumble. Let it reach the bottom of the pendulum. Then it can work out its own destiny in peace.'

I ate supper alone in the outdoor buffet several tables away from a beautiful *citoyenne* and a European visitor, who were eating together in silence, just as she would be doing again the next night, with a different visitor. Someone at the American embassy had lent me a handbook on Zaire put out by our Department of Defense. I started to read. Zaire—the river, the country, and the currency—a Portuguese corruption of the Bantu for river, *nzari*. Area: almost as large as eastern half of US—a good chunk of sub-Saharan Africa. Four lingua francas besides French, the official national language: Kikongo, Tshiluba, Swahili, LiNgala. Two hundred and fifty ethnic groups; the BaKongo, with two and a half million, the largest. Less than five hundred thousand of the country's twenty-six million people have electricity. Twenty-six thousand telephones, seven thousand two hundred television sets.

I closed the handbook and wondered how this trip was going to turn out. I had never even been to Africa. I had no agenda, except to visit an old school friend, now an anthropologist, who had been living with pygmies for a year, and to see as many animals as I could. My return ticket was good for sixty days.

Ten to eight. Time to go to my room and wait for a call. That afternoon I had called on a man in the Zairois government who, a diplomat had told me, was one of the really bright people in Kinshasa, torn between opposition and working within an imperfect structure. The man had agreed to meet me in the evening and to talk about the situation in Zaire, as long as what he said wouldn't be traceable. He was already waiting in the hall when I came up—a powerfully built, very black man in the vibrant prime of his late thirties. He had changed from the dark blue short-sleeved suit, with a button of the Mouvement Populaire de la Révolution in the lapel, which he'd worn to work, into slacks, sandals, and a colorful shirt. In good English, learned while studying abroad, he explained that he hadn't wanted to be overheard telephoning me from downstairs. I showed him into my room and called down for two bottles of Primus, the local beer. The beer came, and pouring himself a glass, he started to talk. 'This is a huge country, four times the size of France, eighty times the size of Belgium, as you've no doubt heard. Its history has been dramatic: colonization, five years of civil war, sixteen of one-man rule. The colonization was too short to have left much of a structure. In the last fifteen years the President has tried to build one, setting up a one-party system, controlling institutions, trade unions, churches, splintering power so no one can challenge him. In the beginning the economic situation looked good. The copper and cobalt factories were booming. The currency was strong. But now the picture is rather gloomy. The cost of living is such that it is practically impossible for an ordinary person to live with his salary. The political picture begins to look unstable. There is opposition out of the country in Belgium, and a lot of discontent within it. The system is now dominated by what the President has called Le Mal Zairois. Corruption is rampant in high circles as well as in low circles. Everyone is engaged in what the French call *l'affairisme*. Here it is called *débrouillardise*. Everyone makes ends meet however he can, mainly illegally. There are unspoken rules that makes up the system. If you want a good room at the Inter, for example, you have to pay for it. You have probably been cheated several times since you came here.

'There is *traffique d'influence* and *traffique de lettres,*' he went on. 'Some mail arrives, some doesn't. If you have a judicial blot on your record, you can make your whole file disappear. *Margoulinage*, the bypassing of rules, is institutionalized.

'The prospects for the university are very gloomy. In the late sixties we had three respectable universities that functioned at the level of universities in the rest of the world. The President made them into one single university because the students caused trouble. In 1960 there were only three hundred graduates from high school in the entire country. Now the high schools are producing thirty thousand graduates a year, but there are only twelve thousand places in the university, and we don't have enough money to send more than three hundred students aboard.

'Health and transportation are similarly deadlocked. There hasn't been a new hospital in Kinshasa since the Belgians were here, when the population was three hundred thousand. Now it's two million. The roads which the Belgians put in have been allowed to deteriorate to the point that many are not passable during the rainy season. People call the Office of Roads the Office of Holes.

'As for agriculture: We import rice, corn, even palm oil, which we used to export. There are shortages of fish and meat. The conditions are here for Zaire to become a world food producer, but who is going to produce if there is no way of getting the goods to market? The palm oil industry collapsed because no one wants to climb trees. They have gone through five years of primary school and can do the four arithmetic processes and feel it is beneath them. So many Zairois have become involved in the lucrative domains: traffic of gold, coffee, ivory, diamonds, cobalt.

'Last April the President said he saw the light at the end of the tunnel. At the beginning of the year thirteen senators from Mbuji-Mayi said in an open letter that he was the only

110

one to see the end of the tunnel. They were arrested and relegated to their area, declared *non-citoyens*, sentenced to *mort civil*. They belonged to the country's most dynamic ethnic group, the Baluba. The Baluba are often 'quota'd' out of positions in the administration and the university. Mobutu is scared of them. They are not his tribe. He is from northern Equateur. The Baluba are from the extreme south. The senators' letter was never published, of course, as he controls the newspapers.

'Everyone wears the button of the party. There is always a big turnout at the *marches de soutien* for the President. But among the marches, behind the façade of unanimity, you will hear rampant criticism. In his speech about Le Mal Zairois, the President shouted the slogan "MPR means serve." and then asked, "Serve yourself?" and the people shouted, "No" But everyone does the opposite.'

He looked beyond roofs and treetops to where the river Zaire widened as it went around two islands. 'Zaire today is a brutal, Hobbesian society where the law of nature is the rule,' he said. 'A very suspicious society in which people are multidimensional, play multiple games, illegal games, supporting the regime and blaming Mobutu for the general failure. And yet you will find a very happy, loving, warm, charming people expressing itself in arts, in music, struggling to live with hope, extremely lively, hardworking, and eager to succeed.'

When I returned to Kinshasa six weeks later I went to the converted colonial villa where this man had been working, but there was someone else at his desk. The whole ministry, in fact, had been replaced. 'Mobutu keeps things moving,' my diplomatic source explained. 'He turns over his cabinet twice a year. Long term stability is not his style. It's frustrating as all get-out to people who think in Western terms. It drives the World Bank and the International Monetary Fund absolutely bonkers. But it's brilliant politically. The constant flux keeps anyone from becoming too powerful, and it gives more people opportunity to enrich themselves, thus winning him more allies.'

I spent five days in Kinshasa. Practical matters like getting on a flight into the the interior and changing my money took a lot of time. The dollar was officially worth only three zaires, but on the 'parallel' market you could get almost ten. One evening at the bar the freelance writer from Los

Angeles told me about some missionaries who were giving the best rate in town. It seemed funny for men of the cloth to be doing this sort of work but they needed hard currency to run their operation, the writer explained.

I went to the missionaries and exchanged my traveller's cheques for a brick of crisp, newly minted ten-zaire notes. The bills were green, with images of the earnest, bespectacled President, a springing leopard, a sinuous black hand grasping a torch, and a warning: *Le contrefacteur est puni de servitude pénale*. They were large and handsome; and in the bush, where you could hire a man for four days with one, they went a long way. I felt nervous carrying so much money around in my side bag, but there seemed to be no alternative. Amony other things, the transaction reduced my hotel bill to a more resonable daily rate of forty dollars.

The city of Kinshasa is divided by a sort of no man's land consisting of a golf course, a cemetery, and a zoo into two sections: the *ville* and the *cité*. The *ville* is the old colonial part, where the Belgians used to live. Now it is inhabited by white businessmen, many of them Belgians who have stayed on, and the country's 'modern elite' You can be sipping Coke by a swimming pool in the *ville* and almost forget that you are in black Africa. The rest of Kinshasa, a couple of million souls, lives on the seething streets of the *cité*. There is no way of being more precise about the population. More arrive each day, perpetuating a hoax that a taxi driver named Misi Masamba explained to me. 'After they've lived in Kinshasa for a year or two, they go back to their villages and lie about how well off they are, about how they always take taxis, when in fact they are *foutus*. The people in the villages see how healthy their children are, and hear how they don't have to walk ten miles for an aspirin or twenty miles for a nurse, and they, too, come to Kinshasa, where there is nothing for millions.' Misi Masamba drove me around one morning. He used to be called Jean-Marie, but like most Zairois, he had given up his Christian name after the *authenticité* proclamation of 1972. He belonged to a local fishing tribe called the Bateke, who had lived on both sides of the Zaire until Independence, when they were driven across the river. Misi Masamba had been allowed to stay because he was born on the Zairian side, but his parents were among those expelled. On Sundays he took the ferry and visited them. The other side

112

is Marxist, the People's Republic of the Congo. 'A lot of diamonds leave the country on that ferry,' he told me.

Misi Masamba showed me the Palais du Peuple, which the Chinese had built, the World Trade Center, which the French had built, and other white elephants of the seventies, when the big powers were courting Mobutu for business, mining, and lumber franchises, and Kinshasa acquired a modest skyline. He took me to the huge central market where you could buy a goat, a smoked monkey, a live crocodile whose jaws were wrapped in vine, or a four-foot-long catfish caught the night before and covered with flies. I bought twenty small shaving mirrors. If the Congo was anything like Amazonia, they would be appreciated in the jungle. The woman who sold me them was striking, with about a dozen shoots of hair standing on her head like antennae and a silver sarong, or *pagne*, with birds and foliage printed on it, wrapped around her body. Misi Masamba said, 'Thank you, *mama*,' and she gave us a radiant smile. You could feel her warmth from several feet away. Misi Masamba told me he could tell what part of the country a woman was from, and often what tribe, from her hairstyle. Sixty thousand *mamas* do business in Kinshasa. The *petit commerce* of the *mamas* is the real economic life of the country.

During my last night in Kinshasa loud booms of thunder rolled up and down the river. When day came it was raining in big, warm drops, pinging on the delicate subleaflets of the mimosa trees around the Inter. I played a last game of squash with Ikilenge, the young pro, after breakfast. The English ball, a better workout. Ikilenge had picked up the game only five months before and moved like a cat. He admired Borg's 'sangfroid terrible.' After we played he asked me for my new blue jogging shoes. I said maybe when I got back to Kinshasa, if there was anything left of them.

Bob Bailey, my old school friend, was with a previously unstudied group of pygmies in the Ituri Forest of Haut-Zaire, within two hundred miles of Uganda and the Sudan. According to an ethnologist I met in Kinshasa who had just visited him, he had cleared about an acre, put up two houses, and was *bien installé*. His camp was near a village call 'Opoku' (to protect its inhabitants from his publicity I have given the village, at Bailey's request, the name of another apparently extinct village in the same region, and have changed some people's names), on a rarely travelled road passable only by truck or Land-Rover. The nearest flights were to places called Bunia and Isiro. Isiro looked a little closer.

The plane took off three hours late, par for Air Peut-être, as the Zairois jokingly call their unpredictable airline. It was the middle of March. The rains were beginning, and the *cuvette*, the central part of the Zaire basin, were socked in. Under the clouds I occasionally glimpsed the smooth green blanket of the world's second-largest continuous expanse of rain forest and the Zaire River itself. It was hard to believe that such a thin ribbon of water could drain two thirds of such an enormous country. I fervently hoped I was going to stay healthy this time. On my last extended visit to a tropical rain forest I had come close to dying from the complication of Falciparum malaria known as blackwater fever.

After about an hour, we landed in Kisangani, the former Stanleyville, and everybody got out for a security check whose real purpose was to give the local customs officials a chance to enrich themselves by finding something illegal. Kisangani is half a degree north of the Equator and was noticeably hotter and steamier than Kinshasa. As Conrad's heart of darkness and V. S. Naipaul's bend in the river, it has a sinister reputation. I planned to stop there on my way back.

We took on some new passengers: *commissaires* of rural zones and their deputies, young coffee bosses and other members of the elite, dressed in short-sleeved suits or blue jeans, carrying attaché cases (some, I bet, with nothing in them) or big radio-cassette players to pass the time in the boondocks. I was the only white aboard besides an old Belgian who was reading the memoirs of Henry Kissinger in French. He had been growing coffee around Isiro since the forties, he told me. In 1973 his plantation had been expropriated, along with about two thousand other foreign-owned farms, businesses, and factories in the country, and turned over to Zairian owners named by the state. 'But Mobutu's Zairianization program was a disaster,' he told me. 'The new owners didn't pay their men. In many cases they sold everything they could, bought Mercedes-Benzes, and moved to Kinshasa. By the end of 1975 the economy was at a standstill, and Mobutu was forced to make his 'retrocession' decree. We were invited to take back what was left of our businesses. But there weren't many takers. There had been *pas mal de* Pakistanis in Isiro. Some of them were formidable badminton players. But none returned to their empty stores. As for me—coffee is the only business I know, so I came back and started over. But I'd never live here again. You never know what these monkeys will do next. I run my plantation from Belgium, fly down twice a year to supervise the shipments. Only eighty per cent of what we ship to Kinshasa arrives, but it's still profitable,' he said. Then he let out a laugh so hearty it was frightening. 'Look. Coffee,' he said, pointing down to a large clearing with rows of glossy shrubs growing in the bare red earth, They were the robusta species, which used to be considered native to the Congo, but now there is some question. Robusta is mainly used for instant coffee.

We were low enough to see here and there a very tall tree—an emergent—poking up from the rest of the forest and spreading a bluish crown above the competition. The writer Tim Cahill, flying over jungle in southern Venezuela, was reminded of 'monstrous stalks of broccoli,' and that is just what these trees looked like. We touched down and taxied up to a small modern building. About a dozen long, curved objects, wrapped in burlap, lay on the runway. 'Tusks,' the Belgian said. 'They belong to the subregional administrator, who seizes them from poachers and buys them from government hunters licensed to shoot nuisance elephants. The slaughter is worse now than it has ever been. They're even poisoning water holes and killing calves for their little nubs of ivory. In ten years I doubt there will be any wild elephants left in Zaire.' These were savanna tusks, judging from their length. The forest elephant has smaller ears and shorter tusks.

A crowd was milling in the buildings, and as the passengers entered, faces lit up with recognition. I stood at a window and watched the baggage being handed down from the belly of the plane and the tusks being brought over on a forklift and slowly raised. The loading of the tusks was a serious operation, and took priority over the delivery of our baggage. It grew dark, but still no one was in any hurry to bring it in. A group of people with a separate pile stood calmly to one side waiting to get on the plane. I took out the cheap Korean guitar I had bought before I left and started to play it. I already knew from the Amazon that a guitar is useful not only for breaking ice with people who may have never seen anyone like you before but for killing time. We waited two hours.

At last an official announced that nothing was going to be done about the baggage, and we were allowed to walk past the soldier in spotted fatigues who had been guarding it with an automatic rifle and retrieve it ourselves. I reached down in front of him and picked up my duffelbag. The Belgian took me in his Land-Rover to some Dominican missionaries who he said would put me up and help me get to Opoku. They were having supper at a long table when I entered. Brother Vincent, the oldest, welcomed me and asked if I had eaten. All eight of them were Flemish. 'The typical Flemish missionary,' a Belgian in Kinshasa had told me, 'comes from a little village and belongs to a large family. The first son inherits the farm, the second joins the army. A daughter is married off. The third son comes to the Congo as a missionary.' There was little talk or eye contact during supper, and when it was over we all stood and Brother Vincent said a blessing. Then he took me into a courtyard and introduced me to three German shepherds who were kept in a shed during the day and were trained to attack intruders. I learned from one of the others that before coming to Isiro, in 1940, Brother Vincent had been a well-known theologian in Belgium. He showed me to my room and brought me a face cloth and towel. He was old to be waiting on people, but as he said to me the next evening when I asked about his beliefs, 'God without the next man is nothing.' My room was on the courtyard, with a crucifix over the bed. I spent the night swiping at slow-moving whines in the darkness.

During the Second World War the Allies built a road from Bumba, on the Zaire, to ship matériel up to the Sudan. Paulis, as Isiro was then called, came into being where they ran out of track (the railroad was supposed to end fifty miles later, at a place called Mungbere). Today about sixty thousand people are crowded in and around Isiro, and two dozen stores line its main street. In most of the stores the goods are laid out on a dirt floor The owners are Greek, as are most of the coffee growers and buyers. In the morning Brother Edward, the mission's red-cheeked business manager, took me to a buyer who would know when a truck came up from the plantation in Digbo, which was a few hours north of Opoku. The buyer said it might be a week or two, but promised to put me in touch with it. 'All you can do is wait,' Brother Edward told me. 'Meanwhile you can stay with us.'

The mission's store was better stocked than any of those in town. All the Catholic missionaries in the subregion of Haut-Uele came and drew from it. I loaded up on things that would soon be as good as money: bags of salt, bars of soap, cigarettes. The local smokes were called Tumbaco and were packed with very strong black tobacco. I smoked them until someone a few weeks later had me exhale a lungful quickly against a sheet of paper and the paper turned brown.

That evening Brother Vincent, Brother Edward, two of the others, and I stayed at the table and talked. I asked about the photographs of eighteen white men and women and one black nun on the wall. 'They were killed right here on the front lawn during the Rebellion,' Brother Vincent said. The Rebellion was started by a man named Pierre Mulele in 1963. During the political chaos after independence, Mulele went into exile and spent several months in China, where he was impressed by the ideas of Mao Tse-tung. He returned and started to assemble a band of guerrillas in the region of Equateur. Many of his followers were only in their teens. They called themselves Simbas, lions. It appears that Mulele wanted to start a classic Third World revolution, that his motives were much like Che Guevara's, but some believe that if Zaire had not been held together by the West, notably the United States, it would have split into five countries long ago, and that the Rebellion was really a war of secession. Life went on as usual in Kinshasa and in the south (where Katanga had already tried once to break away and would try again), but in the northeast, in Haut-Zaire and northern Kivu, the local population suffered terribly as the Rebellion spread. Ancient tribal enmities were revived. In some villages people were eaten. In others young men were forced to copulate with their mothers. Anyone who was white and anyone considered to have been contaminated by the West, who wore eyeglasses or a decent shirt, had a gold tooth or a pencil in his front pocket, was finished. The Rebellion was put down by equally savage mercenaries and national troops. It ended in Isiro. The taxi driver Misi Masamba, when he drove me to the airport in Kinshasa, had

117

described going in with the Red Cross and collecting all the bloated corpses, including the bodies of the missionaries. 'Luckily, I was on leave in Belgium, or my face would be on that wall,' Brother Vincent said. One of the others with us, who was very quiet, had been imprisoned by the Simbas in another town, but miraculously they had only broken his nose.

'What luck!' Brother Edward said when we met the next morning. 'Father Lazaro from Nduye is in town. He only comes every six months or so. He'll be going right through Opoku on his way back.' An orange Fiat truck soon pulled into the courtyard. Father Lazaro, a man of about forty with several days' growth of beard, was in the passenger seat. He was nervous and not friendly. There were several reasons for this, I discovered. He had come from Padua two years before and despised the jungle. He didn't like Flemings either; there was friction between the Flemish and Italian missionaries. I would have liked to know what he was doing in the Congo. He didn't seem the missionary type. But he obviously didn't want to talk about it.

There were only two seats in the truck. I sat on the hump between them, after Father Lazaro agreed to take me. Not that he wanted to, but cooperation among whites is an unwritten law of the bush. He watched the red rutted lane run between the walls of soaring trees and kept to himself. Teo, his driver, was more communicative. He was thirty-six and had five children, he told me. A WaNande from the savanna, he had come to Nduye twenty years before to work for Father Longo, one of the best-loved missionaries in Haut-Zaire, who was killed during the Rebellion.

The truck ploughed along in first and second. I wondered if Teo ever got to use high gears. The road was awful. Our top speed, on the good stretches, wasn't much more than fifteen miles an hour. Twenty-five years earlier, you could have taken the same road at fifty. The Belgians had made the natives build the roads, live along them, and keep them up. According to one story I heard, there was a road superintendent who would drive along with a glass of water on his dashboard, and if any of it spilled he would make the chief in whose *localité* the accident occurred clean his car. According to the *Guide du Voyageur* for the Belgian Congo, published in Brussels in 1958, there were good hotels and lots of things to see and do along these roads: 'Charming waterfall at kilometer 32,' etc—and the natives would let you take their picture for a few centimes.

But for some years now the government in Kinshasa had not been able to provide services into the interior, and there had not been an infrastructure for handling tourists. Some of the roads were actually disappearing, and people were leaving them and returning to the places in the forest where they had lived before. With each new devaluation of the currency, more people were giving up on the cash economy and reverting to subsistence. 'There are corners of the country,' an American who spent his life in Zaire told me, 'that look as if the twentieth century sort of washed in and out and left them high and dry. You can see the high-tide mark, but it isn't there any more.'

The main liaisons with the twentieth century were the missions. They tried to fill the vacuum with their schools and dispensaries. We stopped at several where Father Lazaro had business. There was an almost feudal feeling to the red brick compounds that cropped up every twenty or thirty miles. The missionaries lived well; most of them offered us cold Primus from their gas-powered refrigerators and sausage and cheese that had come all the way from Europe. At the mission in a place called Ibambi we filled six drums with palm oil and rolled them up on planks into the bed of the truck. At Powa we loaded on a cultivator and slept until three in the morning, when we packed up and started for Wamba. The road was bathed in the light of a full orange moon, and every couple of yards a nighthawk was sitting in it. We must have hit dozens as they flew up in the headlights.

At daybreak we were in the country of the BaBudu, an industrious and relatively prosperous tribe, Teo told me. They stood in the doors of small thatched huts and looked at us impassively. Even from the window of a passing truck you felt the strength of their faces. The BaBudu are traders, and often we would overtake a man on a bicycle with a chest full of goods strapped over the back wheel to sell at the next village. Sometimes we would see one of the pygmies who helped the BaBudu with their plantations and brought them meat from the forest. They were a completely different physical type: much shorter, of course, and their skin was light copper brown, and except for their brows, so was their hair; and the pink lips of their large, wryly pursed

119

mouths were thinner. (Pygmies have 'convex and un-everted' lips in the jargon of physical anthropology, as opposed to the 'roll-out' lips of the Negro BaBudu. They used to be described as one of the four original races of Africa—along with the Negroes, the Nilo-Saharans, and the Bushmen—but by now there are so many gradients that many anthropologists wonder if two geographically separate 'races' ever existed.) The men were very muscular, like wrestlers, and some of them were holding little bows and arrows that looked like toys but in their hands were deadly weapons. The women carried firewood, bananas, babies. I could already tell from the way they looked—alert, inquisitive, and full of mischief—and from the little I knew about them—that they are phenomenal yodellers, for instance, and connoisseurs of mushrooms—that I was going to like them. Everyone in Kinshasa who had met pygmies had been charmed by them. 'They are very free, very observant, and terrific hunters,' I was told. 'You ask about their religion and they'll say bah, let's talk about other things . . . They are supple, agile, they can climb any tree, they can squat down right in front of you and you won't even see them . . . Primitive? Now there's a word for you. The pygmies are some of the kindest and most socially mature people on earth!'

At Wamba we met a roadblock. Not that there was anything of strategic importance in the area, but that was how the soldier who came up with his semi-automatic rifle, in the absence of regular pay, made his living—by preying on people whose papers were not in order, or who were smuggling something, as many were. Father Lazaro pointed down to the mission's name on the side of the truck and said nothing to the soldier, who slid back the pole and let us through. Because it was Sunday, we took communion in a small room with several members of Father Lazaro's order, the Combonians. A young Italian novitiate conducted the service in Latin and French. At the same time, another mass was being celebrated nearby in Lingala. Wamba is a good-sized town, and there were about a thousand people in its large church. I could hear the swell of their voices joining in a hymn, together with the sound of quick hands on long drums. I looked in as the congregation was swearing their faith to Mungu, the Christian God, with their hands raised and trembling in the air. A boy who was wearing a T-shirt that said RICH'S EAST STATE SUNOCO turned around and looked at me.

At Lingodo we dropped off two parcels sent from Canada six months earlier, and as we had done at every stop, we collected the letters home. We threw on several sacks of dried fish from one of the big lakes in the Eastern Highlands, and handed up four locally produced armchairs. Their frames were solidly made of *ibuyu* wood from the towering primary forest behind the mission's coffee fields. Then on to Mungbere, past a wet meadow filled with white, red-striped lilies; past an old rubber plantation, with coffee growing between the wrinkled *Hevea* stumps, the bushes bearing clusters of white starlike flowers; past several revival meetings in thatched-roof churches. The worshippers, some of whom had on feather headdresses, belonged to one of the nearby three hundred Protestant sects that have caught on in Zaire. Christianity in all its varieties is doing better in black Africa that anywhere else in the world.

On the way to Andudu we stopped at a coffee plantation, and while Father Lazaro went to find the Greek owner I stood in the yard and watched a noisy colony of Vieillot's black weavers in an umbrella tree. There were dozens of nests, shaped like inverted cups, among the large splayed leaves, and at the bottom of each nest a male weaver was clinging and flapping in some sort of display. The entrance hole was underneath and was indented so the eggs wouldn't fall out.

We clattered over a large river flowing silently through deep forest—the Nepoko. Then it got dark. It was only six-thirty, but near the Equator night falls early and quickly. The days have twelve hours of darkness and twelve of light all year round. Soon the moon appeared and we were hitting nighthawks again. At Digbo we crossed a linguistic divide. From here on Swahili would be spoken. The road became more like a path. Deep erosion cuts slowed the truck down to a barely a crawl. The only motor traffic on it was the Land-Rover of the Catholic sisters who drove up from Nduye every few weeks to give the lepers their sulfa pills.

At Digbo we also entered the country of the BaLese, one of the poorest, least 'developed' tribes in Zaire. The BaBudu and the BaBira, their neighbours, looked down on the BaLese. They say the BaLese are dirty and uneducated and like the forest too much. In most of the BaLese villages everybody had already turned in, but in a few of them the men were still sitting in the *baraza* around a dimly burning fire. Once I heard rumba music from a radio as we drove by. The *baraza* is where the men sit and make things, tell stories, and discuss what is happening in the village. It is usually nothing more than a thatched roof on upright poles. It starts to fill up at noon.

At about eleven Teo stopped and blew the horn. A woman called from the top of a cleared slope to our left, then came down to meet us. She was a handsome British woman of about thirty. Her name was Elizabeth Ross. 'Oh yes,' she said when I had introduced myself. 'Bob said you might be coming.'

During the early nineteen-sixties Bob Bailey and I went to the same boarding school in New Hampshire. Most of the boys who went there were from old families in the East and were destined to work in banks or law firms. Bob came from Tuxedo Park, New York. He was a good athlete—I seem to remember that lacrosse was his best sport—and he belonged to a group that couldn't get too excited about anything—the sort of boy who when we were thirteen or fourteen would turn over your tie and snicker if the label wasn't from Brooks Brothers. He was a real 'sarc'. His humor had a sarcastic edge that made him popular.

After graduation he took a year off and worked on Wall Street, then he started as a freshman at Harvard. I was already a sophomore, and I don't think I saw him more than once or twice there. It wasn't until we were out of college that our lives took a similar direction. We both happened to go to the Amazon.

Two days after I arrived in Opoku Bob came out of the forest, where he had been doing observations in a pygmy camp. We cracked open a bottle of scotch I had brought from Isiro and, lying on the beds in his hut, traced the fates of classmates and looked back on our own lives. 'For most of my undergraduate career I hung out at the P.C.,' he told me. The P.C. was the Porcellian, the most prestigious of Harvard's eating clubs. Bob was elected president his senior year. 'Then I tried to get a teaching job in Massachusetts— I'd gotten my certification over the summer—but there was a glut. It was 1969, and everyone wanted to avoid the draft. I sat on the Cape for six months and finally said the hell with this and went to New York.'

In New York Bob got the highest-paying job he could, because he knew he would only be at it for a year or two— marketing consultant for a major copper smelting firm. Among his responsibilities was to answer the Sierra Club's letters to the editor of the *New York Times*. 'We were going to level a whole mountain chain in Idaho. There was a model of how it was going to look in twenty years—a big lake surrounded by miles of lawn.

'I did very well there. They offered me a big promotion. I could see it all. The big house in Southampton, the family, the kids. I knew I could make money, a lot of it but I just wasn't ready to take the dive. So I just took off. Central America. South America. Maybe on to India. Six months, five years—I didn't know. For the first time I met people who reacted not to my credentials but to *me*, and I loved it. When I got to the Amazon, the beauty of it blew me away.'

In the little wedge of Colombia that comes to a point on the Amazon's left bank at the city of Leticia, Bob got a job with a man named Mike Tsalickis, who shipped animals to zoos and laboratories in the United States. A few years earlier Tsalickis had released five thousand squirrel monkeys on an island in the river. Bob was so fascinated by the monkeys that he stayed on the island for two years. He corresponded with others who were studying New World monkeys and learned how to make scientific observations. It was a completely new direction for him. 'Everything in my life had been oriented to going into business,' he told me. 'Now I wanted to stay in the Amazon forever.' But in the end he went back to Harvard and began to study primates in earnest. I heard he was there and called him in 1977. By then he had been back for several years. I had just returned from the Amazon myself and was starting to write a book about it. He was very helpful on the monkeys.

Then he got into hunter-gatherers. He went to Africa to study the pygmies, who are considered the largest group of hunter-gatherers left in the world. In 1978 he made a survey of their populations in Rwanda, Gabon, Cameroon, the Central African Republic, the People's Republic of the Congo, and other parts of Zaire as well as the Ituri Forest. There are about a hundred and forty thousand pygmies on the continent. The ones who live in the Ituri Forest are called the BaMbuti. No one knows how many BaMbuti there are because they are often on the move. Bailey's estimate was about twenty thousand. While other pygmies grow at least some of their own food, the BaMbuti have shown no interest in taking part in the agricultural revolution that most of the world underwent about twelve thousand years ago (although, as Bob pointed out, they actually get most of their calories from the *shambas*, or plantations, of tribes they work for or trade with). About five thousand BaMbuti are associated with the BaLese. They have lost their own language and speak the BaLese's strange tonal dialect, in which they are known as the Efe. After completing his survey Bob concluded that of the pygmies in Africa the Efe were probably the most tradition-bound and the least likely to be disturbed. Other areas were being invaded by planters and lumber companies, but nothing was happening in this part of the Ituri Forest, and with Zaire's economy in shambles and focused on mineral extraction in the south, nothing was probably going to happen for a while.

In 1980 Bob came back, and as he walked up the road from Nduye with a pack on his back, the Efe slipped into the forest when they caught sight of him, as they had done before, and the BaLese sprinted to their villages in terror. At each village he would find everyone standing together and laughing at the ones who had been scared, and he would tell them in Swahili, which most of them understood, that there was nothing to be afraid of, he had come to learn about them and the Efe and would be with them for two years. 'They're freaked out by *muzungus*,' Bob explained. *Muzungu* is the Swahili word for white man. Like the word *gringo* in South America, it can be a derogatory connotation. I would hear the word *muzungu* hundreds of times in the next two months, mostly from children who would point at me and scream it excitedly as I passed, and from women with dollar signs in their eyes who would call it to me seductively.

'The BaLese are convinced that *muzugus* eat people,' Bob went on. 'I asked a woman in the village, have you ever seen a *muzugu* eating human flesh and she said well no, but I was in a store once and I saw a Belgian woman buy two of the plates that *muzugus* eat black people on.' The conviction is widespread in rural Zaire. It is based partly on stories that are told in the *barazas* about brutal Arab slavers during the last century, Belgians during the colonial period, and white

124

mercenaries during the uprisings of the sixties; and partly on a confusion about holy communion, that people who eat the flesh and drink the blood of their god must be cannibais. Until several generations ago, the BaLese themselves sometimes ate parts of enemies they had slain, and this may have enhanced their credulity.

But Bob was different from the typical muzungu. Tall, bearded, blue-eyed, he laughed with them, danced with them, kept up with them in the forest. For the first time they appreciated how they sounded and looked as Bob played back their songs on a tape recorder and gave them snapshots he had taken with a Polaroid camera moments earlier. They started to like him in spite of themselves. They helped him clear some land and built two huts on it for him and the other muzungus he said would soon be coming. Not wanting to introduce more money than they were used to, Bob paid them what the Greeks up the road at Digbo paid the people who worked in their coffee plantations, two and a half zaires a day. They worked from seven-thirty in the morning until noon, six days a week. The huts were like their own, with baked mud walls and roofs of thatched mangungu leaf, except that tho rooms were bigger. They couldn't understand why Bob wanted such large rooms.

Nadine Peacock, Bob's colleague and friend, came in July, and she started to study the Efe women. Richard Wrangham and Elizabeth Ross, a newly married British couple, came in October. Richard was an old friend of Bob's. He had studied green vervet monkeys in Kenya and had just married Elizabeth, an immunologist. They started to study the BaLese. Now the villagers were building a third hut for Irven Devore and his wife Nancy, who were expected any day. He was a professor at Harvard who had done studies of baboons and the !Kung San bushmen, and was overseeing this project.

Bob spent the better part of that year—a lot more time than he had counted on—setting up the housing. He decided to call the camp Ngodi Ngodi, after the black and white birds that had begun to hang around. Ngodi Ngodi is the BaLeses' word for the African pied wagtail. When I woke up the morning after I got to Opoku—Bob and Nadine were still in the forest—Elizabeth made me a cup of coffee and we sat in the yard, where about a dozen wagtails, bold as bluejays but a little smaller, were feasting on little purple butterflies. The butterflies swirled in dense balls of fifty to a hundred. They settled on moist spots on the red ground and 'puddled'—sucked up the moisture and eliminated it through the anus, perhaps as a thermoregulatory device— and perhaps attracted by a chemical odor completely covered one of my running shoes. One landed on my nose. The yard was a blizzard of metallic lavender flakes. They were lycaenids, a large, complex family with more than a thousand species in Africa, or almost half the butterfly forms below the Sahara. Most seemed to be the same species, but there were a few with copper undersides mixed in. Maybe they were the same kind which Henry Morton Stanley encountered when he passed through the Ituri Forest almost a hundred years earlier on his way to rescue Emin Pasha from the fanatic followers of the Mahdi.

> We saw a cloud of moths sailing up river [Stanley wrote], which reached from the water's surface to the topmost height of the forest, say 180 feet, so dense, that before it overtook us we thought it was a fog, or, as was scarcely possible, a thick fall of lavender-coloured snow. The rate of flight was about three knots an hour. In the dead calm morning air they maintained an even flight, but the slightest breeze from the bank whirled them confusedly about like snow particles on a gusty day.

I asked Elizabeth how her work was going. 'My limited data show that the men sit on their backsides most of the time, and the women do all of the work.' She laughed. 'When I first got here it was maddening, because the women taught their children to fear me. If a child had done something wrong, his mother would pick him up and bring him toward me, and the poor thing would burst into tears. Now the children come up and lean against me. It's funny. Sometimes you think the villagers are just like the folks back home, then one of them turns to you and says, "If you eat this, your backbone will shrivel to nothing." '

Richard came out of his hut and greeted me with a tremendous smile. He had spent a lot of time among Africans and some of their jolliness, as he called it, had rubbed off. He had got up at three that morning to catch termites with some of the men. At this time of year, just before the rains, millions of winged adults emerge from their nests. They are a prized source of protein. 'They're oily and crunchy,' Elizabeth said with a shudder, 'but Nadine likes them.'

I asked Richard if he knew what species the lycaenids were. He said he had caught some for the lepidopterists at the British Museum to identify. 'A few months ago I passed a migration of skippers flying at treetop height along the road to Bunia,' he told me. 'It was four kilometres long. They were heading north.'

When I returned to the States I asked the lepidopterist John C. Downey why one species would occur in such fantastic numbers. He explained that the females of some butterflies, including lycaenids, can lay more than a hundred eggs in the course of their brief adulthood. In most species, the majority of the eggs addle or are attacked by parasites. Some years, however, more of the eggs survive than usual, resulting in a banner crop of butterflies.

Richard and I put some empty oil drums on the back of a pickup truck and headed for the river. It was a brand-new Toyota that had been assembled in Saudi Arabia, he told me, shipped up the Nile to Juba, and driven to the Sudan–Zaire border, where it was exchanged for seven tons of coffee, the equivalent of thirty-five thousand zaires. After paying off the border guards, the man who had bought it drove it to Bunia, where Bob bought it for sixty-five thousand zaires. It was a typical 'parallel' transaction. Most of Zaire's coffee slips out to the Sudan, because the money it fetches that way doesn't have to be repatriated at the official rate, so the profit is three times greater. Most of the country's natural wealth, in fact, and its potential foreign exchange, is seeping out through its borders and quietly accumulating in Swiss bank accounts.

The Toyota was equipped with a tape deck. Richard punched in a cassette of Donna Summer, whose moaning in a heavily mixed disco background fascinated the BaLese. Soul was not so far removed from their music that they could not relate to it. A large bird sailed across the road. Richard said it was a black and white casqued hornbill. He pointed out some *shumbas* to our right planted with bananas, peanuts, and manioc. It was peanut planting time. Most of the work, he said, was being done by Efe women. They would be paid in carbohydrates or marijuana. The banana reached Africa from Malaysia around the year one. Portuguese brought over manioc and the peanut from

Brazil. After it was introduced to the BaLese in the last century by Arabs, they cultivated fields of *bangi*, as the drug is called here, but the Belgians outlawed it. The BaLese now frown on its use, although some of the older people still smoke it and the more politically powerful villagers, who are left alone by the police, grow it to trade to the Efe. 'This is not the affluent society,' Richard said, 'but it's a stable existence. The villagers work hard. They hunt, fish, and set traps. They're closer to the forest, and to the pygmies, than the other tribes. There is much more intermarriage here.'

The BaLese are a Sudanic people who, as well as can be determined, migrated from the savannas of Uganda or the Sudan more than two hundred years ago. They are not Bantu like their neighbours the BaBudu and the BaBira, who arrived in the Congo Valley about the same time as the banana. Richard gathered from stories they had told him that the BaLese had lived in small villages and constantly warred over women—much as the Yanomamo Indians of northern Amazonia still do today—until the Belgians made them stop fighting. 'In a way they are in a fortunate state,' he reflected. 'They came out of the forest only forty years ago. They are not at war, they are not upwardly mobile. The thing that impresses me is how ordinary they are. The other day I saw a man framed by clouds, gazing on his *shamba*. Only a painter could have done justice to the scene.'

We passed a large hut whose roof had fallen in. Richard said it had been a school, but the villagers had stopped going to it about a year ago. They weren't interested in education. Then we passed several huts where people who had been thrown out of the village lived. They were called *mbolozi*, which means ghosts or witches. One was a woman who had slept with her husband's brother. The man had fallen in love with her and then had died, and his jealous widow had accused the woman of killing him with *dawa*, or medicine, which can be either sorcery or actual potions, such as water that has been used to wash a cadaver (which might be put in food). The police had come from Bangupanda, a day's walk, and dragged the woman away to prison. It is a crime against the state to be a witch. She was beaten by all the women of the village, formerly her friends. One of the policemen 'ate' her—bit her arm, making it septic—and she almost died. But the woman had recovered, and now she lived in the outcast community with her mother and four men who had also been categorized as *mbolozi*. The BaLese and the Efe live in constant fear both of being harmed by *mbolozi* and of being accused of witchcraft themselves. The local *mbolozi* tend to be old, unproductive members of the community. 'They have nothing to think about except how their friends and relatives did them wrong,' Richard explained. But most *mbolozi* are not in one's own clan or village, or even in one's own tribe. Richard told me about how a woman had got sick, and her husband had had to walk for a day to the Mamvu, a tribe to the north, to get special *dawa* from their sorcerer, because the *mbolozi* was thought to be from that tribe. The *dawa* was some leaves that, after they had been ground up and brewed to make a tea, compelled the sick woman to name her *mbolozi*, who was, indeed, a Mamvu nobody knew. Only then could *her* witch doctor prescribe counteractive *dawa*—some different leaves—and she got well. The effect of the leaves was presumably purely psychological.

We reached the central settlement of Opoku, a dozen or so thatched huts, some with attached outbuildings, clustered around a bare earth clearing. When Stanley passed through the Ituri Forest the villages he saw consisted of 'a long low wooden building . . . 200, 300, or 400 feet long,' in a clearing 'quite a mile and a half in diameter, and the whole strewn with the relics, debris, and timber of the primeval forest.' But early in this century, probably as soon as inter-village wars were stopped by the Belgians, the BaLese adopted the single-family huts that are standard in much of the Third World.

Everybody in Opoku belonged to the same clan and was related to an old man, now dead, who had had four wives and twelve children. I shook hands with the *capita*, or chief, a young man named Abdullah, who was obviously scared of me and retreated to the other end of the *baraza*, where he stood behind a post and avoided my eyes. Two wicker chaises were brought for me and Richard, who started talking in Swahili with three of the men. The men were very muscular. Richard had compared them with male mud-dauber wasps, who crawl protectively around the nest but do little of the work. I watched two bare-breasted women at the far end of the yard rhythmically mashing nuts of the oil palm *Elaeis guianensis* in a large wooden mortar. As one raised a long stake over her head, the other brought

129

hers down. The oil palm is a native of West Africa; its oil is an ingredient of Palmolive soap and an important source of fat for the BaLese. A bottle of *mafuta*, as the viscous orange oil from the nuts is called, is worth a day's work. On a wall of one of the huts someone had written with a piece of charcoal the words 'Citoyen Mokili le 2-1-81,' which meant Citizen of the World, and under them a little boy was sitting and eating sections of the globular fruit of a *Merianthus* tree.

'I told them you had come to see the Efe,' Richard said as we drove back to camp. 'They asked why is everybody always interested in the Efe and not in us? I said because Americans believe the Efe are closely related to the first man. That's not true, they said. We were farming when the Efe were still living like chimpanzees. They have a story about how they met the Efe. One day an Efe man wandered into their *shambas*, smelled the sweet small bananas, ate some, and fell asleep. A villager found him and, thinking he was a chimpanzee, was about to shoot him when he saw that he was two legged and his eyes were different. The Efe awakened and asked the villager for some more bananas to take to his wife. A few days later, he returned with some meat and honey to give to the villager. The two men became friends.

'The Efe have a different story about the first contact: They came out of the forest and saw a village with some *shambas*. Then they met a black man who gave them some bananas. He said, I live with my wife but we have no children. They brought him some meat and showed him and his wife how to have children. The BaLese agree that it was the Efe who taught them how to make love to their women, and the Efe men are resentful because now the BaLese men often take their women to wife, but they aren't allowed to have a BaLese woman.

'It's hard to figure out what their relationship is. It isn't true symbiosis, because the villagers don't really need the Efe; and it isn't parasitism, because the villagers aren't harmed by it except maybe at the end of April and May when the new crops are growing and there is a shortage of food.

'The Efe bring meat or honey, or they help clear a *shamba*. Often they aren't paid the same day, but everyone remembers that a favour is owed. Sometimes the Efe will ask for something in advance. They come whimpering, but the whimpering is only a strategy—if you give them what they want, they go away beaming. If you don't, they act affronted, as if you're questioning their honesty.

'A few villagers of high status have their own Efe. It's a very amicable, workable long-term relationship. The pygmy's father was his villager's father's pygmy. Often a villager's arrows will be on permanent loan to an Efe. The villager gets a cut of each kill. So does the owner of the dog that cornered the quarry. Then the meat has to be distributed among the other hunters and their families. So there isn't much left for us. We've been eating rice and beans because we don't want to upset the system.

'The missionaries think the pygmies are slaves, and that's why they try so hard to save them, but you wonder who the free ones are. The Efe are like gypsies. They let the villagers think they're dependent on them, but they often don't show up for weeks.'

When we returned to camp, two of the boldest Efe women, who had been planting peanuts, came to check out the new *muzungu*. They were both about eighteen and both called Maria, with their bodies wrapped in colorful *pagnes* like the village women, with black circles of plant juice painted on their arms and legs, and black lines on their faces, much as Amazonian Indians have, their teeth chipped to a point, and their golden brown hair in peppercorn tussocks. Their noses were flat and so broad that the end of their nostril wings were plumb with the centers of their large, lustrous eyes. They weren't much taller than I was seated. Richard said that they weren't married; they had been exchanged several times, but nothing long-term had worked out yet. They stood trembling a few feet from my chair and would not have looked at me for anything, even when I passed them each a Tumbaco cigarette and lit it for them.

The origins of Africa's pygmies and the reason for their smallness—the BaMbuti are the smallest people in the world—are unsolved riddles. Pygmies may have originally lived in the savannas of the Upper Nile and, according to the physical anthropologist Carleton S. Coon, may have been driven into the forest by a drought that affected both their water supply and their hunting. 'Pygmy' is a Greek word. Homer mentions 'ἄνδρες Πυγμαῖοι, 'men a cubit high,' to whom overwintering cranes brought slaughter and death;

131

later texts place these men in Africa. 'Once they were in the forest,' Coon writes in his book *The Origin of Races*, 'one or more mutations for dwarfing, which had already occurred among them outside the forest, now acquired a survival value, and natural selection soon spread this new trait through the forest populations.' Both the size and the anatomy of pygmies are clearly adaptive for life in an equatorial forest. Smallness is advantageous not only because it is easier to move through the low-hanging branches of the shrub layer, and because less food, whose availability in the forest varies seasonally and from place to place, is needed but also because the ratio between surface area and body size increases as size decreases, and the smaller one is, the faster one passes off heat. In the Ituri Forest, Richard pointed out, not only human beings but buffaloes, elephants, antelopes, and giraffids are reduced. The ratio of the pygmies' limb length to their torsos, which is the highest of any humans, is also advantageous for shedding body heat: the larger the limbs, the greater the surface area, in proportion to body mass, from which heat can be lost. The relatively small development of their bodies—pygmies tend to be fifteen per cent smaller than other Africans—was at the time of my visit thought to be due to a 'peripheral subresponsiveness to the human growth hormone, which occurs in normal amounts,' as Richard explained; it has since been found to be caused by a lack of the somatomedins, the hormones that mediate between growth hormones and organ development. This lack seems to be programmed into every pygmy, although the exact genetic mechanism by which the trait is transmitted is not known. Whether the body develops normally until a certain age, and then its development slows down or stops altogether, is not known, either. Perhaps at some point very long ago, one or, more likely, several mutations took place in the parent race of the pygmies, whoever they were (Coon suggests that they may be descended from Rhodesian man, but this is a highly speculative theory that is based on only one skull); and because these mutations were adaptive for forest people they gradually became a 'trend in evolution,' and ultimately a character. The evidence that such a process did indeed occur, however, is purely circumstantial. Nothing has been proved at the molecular level.

In the afternoon, at about four o'clock, I walked down to

the river with a bar of soap. The path led through several minutes of primary forest. It was a world of overpowering vegetable intensity. Huge buttresses flared at the bases of ancient trees; vines streamed down in cool green galleries; ferns and air plants encrusted branches. A large butterfly, flashing creamy turquoise, rose in front of us and, after several dozen yards of erratic flight, landed in a patch of sun and let the light pour through its half-open wings. It was a member of one of Africa's most spectacular genera, *Charaxes*. A large brown moth settled on the pungent, leaf-strewn floor and blended in so closely that I could see only the faint outlines of its wings, like the edges of a jigsaw puzzle. The canopy was coming to life: I could hear the huffing and groaning of hornbills flying over, and their raucous contentment as they settled in a tree. The hornbill is a large bird of the treetops which resembles the South American toucan in its behavior and appearance. During incubation, the female hornbill imprisons herself inside her hollow-tree nest by plastering the edges of the entrance hole until it is just wide enough for the male to pass food through. Africa has forty-five species; these were probably white-thighed hornbills, the most common of the four larger kinds in the Ituri Forest.

Some of the plants looked very familiar. Many of the most abundant ones, whose leaves, on long stalks, stood like pennants in the understory, were in the arrowroot family. The arrowroot known as *mangungu*, which is used to thatch roofs and for many other purposes, was all over the place. The arrowroots are also well represented in the Amazon, as are other plant families found in Africa. The floras of the two great rain forests overlap a lot at the family level, and considerably at the genus level, and they even have a few species in common. There are also cases of convergent evolution—plants in completely different families which, in filling similar niches on different continents, have come to look alike. The cacti of the New World and the succulent euphorbs of Africa are ready examples of this type of morphological convergence (to which animals—like the hornbills and the toucans—are just as prone), while the cecropia tree of Brazil and its Zairian counterpart, the umbrella tree, *Musanga cecropioides*, which both have palmately cleft foliage and flourish on disturbed sites, are an example of parallel evolution—morphological convergence between generically separate members of the same family.

The flora of the Zaire forest is less than half as rich as that of the Amazon, however. Africa and South America began to separate soon after higher plants evolved, about a hundred and twenty million years ago. Interchange was still possible through the Oligocene epoch. About twenty-five thousand years ago, Africa suffered a widespread desiccation. The forest contracted to a few small refuge areas, and it is thought that many kinds of plants were wiped out. The whole continent has no more than twenty thousand species, while the Amazon alone has between twenty-five and fifty thousand. In the higher parts of the Zaire Valley, trees form almost pure stands. But the Amazon is so diverse that you can walk for hundreds of feet from one tree and not find another like it.

I sidestepped a column of driver ants, relatives of the famous South American army ant. They were small and brown, and looked harmless enough, but they could make quick work of a nestling bird or a small injured mammal; the reputation they have for tearing down people is a Victorian exaggeration. I watched two medium-sized butterflies with long narrow orange-and-black wings—mating acraeas—whirl up a shaft of sunlight that had pierced the canopy. Thousands of butterflies were skipping along the river. Where the path came to it there was a moist sandbar which several hundred lycaenids had found to their liking, and every so often several dozen large white pierids would fly past. Something downstream must have held their attention, because they did not return.

The river was called the Uala, and it ran into the Nepoko. It was twenty feet at its widest. The water was clear amber in the sunlight and sooty blue in the shadows, and its reflection flickered on the undersides of the branches that overhung it. It was an acid, relatively sterile blackwater river, steeped to the colour of tea by leaf tannins and safe to drink from. There were bilharzia parasites in the river near Isiro, but the Uala came out of the forest, and no one lived on it. I took off my clothes, eased in, and lathered myself to a loud hum of bees and all sorts of bird sounds: the lugubrious coo of doves, the cracked-whip calls of a wattle-eye flycatcher, the clear, liquid fluting of an ant-thrush, the whistles of an African golden oriole, which had the same clarion richness as a Baltimore oriole's song. As I sat turtle-still on a tree trunk that had fallen into the water and let the sun dry me, something big thrashed in a tree upstream, and then, forcing air from its chest, made a sound that was definitely mammalian. Moments later, a large dark monkey appeared, perhaps a hundred feet above the ground, and holding on to a branch with one hand, called again across the river. From a thicket on the other side the call was answered.

Richard said they were two blue monkeys at the edge of their territories, warning each other to stay away. The river was on the boundary. We took a walk on the road at dusk and were followed by several red colobus monkeys, who are smaller, more active, and more insectivorous than blues. We also surprised a band of black-and-white colobus, a slow-moving bovine species that eats leaves and fills approximately the niche that howlers occupy in neotropical forests. They moved along quite fast because they were startled, and went deeper into the forest until we could no longer see even the flashing of their white-tipped tails. Richard said he had also seen mona and red-tail monkeys, both gray-cheeked and crested mangabeys, chimpanzees, and baboons in the vicinity. I was exhilarated because I had never seen so many different monkeys in such a short period of time. Richard said there were quite a lot here, but it didn't compare with forests he knew in Kenya. On the way back we passed a shrub whose flowers—white trum-pets the size of light bulbs—had been hanging limply folded half an hour ago. Now they were open, exposing orange sex organs to the pollinators of the night. It may have been one the night-shades which bloom on alternative full moons.

A few hours later, in darkness quaking with frog and insect din, bloodcurdling screams, as if a woman were being strangled, but repeated every minute or so, started to come from the crown of a tree near camp. Their perpetrator was the tree hyrax—a small, edible gray mammal with a white dorsal tuft, whose family is most closely related to eleph-ants. The BaLese (except in clans that have a taboo against eating hyrax) mark the tree in which a territorial male is calling and, returning in daylight, chop it down and find the hole to which the hyrax has retired (just as Amazonian Indians do with owl monkeys). The hyrax kept screaming until after midnight, then in the hours before dawn a troop of black-and-white colobus started calling to each other. They sounded like several motorcycles being revved.

Nadine came in that evening—a good-looking and very sharp young woman who would be considered black in the States, although she was not significantly darker-complected than the four of us, and here was considered a *muzungu*. She and Bob had not seen Richard and Elizabeth in several days, and I listened as they caught up and bounced ideas off each other. That morning a child had died in the village. A nasty diarrhea disease, a *Shigella*, had been going around choleralike and killing people. Three babies had died of it in the past month, and three adults since July. No one had been blamed yet for the death, but the villagers could not deal with tragedy without pointing the finger at someone. Richard said that their belief in witchcraft arose from a natural need to explain things that happened. 'It's like the superstitiousness in every society. Why did the snake bite you? It's much easier to lay it on an enemy than to face your own karma.' Nadine told me about a woman in the Efe camp who was ill, perhaps schizophrenic. She would suddenly start eating dirt and erupt into high-pitched, hysterical laughter, and her companions would have to restrain her as she ripped off her clothes and tried to throw herself into the fire. 'They say it's the Efe of Mamvu who gave her medicine,' Nadine said. 'She was supposed to marry one of them.' A finger cut while fishing with some Efe women had cost Nadine a month. The cut had infected to the bone, and the microbes had proved immune to penicillin. To save the finger she had had to go to a mission hospital near Bunia until an antibiotic that worked was found.

Another problem, graver in the long run than the dysentery epidemic, was gonorrhea. 'This is a sociobiological study concerning factors like nutrition, energy expenditure, time allocation, and patterns of cooperation and their effects on reproductive success in both populations,' Bob said, 'but the widespread venereal disease, which we hadn't anticipated at all, has thrown a wrench into the works. The fertility rate in both the village and the Efe camp is two live births per woman. The mortality rate is twenty-six per cent before the age of fifteen, so the population is declining at the rate of fifty per cent per generation. Twenty-four of the fifty-eight Efe women beyond menopause have never had a live birth, so the disease has probably been around for several generations. Those two girls who came to see you—they've been having relations for three years. By the time they marry chances are that their fallopian tubes will be hopelessly scarred and they will be infertile.'

The four scientists had done anthropometry (measurement of height, weight, subcutaneous fat, and other body characteristics) and demography (data about age, residential history, kinship, birth and death rates) on twelve hundred people, and they had completed hundreds of hours of 'focal samples.' 'We follow a person for an hour,' Bob explained, 'quantify what they eat, who they talk to, who they sit next to, who they fight with, who they laugh with, how much time they spend working; we observe about a hundred of their activities. It's based on primate-observation techniques.'

Bob was also concentrating a lot on hunts. 'The other day the men made two hundred sixty-seven poison arrows,' he said 'Eight monkeys came into camp. They don't fire at anything over thirty feet away. Most of their targets are moving—little antelopes motoring through the forest. Only one arrow in eight hits an animal, and half of those get away.' Bob had a scar on his shin from when he had tripped on a root while running with a hunting party. He seemed to have a sure sense of pygmy motivation and to be wary of the overintellectualizing that some anthropologists, especially those under the influence of Claude Lévi-Strauss, get into. We talked about how the Efe attach a small tree to the roof of their hut when a baby is born. 'The tree of life? Homage to the forest?' I suggested. 'Come off it,' he said. 'It's just an announcement with the most convenient thing at hand.' Like the way suburban people tie balloons to their mailbox.

Richard described how some of the BaLese had been leaving the road, giving up on the undelivered promise of a better life that it held out, and returning to their ancestral village sites deep in the forest. The four of them had visited some villages that were five days from the road, but there were more, farther in, which no muzungu had been to. 'That part of the Ituri has to be one of the wildest places in Africa,' Richard said. 'There are mountains in there, with savanna grass, elephants, and buffalo.' According to his information, the last village, called Moto Moto, was ten days in, and gold had been found on a nearby stream. On the eleventh day you came out on the 'big' road to Kisangani. I asked how long it was from Opoku to the Kisangani road. Bob said about a hundred miles. I asked if there was any chance of my making the trip. He said we could see in the morning if anybody in Opoku was interested in going with me.

In the morning Bob took me to Opoku and introduced me to two of the younger, more progressive men there, who weren't so afraid of muzungus. Their names were Baudouin and Gamaembi. Baudouin spoke a little French—the official language of Zaire, which few BaLese and no Efe speak or understand—and Gamaembi knew it quite well, so we could communicate. They also spoke their own language, KiLese, as well as Swahili, the lingua franca of the region, neither of which I knew. Like many male Zairois born in 1955, Baudouin had been named for the King of the Belgians, who had toured the Congo that year. He had another, 'authentic' name, Apabu, probably given by his father, but Baudouin was one of many who had not got the word about Mobutu's 1972 authenticité decree. He was about five feet tall, with a large head, a high shiny forehead, and lighter skin than most of the villagers. He thought he had pygmy blood, although his father was a Lende, from near Uganda, and his mother a Lese. He had grown up with her in her village—his father had abandoned them when he was little—and his strongest connection to Opoku was a leprotic aunt, whose claw hand I shook, reaching into an enclosure where she and two other women were gaily shelling peanuts. People liked to employ him, but they did not feel obligated to him, because he was an immigrant and not in their fungu, or clan—the patrilineal kinship group to which every Lese's allegiance is unquestioning. In many ways, he was more like a pygmy than like a villager. His best friend, Manuele, was an Efe. So was his wife. It was a mark of his low status that he didn't have a BaLese wife. His personality—the air of mischief, the spoiling for fun, the way he dissolved into laughter at the slightest provocation—was Efe, and, like the Efe, he loved marijuana.

Gamaembi (ex-Dieudonné—the European name, it seemed, of every third man in Zaire) was twenty-two, four inches taller than Baudouin, darker-skinned, and well built, with broad shoulders, strong arms and legs, a slim waist, and not an ounce of fat. 'Gamaembi' means 'the man without a chief.' He was the last son of the late capita, or headman, of Opoku. One of his brothers was almost sixty,

138

one of his sisters was married to a son of the chief of the *collectivité*, and some of the *capitas* of the villages in the forest were his relatives. Besides being well connected, he had walked to Epini a few years earlier and knew the way, so I couldn't have had a better guide. He was about to plant a peanut *shamba*, but when I offered to pay him five zaires a day, he decided to come. Five zaires was then officially worth about a dollar-fifty. At the 'parallel' (black market) rate—the one that mattered—five zaires was worth only fifty cents, but that was still good money to Gamaembi: double what the Greek coffee planters in Digbo, twenty miles up the road, were paying. He and his half brother Kuri were raising money to open a store in Opoku. (The nearest store was in Digbo.) I made the same offer to Baudouin, and he accepted. The three of us shook hands and agreed to set out in the morning.

Later in the day Baudouin appeared in camp and asked if I could advance him some of his pay so he could buy some *bangi* for the trip. Richard advised me to hold the *bangi* for Baudouin, or he would smoke it all at once. I gave him ten zaires and in the evening he turned over six little balls of the herb, wrapped in *mangungu* leaf.

That night, I made a final inventory of my gear. For clothing, I had shorts (long pants are cumbersome in the jungle), jogging shoes, heavy knee socks, a couple of T-shirts, a blue cap, a poncho that doubled as a ground cloth, a sweatshirt to put on at night, flannel pajamas, and bedroom slippers. I had a bottle of alcohol to rub down my arms and legs with; cuts and insect bites infect easily in the humid tropics, and alcohol not only disinfects them but reduces the urge to scratch. My medicine chest—an empty coffee can—contained Merthiolate; a course of the broad-spectrum antibiotic ampicillin; paregoric and Lomotil for diarrhea; chloroquine and primaquine for malaria; effervescent Vitamin C tablets; and gamma globulin, which offers transcient protection against hepatitis A (but does nothing for hepatitis B, which I eventually came down with), and a syringe to inject it with. I had already given myself a shot that was good for thirty days. Elizabeth supplied me with a handful of aspirin for 'public relations,' and some little white pills to be taken twice a week against African river blindness, which is transmitted by black flies. Richard lent me a lightweight sleeping bag, and Nadine told me three good sentences to know in Swahili: *Kwenda nzuri* (Go well); *Bakie nzuri* (Stay well); *Lala nzuri* (Sleep well). I had field guides to the birds, butterflies, and large mammals of Africa, and a stack of empty notebooks. All this fit into a long brown canvas duffelbag whose strap I put over my forehead as a tumpline, letting the bag hang behind. Once your neck muscles have got used to it, this system—which most of the people in South America, Africa, and Asia use to carry heavy loads—works better in the forest than a backpack, because your shoulders aren't pinned down and it is easier to raise your arms to negotiate vines and branches.

The guitar was in a black vinyl case, and in my side bag were a Nikkormat camera with a macro lens for close shots of butterflies and flowers; a small Sony tape recorder; a small pair of six-power Nikon binoculars; my passport, traveller's checks, return air ticket, and the brick of zaires. I also had a large, lethal-looking folding knife, such as the carpenters in my hometown wear in cases on their belts. I figured I owed it to my family to have it along. The provisions and trade items—the hand mirrors, salt, a dozen bars of soap, and a carton of Tumbaco—were in a burlap sack, as were two cans of sardines and enough rice, beans, peanuts, and plantains to last the three of us two days. After that we would be dependent on hunting and gathering and on trading with the people in the forest. For cooking, I had a small aluminium pot with a lid and a detachable handle; for illumination a flashlight, a dozen candles, and several hundred matches. I had also brought a dozen plastic Ziploc bags. They didn't weigh much and always came in handy for sequestering things.

At three o'clock the next morning—it was a Thursday—I tapped at the small wicker door of one of the huts in Opoku and whispered 'Baudouin.' He came out rubbing the sleep from his eyes, and we set off walking through the misty *shambas* behind the village. It was oddly quiet, the lull before dawn. Not a frog, insect, hyrax, colobus, or bird to be heard.

At daybreak, amid a growing bee hum, with more and more birds coming in, giving their position, from every direction, we reached Ondikomvu, a suburb of Opoku, consisting of three huts, one of which was inhabited by Gamaembi and his wife, Anna. He came out looking dapper

140

in red shorts and a red T-shirt, with a red vinyl side bag that contained a toothbrush, a comb, and a change of clothes. He contributed some palm oil and some peanut butter that his wife had ground the night before. Baudouin put the oil, which was in a plastic bottle, and the peanut butter, which was wrapped in leaves, into the burlap sack. He wore a white shirt and a pair of long brown pants, which he stooped to roll up over his strong thighs when, soon after leaving Ondikomvu, we entered the forest.

'Do you have forest like this in America?' Gamaembi asked. He was in the lead, carrying my duffelbag and holding a small bow and about a dozen arrows. Baudouin was next, carrying the burlap sack by a tumpline he had made from the inner bark of a tree. I followed close behind, with my side bag and Gamaembi's and the guitar.

'No, not exactly,' I said. 'It isn't as thick with shrubs and vines. There aren't so many kinds of trees, and it isn't so green.'

Gamaembi's response was to turn over a leaf with a silver underside. 'This is another leaf,' he said.

Baudouin and Gamaembi walked with slightly bowed legs, gripping the ground with spread toes. I said I envied them that contact. 'Of course, we would like to have shoes if we could afford them,' Gamaembi told me, 'but in the forest we prefer bare feet.' As we passed through a slanting shaft of light, I was for some reason reminded of an incident in my early childhood. I could almost bring the specific place and time into focus, but at the last moment they faded into only a sensation.

After a while, we came to a smoky clearing with half a dozen domes of mangungu thatch in it. They were the smallest dwellings I had ever seen, like tropical igloos or the nests of some gregarious ground creature. I could not quite have stretched out in one. Two Efe women, squatting before a little fire that smoldered at the meeting point of three logs, got up and, without daring to look at me, bravely took my extended hand. A man and another woman came out of one of the huts. The man was very muscular, like a wrestler, and his arms and legs looked slightly long in relation to his torso. He stood about four feet nine and, except for a rag tucked through a vine belt, he was naked. The women, who were a few inches shorter, wore similar loincloths. They had black circles of plant juice painted on their arms and legs and black lines on their faces, much as some Amazon Indian women have, and their teeth were chipped to points. Two of them were old—over thirty—with wrinkled breasts sagging over their bellies. The average life span of an Efe, with infant mortality taken into account, is forty, although some live to be eighty. I passed the man and each of the women cigarettes, which they took, still not looking at me. I took out my guitar and played them a high-stepping rag called 'The St Louis Tickle.' Their reaction was guarded, but they understood that it was music. The man went to his hut and, returning with a little five-string harp, plucked a single open minor chord over and over for about a minute. I recorded it. Then I recorded the woman, who, after much giggling and several false starts, broke into a haunting three-part yodel to a cross rhythm that one of them kept by slapping her thigh. 'It is a song of joy,' Gamaembi explained when they had stopped, 'about their child being old enough to be sent to his hut for the first time after disobeying his mother.' They listened intently as I played it back to them, and when it was over they looked at each other with sly, knowing smiles, burst into laughter, and slapped each other's open palms, like basketball players who have just scored. I had always thought that 'giving skin' was something American blacks had invented—part of a routine that the members of a particular oppressed minority had made up to support each other. It is equally intriguing that the BaLese use the word 'bad' in the approving way, and 'brother' in the loosely fraternal way that some American blacks do.

We crossed a little river called the Afalabombi. Baudouin's tumpline had frayed and was coming apart, and while he was off peeling a new one Gamaembi picked a nearby mangungu leaf, folded it into a cone, dipped it in the river, and passed it to me. Baudouin returned with a long strip of bark and wrapped it around the neck of the burlap sack, leaving a loop that he slipped over his head, and we started out again.

After several hours, we reached the top of a viewless hill. 'This is where we stop and rest whenever we are here.' Gamaembi informed me. He spread out a few handy mangungu leaves for me to sit on, while Baudouin tore a square from an old, khaki-colored mangungu leaf, sprinkled Tumbaco and bangi on it, and rolled himself a joint.

142

The leaf had the body of a thin sheet of paper etched with tough little fibres. *Mangungu* seemed to have a thousand and one uses.

We were sitting in a grove of hundred-and-fifty-foot strangler figs. The species, *Ficus thonningii*, is partial to high, well-drained sites. Each tree had started as a seed dropped by a bird in the crotch of a different species of tree which had originally occupied the site. Like wax melting down the side of a candle, the roots had descended from the seeds, mingled and merged, and eventually smothered the host tree out of existence. At the same time, usually about thirty feet from the ground, a trunk had ascended from the seed and shot up for a hundred feet or so before finally branching into a crown. Gamaembi cut into a huge buttress of anastomosed fig root with the edge of an iron arrowhead, and a sticky white latex bubbled out. 'Along the rivers, we line traps with the milk of this tree and bait them with seeds,' he said. 'Birds walk in and get stuck.' He said the tree was called *popo* and was one of those whose inner bark the Efe and some of the older BaLese pounded into loincloths.

We sat eating peanut butter with our fingers. I noticed that Gamaembi had both metal-tipped arrows and arrows with plain, sharpened shafts which had been dipped in the sap of a vine of the biologically active genus *Strophanthus*— a sap that paralyzes monkeys and makes them release the branches they are holding. I asked if he was a good shot, and he said, without a trace of ego, 'We are all good shots.' I never got to see him in action, although we ran into quite a lot of game. He carried the bow in case of attack from animals or spirits, not for hunting.

When we started walking again, Baudouin pointed out on the edge of the path a bent-over branch with a noose on the end of it for snaring little forest antelopes. Most of them are duikers, six species of which inhabit the Ituri Forest. The smallest and most abundant, the blue duiker, is not much bigger than a dachshund. There are also Bates's pygmy antelope and the water chevrotain, a diminutive relative of deer which has some affinities with pigs. Of these, the wildlife ecologist John Hart, who has spent five years in the forest, has told me, only the pygmy antelope, which frequents the edges of *shambas*, subsists on leaves. The rest browse on fallen fruit, seeds, flowers, and mushrooms.

There are very few deep-forest leaf-eaters in the Ituri. All the monkeys (except the colobuses), and even the forest elephants, are frugivorous. The reason for this may be that here the cost to a tree of losing its leaves is tremendous. Most of the trees are not deciduous, and because they do not flush a new set of leaves each year their foliage is heavily protected—in most cases by toxic or indigestible secondary compounds, but sometimes by thorns or prickly hairs or by sophisticated symbiotic relationships with stinging insects. A few species have evolved extra-floral nectaries, which attract fire ants; no one would want to brush against these leaves, let alone try to eat them. Life for a tree in such a forest is not easy. Many trees spend years, or even their whole lives, no more than a yard tall, waiting for a gap to open in the canopy, and at this stage they are most vulnerable. When an opening does present itself, they shoot up with amazing speed.

Gamaembi picked some white-gilled mushrooms with light-gray caps and foot-long taproots. He said they were called *imamburama* and were good to eat. That evening, we ate them sautéed in *mafuta* with rice and sardines, and they were good. We would sleep on *mangungu* pallets in a lean-to on the Afande River which two men from Opoku had recently built as a fishing and trapping camp. After supper, I tried one of Baudouin's joints. The *bangi* was very smooth and relaxing, but it wasn't conducive to clear thought, and when I got up to poke the fire back to life I discovered that it made tedious demands on motor coordination. Gamaembi didn't touch the stuff. 'For me, life is already wonderful,' he explained.

He and Baudouin were fascinated by the color plates in Jean Dorst and Pierre Dandelot's *Field Guide to the Larger Mammals of Africa*, which we pored over with a flashlight. I wrote down in phonetic spelling the Swahili and KiLese names of the animals they recognized. I asked about leopards. Gamaembi said that a day in from the road they were quite common—especially along rivers. 'We can hear him sing, cry, *être dans la folie pour rien*, purr happily after killing an antelope,' he said. He told me that you could hit a giant forest hog with a hundred arrows before it died, but that with a spear it only took once or twice. I asked about butterflies. The BaLese have many names for bees, but for butterflies they use only the general Swahili word, *kipepéo*.

'Butterflies are bad for us, because we have no use for them,' Gamaembi said.

'To me, the butterfly is the insect that climbs trees and eats the leaves,' Baudouin remarked.

'Butterflies are metamorphoses,' Gamaembi said. 'We eat the caterpillars but not the butterflies.'

'I love the forest, monsieur,' Gamaembi said a little later, as we lay in the darkness. 'To know its situation, to find all the marvellous little things and the mountains in it.'

Late in the night, it started to pour, but the roof was good and we stayed dry. In the morning, the river was muddy and swollen, way up over the rocks and prostrate trees I had walked out on the evening before. 'Friday the twenty-seventh. The quality of our drinking water has taken a turn for the worse,' I entered in a journal I was keeping. 'We can look forward to a day of gray dampness.' The river was now as wide as the trees along its bank were tall. If one of the trees had fallen over, it would have been just long enough to cross on. I noticed several pendulous socks hanging in a tree on the other side. They were the nests of malimbe weavers and looked much like the nests of the yellow-rumped cacique of the Amazon. The malimbes were already off somewhere, perhaps flocking with greenbuls, bulbuls, and flycatchers. Africa has at least ninety kinds of weaver.

We were ready to go at 6:30 A.M., but as I was zipping up the duffelbag the side caught on my pajamas and, trying to free it, I forced it off one of its tracks. 'What are we going to do now? I asked Gamaembi. He started to work—removing the staple at the base of the track, rethreading the slide, putting back the staple—and in five minutes it was fixed. I was impressed, having operated hundreds of zippers but never having come to terms with one. I tended to take the mechanisms in my life for granted—even had a slight aversion to them—but Gamaembi approached them with deep respect and curiosity. If in the United States the zipper in my pants had broken, I reflected, I would probably have thrown them away and bought a new pair. But this was not a throw-it-away society. There were no spare parts, no convenient repair shops. If something broke, you had no choice but to try to fix it.

We crossed the Afande half a mile downstream, inching along a partly submerged log. Almost at the end, I lost my balance and fell into furious brown water; I expected to be

145

swept away, but it was only knee-deep. The three of us laughed, realizing we could have just waded across. Soon afterward, we crossed another river—the Afalu—and then we reached the first village in the forest: Zalondi.

Gamaembi had been explaining as we walked that in 1942 the men of his tribe had been forced by the Belgians to come out of the forest and build the road that went past Opoku. The road was needed to bring up war matériel to the Sudan, and after it was built the men were sent out to collect wild rubber, which was also needed. It was a period of great hardship for the BaLese. The men were separated from their wives and their *shambas*. There was little to eat. If they did not bring in their quota of rubber, they were beaten. After the war, the BaLese men were forced to live near the road— where they could be kept track of—to keep the road in repair, and to grow cash crops like peanuts, rice, and cotton. Their women joined them, and the villages in the forest were abandoned. Maintenance of the road stopped abruptly with independence. Some of the BaLese immediately went back to their *matongo*, their *ancienne place* in the forest, and started new villages, but most of them remained on the road. It was disappearing, becoming not much more than a path. Because of the widespread gonorrhea and other diseases, the population along the road was in decline. More BaLese were giving up on the promises of the road and were returning to their *matongos*. In the past few years, a dozen new villages had started in the forest. The *collectivité*, like much of the country, was in a state of active regression.

Zalondi was a recent recolonization of one of the ancestral village sites. It consisted of three huts in a clearing surrounded by immense banana trees,. The *capita*, a young man who was a friend of Gamaembi's, welcomed us warmly. In broken French, he told me that he had come to Zalondi a year ago, 'for a rest.' He went on to say, 'There is too much *dérangement*, too many thieves. I was getting tired of the police taking my chickens, and officials of the *collectivité* dropping in and expecting to be fed.' Thirty Efe had a camp nearby, and a group of women and children from it were sitting in a doorway of one of the huts, all heaped together, nursing babies, combing each other's hair, enjoying each other's warmth. A sweet lanolin smell emanated from them. The oldest woman, a withered grandmother, puffed marijuana in a wooden pipe whose stem was the hollowed three-foot midrib of a banana leaf. The Efe like to smoke a lot of *bangi* before they go hunting, Bob told me—especially when they are going for elephant—or before they climb a honey tree, but sometimes they smoke so much it leaves them dazed and their projects are abandoned.

We traded a bar of soap for a hand of pudgy bananas that were only a few inches long, and traded some of Baudouin's *bangi* for a comb of thick, dark honey. The bananas were wonderfully sweet, and the honey was so strong I felt a surge of energy from it almost immediately. Bob had told me that during July and August, the wettest months, the Efe roam the forest and eat nothing else. The start of the honey season is signalled by a long, woeful, high-pitched cry that is heard in the distance. The Efe say the sound is made by a newt who is about to lay her eggs and die, and that that is why her cry is woeful; but it is actually made by a crake. No later than five-thirty in the morning, before the bees have left their hives, the Efe men fan out in groups of five or six, approaching trees and tilting their heads. When one of them hears a tree humming with the promise of honey, he blows a flute made from a sapling, as a joyous announcement to the others, and breaks branches around the bee tree to mark the site. After a man has found three or four such trees, he goes back with his companions (not necessarily right away but within several weeks) to get the honey, a procedure that may require daring feats of engineering, since the hive is often a hundred feet up and a bridge from a smaller tree—sometimes several bridges—must be built. On the spot, the men weave from *mangungu* two baskets—one for the honey, the other to fill with burning wet leaves—and the man who found the bees' hole climbs to it, and smokes the hive; after waiting for the bees to go into a torpor, he widens the hole with an axe and chops out the honey. When he returns to the ground, more often than not he will eat several pounds of honey and get on a sugar high—becoming excited to the point of screaming about the next tree he is going to raid. (The Efe seem immune to the nausea and chills of hyperglycemia.) A good hive can yield from twenty to twenty-five pounds of honey, and what the finder does not eat he brings to his wife and relatives. At the start of the honey season, the BaLese villages give the Efe big *chungus*—aluminum pots capable of holding forty pounds of honey—which the Efe bring back full and trade for cloth. One year, there may be a bumper crop of honey, the next almost none, whereupon the Efe become uncharacteristically sad for that season.

The village clearing was swarming with bees (one stung me on the neck when I brushed it accidentally with my hands) and with skippers that had dull brown wings and stout green bodies—a species known as the striped policeman. Several chickens and emaciated dogs were snapping up the butterflies. The dogs were small, with curly tails, and were mostly hound. The breed is called the African barkless dog, because they don't vocalize as much as other dogs; they are thought to be like the first dogs that lived with man. Dogs are very important for driving game. Before a drive starts, Bob had told me, the Efe tie wooden clappers around the necks of the dogs, about half of which belong to the BaLese villagers. One man, the beater, sings and shouts continually to keep the dogs moving. Four hundred yards from where the drive begins, the other men wait in a semicircle, very still, for panicky duikers to streak within bowshot. The hunters do not shoot at anything over thirty feet away; it is too chancy through the trees. Once an animal is hit, the dogs keep it on the move until it drops or passes by another hunter, who is waiting motionless to finish it off with another arrow.

I took out my camera and aimed it at three teen-age Efe girls, and they ran in mock terror behind a hut, where I could hear them giggling. I tried to photograph another Efe woman and her children, but she shooed them from the man-eating muzungu, so I gave up on taking pictures and turned on my Sony. When the girls behind the hut heard the three women I had recorded the day before, they returned and, not to be outdone, launched into a three-part yodel, breaking their voices on throaty aOO's that came with the haphazard timing of frogs in chorus or katydids in late August. The girls were as shy as birds, and their music was cosmic; their yodels seemed to resonate indefinitely. The way each took a different note is called hocket singing, but their collective sound, unlike contemporary Western music, came out in a pentatonic scale; it was based almost entirely on the dominant, with the occasional addition of sevenths, and was nearly always in a descending pattern. Every few seconds, another rhythm, another melody blended in. The Belgian ethnomusicologist Benoti Quersin has described the pygmies' music as '*polyphonie en cascade.*' There is nothing quite like it elsewhere in Africa or in any other place.

The *capita* of Zalondi told Gamaembi of a village that had been started since his last visit. It was up the Mubilinga River, and we could go to it instead of to three villages that Gamaembi was already familiar with. I said it sounded like a good idea. When we were back in the forest, I asked to go first, so I could learn to find the way. The path was well worn and about a foot wide—twice as wide as an Amazonian footpath, because the Indians put one foot directly in front of the other as they lope along. Sometimes it had lots of little offshoots. It wasn't easy to tell the ones that were shortcuts from the animal trails that petered into nothing. The elephant trails, which crossed the path from time to time and sometimes followed it for a stretch, were deep and especially confusing. Sometimes the path would split in two, which meant that up ahead a tree had fallen across the original route. You took the newer-looking detour. Snapped saplings always meant something—usually that someone had rights to a nearby honey tree. Once, we came across a message carved on a tree in Swahili. It said, according to Gamaembi:

I came by here in December, when you had gone in search of honey. Bring me some quickly.

Sekuri

In time, I learned to let my feet make the decisions, and they were usually right.

The forest was quite hilly, and its physiognomy varied with the elevation. In some high places, it was as open as the woods in my native Westchester. In seasonally flooded places, we had to fight through vines and *mangungu*; it was like *mata de cipó*, a dense vine thicket in the Amazon. But it was never evil or teeming with danger, as writers brought up on Stanley and Conrad feel they should make 'the jungle' out to be. It was just intense. Maybe for me it was an adventure, but for Gamaembi and Baudouin it was home. There were few mosquitoes, and in eleven days we didn't see one snake, although the Gabon viper is said to be fairly common. Knowing how slim the odds were of running into a

149

snake, let alone being bitten by one, I had not brought any antivenin.

We passed through a stand of shrubs with glossy leaves and small, fragrant, starlike white flowers—robusta coffee, either a natural stand or escapees from an abandoned village. Gamaembi did not know. Moments later, we stampeded a sounder—as a herd is called—of ten or so bright-red bush pigs with long white dorsal crests. Gamaembi and Baudouin dropped their baggage and took off after them. '*Restez donc que nous partons,*' Baudouin told me, in solemn, antiquated French. In a little while, they came back, empty-handed. When we reached the turnoff to Mubilinga, the new village, Baudouin dropped three *mangungu* leaves in the path as a courtesy to other BaLese and pygmies in the forest who might be interested in our movements. Minutes later, we surprised an okapi, an aberrant forest giraffe so secretive and sharp of hearing that it was one of the last large mammals to become known to science; a complete skin was not obtained until 1901. Though its habits are still largely unknown, it has become the unofficial faunal symbol of Zaire, lending its name to a hotel, a filter cigarette, and the folding knife that is carried by policemen. An adult male okapi stands eight feet tall and elk proud, with a coat of mauve velvet as shiny as a curried horse's and with white slashes across the rump and forelegs —disruptive coloration, such as zebras have, perhaps to confuse leopards. It has large, nervous ears; short, furry horns pointing backward; a long tongue, for licking its eyes clean and for pulling down foliage (it is the only deep-forest terrestrial leaf-eater in the Ituri); and an elongated head and neck, which also relate to its eating habits but which are not nearly as long as those of its gregarious cousin of the savanna. The female has no horns and is larger than the male—one of the few such cases among large mammals. The okapi inhabits only the Ituri Forest and is thus a rare animal, though in the forest it is common. It tames readily. This okapi bolted before I could even determine its sex. A bit later, Gamaembi flushed a family of blue duikers by hissing into a thicket, but they, too, to my secret delight, ran off, as silently as fleeting shadows, before Gamaembi could even feather his bow. 'They wait for the cover of night to appear in the open. You can't see them at all when they're still,' Gamaembi told me.

We had better luck with mushrooms. The forest gave us seven more *imamburama* that morning, and Baudouin spotted a colony of edible white *ikiangi* fastened to a mossy fallen tree. Their stalks were shaggy, their caps depressed at the centre and spattered with little gray squamules. I had never seen such woods for mushrooms. Racks of yellow-gilled shelf fungi hung twenty feet up. Tiny, purple-striped parasols stood on mildewed green slivers of wood, and there was a violently poisonous off-white member of the genus *Phallus* whose cap was surrounded by a mantle of delicately reticulated deliquescent tissue. I asked Gamaembi how many kinds of mushrooms were good to eat. He started to tick them off on his fingers, then gave up and said, 'More than I can count.' Bob Bailey knew at least sixteen.

After about half an hour on the new path, Gamaembi and Baudouin heard voices in a gully and went off to see whose they were. 'There are men talking and women singing down there,' Gamaembi said as he left. I couldn't hear a thing—only birds. One had a descending whistle that sounded like a bomb dropping. Others pulsed in audibility. A robin chat sang a quotable theme, which I whistled back. It answered with the theme again, then mocked it in half a dozen brilliant variations. After a while, I heard dogs howling in the gully, then Gamaembi and Baudouin shouting to identify themselves, then a great shout from the people they had startled, then silence. Soon Gamaembi and Baudouin returned with two Efe men and their wives, who had been looking for honey.

Half an hour later, we met on the path two BaLese men and two women who looked to be pygmoids—BaLese-Efe mixes. The pygmoids are raised by the villagers. A BaLese man will not permit an Efe woman to go back to the forest with their child, and the BaLese fight over the right to bring up even children who are not their own. In society without writing, children are perhaps the most precious commodities, because the only way to achieve immortality, to have your name continue for several generations, is through them. If the child is a girl, she represents eventual bride wealth; if the child is a boy, he means another man in the clan, and the larger the clan, the greater its importance and power.

One of the men carried a long spear and wore the sleeveless brown flannel liner of a winter coat, which seemed on him like an elegant robe. His name was Joaçim, and his father was the chief of the *collectivité*. Joaçim was, at twenty-eight, in his vibrant prime. He walked very straight, conscious that he was the local royalty, and spoke in a husky voice. I asked what the spear was for. Buffalo, he said. He took us up to a weathered brown dome of basaltic rock which looked over the forest for twenty miles around—the first and only view of it we would have. We were about three thousand feet above sea level. Here and there, the bluish crown of an emergent stood up above the canopy. The botanist Ghillean Prance looked at my slide of this vista of treetops and judged from the architecture of the emergents' crowns—the way branches had been born at different levels, the way gaps of light often appeared between the racks of foliage—that they were probably in the pea family. Another, white-flowering legume, *Cynometra alexandri*, was in bloom all over the forest. The bushy crowns looked as if they had been caught in a heavy snow. *Ató*, as Gamaembi called it, is one of three trees—all in the pea family—that form nearly pure stands in the Ituri Forest. The honey we had eaten in Zalondi was from *ató* blossoms.

I took a picture of Joaçim and his entourage lifting a boulder together. It was Joaçim's idea that they should be doing something instead of just standing there. Then, as he stood in the sunlight, his robe fluttering, he became serious. 'After independence, we lost our happiness,' he told me. 'We are free, but we are not well.' I asked how many people live in the *collectivité*. 'About four thousand BaLese men and fifteen hundred Efe men,' he said. How bad a problem was veneral disease? He said that the main reason for the decrease in fertility was not gonorrhea but a plant abortifacient that women took because they were tired of having children, although occasionally jealous wives of the same man slipped some to each other. He himself had eight children by six wives and half a dozen illegitimate children whom he helped support. His senior wife was Gamaembi's sister.

As we descended into the forest, it started to rain a little. Hardly any rain penetrated the canopy. 'We already have umbrellas', Joaçim joked. We exchanged addresses and promised to correspond, then went opposite ways. When he had gone, Gamaembi said, 'Joaçim's father is getting old, and he will be the next chief, because no one else in the *collectivité* is as intelligent or as educated. Only he and his brother can afford shot-guns. He hunts on this side of the road, his brother on the other. When he kills an elephant, he takes the ivory and leaves the meat for his people. He brings news and tetracycline. Some of his friends are soldiers.'

I asked if it had been hard for his sister when Joaçim took other wives, and Gamaembi said, 'The first wife always complains.'

A littler later, Joaçim came running up behind us. 'My friends are probably wondering where I am,' he said, with a grin. 'I left without telling them. I will go to Mubilinga with you.' Gamaembi told me later that it was a great honour for Joaçim to have returned. On the way, Joaçim showed me a golden vine with asperous bark, rough to the touch, like sandpaper, that would give you a nasty scrape and was to be avoided. He had the coat liner on inside out, and I could see a label at the nape; it said 'Winflite'. I asked where he had got the garment. From a trader, he said. Big bundles of clothing donated by American church organizations arrive in Kinshasa, and by the time they reach the Ituri Forest— having ascended the Zaire by riverboat, been transferred to trucks, and finally to green wooden chests strapped over the back wheels of bicycles, which BaBudu traders walk from village to village—they have to be paid for. Once in the middle of nowhere Bob had run into a T-shirt that read, LABORATORY OF NEURO-PHYSIOLOGY DOWNSTATE MEDICAL CENTER CREW TEAM.

After half an hour, we came to a pygmy camp, but its eight huts were empty. In the middle of the clearing was a large stone for whetting arrows and a small stool made of four crossed sticks lashed together with vines. I could find no water in the vicinity. The Efe do not camp along rivers, because malaria- and filaria-bearing insects breed there. The women have to bring the water in pots to camp. They do not bathe every day and can do with a very small trickle. I asked Joaçim why the Efe didn't grow things. He said that it was because they didn't like to sit in one place for the whole year, and because they didn't like sunlight. 'The Efe come to you with meat and say they have a friend who wants bananas, when it is really they themselves,' he said, with a laugh. 'They say they will come early and work in your *shamba*, and it is afternoon and they haven't come yet.'

After another hour, we reached Mubilinga. As soon as

they saw us, a man of about forty and two women quickly gathered some things and left. An old man standing before one of the huts with his knees shaking and his eyes on the treetops said that they had gone fishing. Gamaembi said the old man was cold, so I gave him some aspirin. He told us that the village had been started two years earlier, and that there was three men and two women in it, and twelve Efe who came and went. Richard Wrangham had asked me to make a census of each new village, so I took down the name, age, and clan of each resident. The ages that the old man gave me were very approximate. Few BaLese born before 1960 know how many years they have been alive. They speak of being born before the road was built or before a certain man became chief or after the Belgians went away or during the Rebellion.

Joaçim stayed for a while and talked with me in the *baraza*. He followed world developments on a shortwave radio and had a theory about why Israel always beat Egypt. Maybe an Egyptian woman got pregnant in Israel, went back to Egypt to have the baby, sent him to the best schools, and he grew up to be a general. Then she told him that his father was an Israeli, and he became a mole.

After Joaçim left, we had the village to ourselves except for the old man, who stood where he was until it got dark, and another old man, in one of the huts. I finally realized that the people of Mubilinga were terrified of me. Gamaembi later confessed that the others had not gone fishing— they had fled. The old men who stayed would have fled, too, if they had been able to. The one with shaking knees had not been having a malaria attack. He had been waiting for me to kill him.

The village was immaculately swept ('Très *soigné*,' I remarked to Gamaembi), probably with the broom, a cluster of dry berries, that was leaning on a post of the *baraza*. Hanging from the rafters were several gourds and a calendar that looked like a clip of firecrackers, with numbered wooden slats that were brought down on a string. (The date it indicated was two days earlier.) Various things were wedged in the thatch—a few smoke-blackened ears of seed corn, a buffalo horn, a wooden spoon, a rattle of dried seeds in a ball of woven vine. A game of *mangola*, in which seeds are moved along four rows of pockets in the red earth, had been left in progress.

154

The next morning, Gamaembi again demonstrated his handiness, melting one of my Ziploc bags with a match and sealing with the liquid plastic a crack that had developed in the *mafuta* bottle. Soon after leaving the village, we crossed a stream full of milky quartz pebbles that puzzled him. 'This stream has too many stones,' he said. There was no obvious source for them nearby, and many seemed too large for such a small stream to have borne them any distance. He showed me some large, round depressions in the soft, miry leaves—elephant prints. We passed a place permeated with the smell of crested mangabeys, who had slept there. We picked some edible yellow gilled mushrooms called *lobo-lobo*. I photographed a lily with a clustered inflorescence of pale-orange flowers, each with six petals and six exserted stamens. I also photographed white, trumpet-shaped blossoms that dripped from a twining liana in the birth-wort family. Flies were induced to enter the trumpets by a carrion smell; were trapped inside, by retrorse hairs; and were released within twenty-four hours, smothered with pollen, when the hairs wilted. But these were rare splashes of color in an otherwise drab green understory. It was the wrong time of year for flowers, and even at the right time the lower strata of the Ituri Forest are relatively poor in showy flowers; nor are the sunbirds, which drink their nectar, as numerous as humming-birds are in the Amazon. Heavy taboos protect such blooms as there are from would-be pickers. There is an orchid, for instance, that the pygmies believe must never be touched, or a heavy rain will come and make branches fall on them—perhaps the greatest danger to someone walking in the forest. Conservation may have had nothing to do with the belief; there is often no functional explanation for what the Efe think and do.

We found a lime tree—all that was left of a BaBudu village—and helped ourselves to half a dozen limes. We were on the edge of BaBudu country. Gamaembi said we would visit three villages that day—Matiasi, Selemani, and Azangu. Men named Matiasi, Selemani, and Azangu were the *capitas*. As often as not, a BaLese village is known by the name of its *capita*. Opoku, for example, is also known as Abdullah; Opoku is the stream that runs by. The BaLese generally name their villages after the water they drink. But the other name of the village of Matiasi was Pumzika Un, which meant Resting Place One, and Selemani was Pumzika Deux. I was reminded of a hamlet called Rest-and-Be-Thankful, in the mountainous interior of Jamaica, which I once passed through. The village whose *capita* was Azangu was also named for a certain kind of fly.

When we reached Matiasi, Gamaembi guessed it was nine-thirty-five, and it was. He had once had the use of a wristwatch, and his sense of clock time was uncanny. The *capita* Matiasi was Gamaembi's maternal uncle. Two of his little cousins ran up and hugged him. Several hundred large pierid, or White, butterflies had congregated in the middle of the village. Through their shimmering wings, I could see a young BaLese mother in a doorway looking deep into her baby's eyes and stroking its forehead as it fed at her breast. A constant humming of voices, most of them pygmy women's, filled the clearing and occasionally broke into song. 'They are singing, "Why do you come each time with a *muzungu*?"' Gamaembi told me. Two Efe boys came up and asked for a cigarette. A while later, they returned with six small fish. 'The Efe are like that,' Gamaembi explained. 'You give them something and they give you something back.' Baudouin beheaded and plucked and cut up a chicken we had bought for ten zaires, holding my pot between his feet as he threw in the pieces and added manioc greens and *mafuta* to fry them in. The boiled greens are called *sombe*, and are a Zairian staple. Fish or the meat of antelope or elephant can also be added . The spinachlike greens are very nutritious, being rich in Vitamins A and C and containing adequate quantities of seven of the eight essential amino acids. Manioc is native to Brazil and was brought to Africa by the Portuguese. It is puzzling that the Amazonians eat the starchy roots but do not eat the leaves as often.

In Selemani, an hour farther on, we met a family of BaBudu who had come from Wamba, two days to the west, to trade clothes and *mafuta* for meat. The proximity of Wamba was another good reason for the BaLese to move into the forest. I noticed a net stuffed in the rafters of the *baraza*. Hunting nets, which are made from a vine in the spurge family called *kusa*, are used by the pygmies of the BaBudu and the BaBira but rarely by the Efe, to whom this one was probably on loan. It is much more efficient to drive game into a net than to hunt it with a bow, but the Efe have not adopted the method, perhaps from pride or perhaps because it would force them to live in larger groups. Three or four families are not enough people for an effective drive.

At two o'clock, we reached Azangu. The *capita* was Gamaembi's father's 'brother,' or *ndugu*; he was from the same *localité*, though not from the same clan. An old man with a sly, humorous face, he was wearing a purple shirt and sitting in a wicker deck chair weaving a shallow basket for winnowing rice. The chair, a far more finished piece of furniture than the BaLese produce, was made by the Mangbetu, a tribe to the north; such chairs are a popular trade item. After studying me for some time, Azangu thanked me for coming and said, 'You are big, as our people used to be.' (I am six feet tall and was about twenty pounds overweight.) Excess body fat, implying that you have plenty of food and have other people to do your work for you, is a status symbol in black Africa. The only men in the *collectivité* who were in my league were Joaçim's father and the judge. Azangu must have thought I was an important person. I spent the afternoon conversing with him through Gamaembi, after bathing in the river and painting with Merthiolate the cuts and open sores of several Efe, whose camp was below the village. I told my patients that it would sting for a moment, and afterward they would feel better. They sucked in their breath, as if in pain, even before the applicator touched them.

I dropped a tablet of effervescent Vitamin C into a cup of water and passed it to Azangu, who screamed 'Ow!' with delight before he drank. Later, when I played the guitar, he stood up and did a little shuffle, which everybody had to come and watch. When he had sat down again, he tapped some snuff from a Coca-Cola bottle, inhaled it, and dictated into my Sony a letter of introduction to Moto Moto, the most important chief in the southern part of the forest: 'This is Alex. He spent the night here. I need a shirt and some pants.'

'Azangu is the biggest village around here,' Gamaembi explained. 'Moto Moto is the capital of all the little villages *de ce côté là*.'

We stayed that night in a small hut without windows. Gamaembi barred the door on the inside, and I asked why we needed so much security. He said, 'It is our custom.' It was not attack from another village he was worried about. Fifty years ago, the BaLese had raided each other's villages for women, as the Yanomamo of northern Amazonia still do today, but the Belgians had put a stop to the practice. Nor was it spirits, who could walk through walls, that concerned him. It was *enemies*, who could change into leopards through sorcery and kill you as you slept. Metamorphosed enemies were not afraid of fire, as real leopards are.

Outside, still sitting in the *baraza*, Azangu told stories about mean Belgians in a voice the whole village could hear. I slept deeply in the pitch darkness. In the morning, Azangu asked to see another Vitamin C tablet dissolve in water.

Soon after crossing the Angu River, we met an Efe man and his wife. Using an iron arrowhead, he was whittling the shaft of another arrow to a point, for hunting monkeys, and he had a round wooden plug in the pierced philtrum of his upper lip. The labret may have been a vestige of the large lip disc that used to be in vogue, which may have served to emphasize the sexual function of the mouth. This was a rare sighting, as Efe men carve lip plugs for their wives but seldom wear them themselves. This man's wife was carrying a smoldering faggot to start their next fire with and an empty bottle of Primus, the most popular beer, to put honey in.

We reached the village of Adremani by midmorning. The *capita*, Bernard, bore an amazing resemblance to the young Harry Belafonte. He was sitting in the *baraza* with a policeman in ragged, epauletted green fatigues and worn-out sneakers who had come to collect the annual head tax from the people in the forest. The policeman, who had an Okapi-brand folding knife for a weapon, had brought a prisoner as his porter. The man, whose hands were tied, had been arrested in Digbo for making alcohol from manioc, which is illegal—although all the Zairois, and especially policemen, drink it. Somebody must have wanted the man arrested; perhaps it was the policeman himself, knowing that he was going into the forest for several months and could use a porter, and that the man would never be able to come up with the three-hundred-zaire fine for making home brew.

In the afternoon, farther up the Angu River, we came to a village of four huts, named Angu-Kinshasa, after the capital of Zaire. The *capita*, Sadiki, was forging a curved brush hook, pumping with his foot a bellows made of the endlessly useful *mangungu*. As I was going through my duffelbag, his eyes fell on my blue cap, and he asked me for it. I asked what he would give me in return. He went into his hut and brought out a cup carved of very hard gray wood, and we made the trade—both of us thinking we had got the better of the deal. In the clearing, his fifteen-year-old daughter, already a sultry young woman and pregnant by a BaBudu trader, was pounding the hulls off some rice in a mortar. A boy led me to a stream. As I washed in a pool, a huge velvet-brown swallowtail butterfly with luminous lemon-green wing bands—it flew so strongly I thought at first it was a bird—patrolled the streambed possessively, disappearing upstream and returning every few minutes. It was the largest of several brown-and-yellow species in the genus *Graphium*. Downstream, the boy was checking traps for catfish. He came back with two freshwater crabs that had walked into them. Suddenly, I was in a whirl of smaller butterflies—hair-streaks which changed from dull purple to brilliant blowtorch blue whenever sunlight hit their wings. I watched one land on a leaf and rub its long, slender tails together, perhaps to make them seem even more like its antennae. On its folded hind wings, black spots, mimicking eyes, ringed with orange and shot with a zigzag of opalescent green, furthered the illusion that the insect was resting face down. The purpose of the illusion was probably to fool predators into striking at a part of its body which it could better afford to lose than its head.

When I returned to the village, Sadiki was drunk on banana wine—*le whisky zaïrois*, Gamaembi called it. After dark, the whole village, roused by Sadiki, had a dance in our honor. An Efe man tapped a brisk contagious rhythm on a drum, three Efe women yodelled, and all the others joined in a BaBudu chant they knew. Tramping in a circle with our hands on the next person's shoulders, we hopped to either side with both feet together, like downhill skiers, or stood and watched as two people on opposite edges of the circle jumped in, acted spooky for a few seconds, then dropped back to their places. I spotted two new uses of *mangungu*, of which I had begun a list: one of the Efe women wore an upright leaf, like a feather, on a head-band; another had a bracelet pouch, rather like a disco bag, on her wrist.

In the morning, all the villagers put on their best clothes for an official photograph. Some of them went with us for a little way into the forest.

Soon after they had turned back, we could hear the Mambo River rushing through a gorge to our right. After following it for four and a half hours, we reached Salumu, the last village that any muzungu had ever been to. Sadiki had told me that he talked regularly to Salumu with drums, although all he could say was 'Come here.' In other parts of Africa, drummers can communicate full paragraphs.

In Salumu, several magnificent roosters paced the clearing, and a young man with a T-shirt that said HOUSTON 38 was strumming a homemade stringed instrument carved in the shape of an electric guitar. We were offered, as a special treat, some smoked elephant meat. I put a chunk in my mouth but could not bring myself to swallow it. It was as tough as rubber and it smelled and tasted weeks old. Gamaembi, talking with the villagers about where to go from here, learned of a new village called Pereni, which some of their people had started. A pygmy named Sabani offered to take us there, but his wife wouldn't let him go, so we went on by ourselves.

We crossed the Ngawe River almost immediately. It flowed south; the other rivers we had crossed flowed north. After three and a half hours, we came to Pereni, which was not really a village but a still. It owed its existence to a grove of raffia palm trees, whose juice becomes alcoholic within a few hours of being tapped. Two young men named Mosalia and Shafiku and their women ran the still, which was not legal. Mosalia was wearing a Wonderknit shirt with a label that said, 'Washing instructions: only machine wash— warm tumble dry—no bleach.' Shafiku was an Efe-BaLese mestizo. That night, passing around halved calabashes full of palm wine, we made up a song that consisted of one line in Swahili, 'It is just us here,' and shouted it again and again in the darkness, like dogs howling at the moon.

In the morning, we were given a tour of the works. Since their arrival, Mosalia and Shafiku had cut down seven trees, and they were all still exuding juice, or wine, which the two men collected every twenty-four hours from homemade clay pots they had left beneath the dripping ends of the fallen trunks. 'It flows day and night,' Mosalia told me. The wine was slightly hard, like cider or birch beer, and very drinkable. It is a beverage of great antiquity, mentioned by Herodotus. We tasted wine from a tree that had been cut down a month earlier and was still dripping, and wine from one felled only the day before. The fresher stuff was more acid and carbonated, the other calmer and smoother, rather like Beaujolais. As we drank, we sat and watched two white lines way above the clouds trace themselves across the sky. Gamaembi, who had never been near an airplane, said, 'That one holds four hundred and fifty people.'

After collecting the wine from the trees, Mosalia and Shafiku poured it into an oil drum, heated it while it evaporated up a length of hollowed bamboo, and bottled the distillate as it condensed and ran down another bamboo tube. The final product, known as *kaikbo* (it is also distilled from corn, bananas, or manioc), was as strong as gasoline, Mosalia claimed, and exploded when you threw it on a fire. They were making thirty bottles a day and selling them to BaBudu traders. He offered to sell us some, but Gamaembi, looking anxiously at Baudouin, shook his head. Baudouin was already drunk, and it was only eight o'clock. With great difficulty, we got him to his feet and on the path. He didn't want to leave at all. '*Pereni c'est matata*,' he said. *Matata* means 'trouble,' in a positive sense. He managed to stagger along for about half a mile; then, overcome by a mixture of wine and pot, he vomitted and passed out. As he slept, half a dozen huge cicadas, each blending with the mossy bark of a different tree, droned around us.

We waited for Baudouin to come to, and Gamaembi talked about the store he was going to start with his half brother Kuri. He would bring the goods by bicycle from Digbo: simple things at first—cooking pots, flashlights, drinking glasses, soap, needles, cigarettes—slowly building up to more expensive items, like radios and wax-printed cloth. Then he would put a tin roof on the store. Then he would buy a truck. He already had a bicycle. Bicycles were not cheap in Haut-Zaire. Even a beaten-up wreck cost six hundred zaires. But he and Kuri owned a coffee *shamba* together. With three hundred zaires they had made from selling the beans, they had paid some Efe—in soap, shirts, and pants—to kill an elephant with spears. A local *fraudeur*, or smuggler, had bought the tusks and the teeth for two thousand zaires. He would sell them to the next level of *fraudeur*, and from then on they would be the focus of numerous illegal dealings. Perhaps the subregional administrator in Isiro, the nearest large city, would acquire them.

They would probably end up in Hong Kong, to be carved into coffee-table objects and jewelry for consumers in the West. Gamaembi figured he had enough to start with—nine hundred zaires for the merchandise, two hundred for incidental expenses like keeping the police off his back. I thought how unfortunate it was that the only way a young man in Gamaembi's position could get ahead was to kill an elephant.

By eleven, Baudouin was ready to continue. We crossed the Ngawe again—on a fallen tree, and a vine railing along which a column of small red ants was moving. They jumped on my hand instantly and covered it with bites. We saw dragonflies with dazzling blue wings, and an elongated black-and-white butterfly that was hardly distinguishable from the dappled shadows among which it was lazily flapping. We arrived at Dulungu by midafternoon, stayed long enough to take a census—Dulungu was seventeen years old, one of the oldest of the new villages in the forest, with a population of eight—and pushed on to make Sandiki by nightfall.

From Sandiki, it was eight hours to the next village, Mangiese, by a path that went along a shrubby ridge most of the way. Mangiese was on the Isolo River, and four families lived there. Eight prospectors from Mambasa, a relatively large town on the Kisangani road, which was the capital of the zone, were lodging there, too. Gold had been found in a stream near Moto Moto, about fifteen miles away, and the discovery had sparked a small gold rush in the southern Ituri Forest. I photographed the prospectors, with their picks and shovels. 'They want to get rich without working in shambas,' Gamaembi said, perhaps a little enviously. If gold was found near Mangiese, it would no longer be a quiet village in the forest. Already, the doors of its huts were padlocked.

Andalita, the capita of Mangiese, was the son of Gamaembi's aunt, and he received us as family. He mended Baudouin's torn pants on his sewing machine and fixed a broken buckle on my side bag. He was not one for lounging in the baraza. It had taken him only a week to clear a large shamba we had passed on the way to the village. As the bees died down and daylight faded and a flock of green forest ibises, hurrying to their roosts, flew over and filled the sky with trumpeting, he chipped weeds in the clearing with a

162

hoe. 'This has to be done every two weeks,' he said. His two-year-old daughter, Molai, followed him with a little hoe, stabbing at weeds, and in a vinegrown *shamba* behind them his wife, Ubolubu, of a delicate and sensitive beauty, picked leaves for a flyswatter. They seemed a happy family.

After dark, Ubolubu came to the *baraza* with boiled bananas and chicken and *sombe* on a real silver platter. (Andalita must have been panning a little gold himself, I thought.) Molai, with coils of thread in her pierced ears, sat on my lap and looked up at me with wonder. She had never seen a *muzungu*. I couldn't get a smile out of her. I played a little to her on my guitar, but one of the strings broke. The villagers and the prospectors sang the Zairian national anthem, which was in French, for me; then they fell into their own language. On the edge of the sky, flickering flashes of lightning momentarily eclipsed the stars and the fire's glow, and illumined clouds, looming trees, tattered banana leaves, a battered pot in the middle of the gray clay clearing, and Molai, who had moved to a little chair against a post but was still staring at me with her mouth open. I thought of how Gamaembi had promised that afternoon to give me his bracelet, woven from the black hair of an elephant's tail, to commemorate our friendship. But he still did not quite believe that if a well-cooked plate of human flesh were put before me I would be able to pass it up. 'A few years ago, my cousin bought what he thought was a can of sardines at a store in Kisangani,' he had told me. 'He opened it, and there was a hand inside. The owner of the store, a *muzungu*, begged him to keep it a secret." The basis of this story probably went back to the First World War, when the natives of the Congo were first forced to collect rubber, and the Belgians sometimes cut off the hands of those who had not collected enough. To the BaLese, the most logical motive for the amputations was that *muzungus* were cannibals, as the BaLese's other enemies were.

I started to fade, listening to wonderful-sounding stories I couldn't make head or tail of, but suddenly there was a great shout and everyone in the *baraza* jumped up. Andalita grabbed a burning log from the fire and clubbed something on the ground. It looked like a scorpion, but was another arthropod—a long-tailed thirty-legged centipede. Gamaembi said that it had been attracted to the fire, and that its bite could paralyse you for days, or even kill a child.

163

When we hit the trail for Moto Moto the next day, Gamaembi, who was in the lead, and was breathing faint, evanescent plumes of steam into the morning coolness and parting wet cobwebs with his forehead, turned around and said, 'There will be a story in Mangiese about the *muzungu* who came and played the guitar and one of his strings broke.' I had given Andalita a roll of nylon cord, although Bob Bailey had advised me to go easy with presents, saying, 'Your presence will be enough of a gift.'

I was bushed. I had not recovered from the long day before. Gamaembi said it was only four hours to Moto Moto, but every step was an effort. I kept asking when we were going to get there, and Baudouin would say gently, '*À peu près, monsieur. Un peu plus près.*' To aggravate matters, I was stung by nettles on the back of my right thumb. Too late, Gamaembi showed me the vine, whose innocent-looking, heart-shaped leaves were covered with minute, prickly hairs. The thumb quickly swelled, and for the next few days it itched incessantly. But my malaise was more than physical. I wondered if it had anything to do with the 'mental strain' described in a pamphlet, *Preservation of Personal Health in Warm Climates*, which I'd read in preparation for the trip. It was published in Great Britain, for people planning extended stays in the tropics, and stated:

> The condition at present responsible for many cases of Europeans having to be invalided from the tropics is mental health, which commonly takes the form of lack of self-confidence and anxiety. Some of this ill health is associated with physical illness but most of it arises from a temperamental incompetence—an inability to adjust outlook and habits to the strange people, customs, social life and climate of a tropical environment. Inflexible people and those with definite racial or cultural prejudices find this adjustment most difficult, and those to whom the glamour of tropical life seems an escape from competition 'at home' are sure to be disillusioned. Persons of a highly nervous disposition or with a family history of mental disturbance react badly to the life in the tropics where the heat and the humidity tend to magnify the petty irritations that would pass unnoticed in more temperate regions.

The pamphlet went on to say that many people had found a glass of gin in the evening an antidote.

At eleven, we met some pygmies on the path, and they told us, 'You will get to Moto Moto before we get to Mangiese.' One of the women, whose face was scored with black lines, had an enormous bottom. This condition, known as steatopygia, is common among pygmies. Since pygmy women with bulbous bottoms are the most attractive to pygmies and to BaLese, whose women also have the trait (though nowhere nearly so conspicuously), sexual selection may be at work. (An equally interesting question is why *muzungus* have comparatively flat, compact bottoms.) An hour later, we walked into Moto Moto. In contrast to Mangiese and the butterflies that haunted it, it was a filthy place. It hadn't been swept in days, and all kinds of putrid scraps and leftovers were lying around, attracting flies by the thousands. I went to the river as quickly as I could; that was always the best part of the day. Three Efe girls, waist-deep in the water, were pounding it with cupped hands, making a staccato clopping sound, like horses trotting on pavement. Baudouin called to them teasingly, 'I am your husband,' and they screamed with frightened delight. A little later, one of them came over shyly to borrow my soap.

When I returned to the village, Gamaembi told me there were some Efe who needed medicine. One was an old man who complained of pain in his chest. I asked if he smoked a lot, and he said he did. I gave him some aspirin and told him to stop smoking until the pain went away. That was all I could do for him. Then we went to a woman sitting in front of a hut. She called her son, who was lying in the darkness inside, and he came out, so weak he could barely stand. He was about six years old. His face and back were covered with purulent warts the size of nickels and quarters. They looked like little cauliflowers. She pulled away his loin-cloth, and what I saw made tears rush to my eyes. On the inside of both thighs the flesh was inflated and white, like whale blubber, and the infection was eating into his scrotum. Whatever he had, it was advanced. Something I had read rang a bell, and when I got home I found the following passage in a book by Sebastian Snow, who reached the source of the Marañon River, in Peru, early in the nineteen-fifties:

Inside the shelter, with his head against a large earthenware cauldron, lay an Indian boy, his legs covered with *verugas*, or warts. They were hardly distinguishable because they were so covered with blood and flies, with hundreds of mosquitoes circling above . . . His legs were like matchsticks, his cheeks hollow and his eyes large and brilliant. He seemed remarkably philosophical about his condition and accepted his fate with a stoicism which I greatly admired and envied. He had no fear of death; he certainly had little will to live.

This was not *verruga peruana*, however, but another tropical disease, called yaws, or frambesia. I did not know the French word for it, and neither did Gamaembi. 'Young children get it, and it comes again in adolescence,' he said. 'He needs penicillin.' The antibiotic I had with me had almost the same spectrum. It might raise the boy's chances to fifty-fifty, but if I gave it to him I would be unprotected. And if I didn't give it to him his chances were probably zero. Emotionally, almost shouting, I explained to the woman through Gamaembi that I was giving her this medicine, but it would not save the boy, and if she did not take him to the dispensary in Wamba, which was three days' walk, he would probably die. And if she did not follow the full course, and give him one pill three times a day for nine days, the medicine would do no good. She nodded, but I doubt whether she understood any of it.

As we walked on through the village, Gamaembi stopped a woman he knew, and she said she would go with the mother and her son to Wamba. In one of the most interesting of the *mba*, the plant and animal taboos that protect the capacity of the forest to provide for them, the pygmies believe that if they kill and eat a baby blue duiker their own child will get sick and die unless they find a certain plant in the arrowroot family, pound its root, boil it with salt, and feed it to the child. To their way of thinking, something awful could have happened to one of my sons if I had allowed the boy to die by not giving him the medicine. What you did mattered in the Ituri Forest, as it did anywhere. All sorts of taboos and fetishes held you responsible for your actions.

I sat for the rest of the day in the *baraza*. Moto Moto, the degenerate old *capita*, was there, in a chair that was slightly higher and fancier than the others. A wire in the Sony had come loose, and the complex circuitry was beyond Gamaembi or me, so I could not play Moto Moto his message from Azangu. Moto Moto was a member of the same clan as Gamaembi's wife. His mother was an Efe. He wore sandals, and also owned a pair of yellow rubber boots, which were drying in the yard. Lighting a marijuana pipe, he asked me through Gamaembi, who sat at his feet, if it was possible for him to marry a woman of my race. I said yes. 'Well, bring me one the next time you come,' he said. 'And what about the bride price?' he asked a bit later. I said there was none. 'What? You mean I can get a woman for nothing?' he asked with astonishment. Not only that, I said, but her father would probably pay for the wedding.

For the better part of the afternoon, I sat across from a tall policeman with a goatee, who had come from Mambasa to collect the annual head tax. He was reading a pamphlet, in French, about pregnancy. His two young associates were reading a paperback called *How to Realize Your Life* and an excruciatingly theological biography of Mary of Nazareth, both of which were also in French. Each of the two had a radio to his ear, and the radios were tuned to different rumba stations. I found it hard to hear myself think, but everybody else was oblivious of the problem. 'French is the national language, but not many people in Haut-Zaire know it,' the policeman told me. 'Only five per cent really speak it. Maybe fifteen or twenty per cent get along, and thirty per cent understand it.' He said he was resting that day, but, beginning the next day, he and his associates were going to spend about five days hunting down prospectors and getting six zaires from each of them. He reckoned there were about thirty prospectors in the area—BaNdaka from Mambasa, and WaNande from the highlands.

Like the policeman in Adremani, he had an Okapi-brand folding knife for a weapon. His symbol of authority, instead of a badge, was a set of keys. He told me that two of the keys opened desks at the police station, one was to his house, the fourth was a skeleton. I had the impression he could have been bought with little trouble. In the course of the afternoon, he bummed a dozen cigarettes, two candles, and a box of matches from me, and asked for but did not get my felt-tip pen, my guitar, my running shoes, and my knife. I felt I got off lightly.

Toward evening, a low, sullen, but beautiful raft of steel-grey clouds moved in from the north. Gamaembi said we should get an early start tomorrow, or we might not be able to cross the river. I changed the string on my guitar and played a few licks for Moto Moto and the policeman, who eyed me wordlessly, trying to decide what to ask for next. An old man from the village who was sitting next to him also studied me intently. I thought he was interested in the music, but he finally saw his moment and asked, 'Soap, monsieur?' When we turned in, the policeman had a last request: my address. I asked what for. 'So we can correspond.'

It rained all night, but in the morning we waded the Ngawe without trouble. It was only up to our waists. We passed a buffalo pit trap and then some small, capped termitaries that resembled two-foot gray toadstools. We surprised a large troop of gray-cheeked mangabeys feeding on the ground. Compared with blue monkeys, which stay in a small, fixed home range, mangabeys are seminomadic; they move for several weeks into an area where a particular forest fruit is abundant, then go somewhere else. As the troop scampered along, with clucks of alarm which turned into panicky shrieks as they climbed up leafy lianas, I spotted several males. (The females of most of the monkey species in the Ituri Forest are usually accompanied by only a single male.) A bit later, some monkeys that were more arboreal—probably Angolan colobus—brayed at us from the crown of an emergent, sucking in air with excited *hoos*. One of them threw down a dead branch, which just missed me. I was exhilarated. Farther on, I stopped to pick burrs from my socks, and Baudouin plucked a vine stretched taut between two buttresses; it resonated deeply, like a bass. We came to two empty Efe camps. The Efe were always somewhere else, it seemed. The second camp had eighteen huts, and several healthy *bangi* plants and a creeping cherry-tomato vine were growing in the clearing. 'So they do grow things,' I said to Gamaembi, and he said that these had probably not been planted but had started spontaneously from fallen seeds.

That night, after ten hours of walking, we slept in a streamside lean-to. When day came, Gamaembi noticed a tree even he did not know, with long, linear leaves in the crown, almost like pine needles. I asked if he could climb it. He said '*Mais oui*' and proceeded to swarm up it, grabbing the straight branchless trunk, as big around as a telephone pole, in his hands, and bringing up his feet—measuring it like an inchworm. The sprig he threw down, which I described a few days later to the botanist Terese Hart, who was doing an ecological study in the forest, was probably from a species of dracaena called the dragon tree.

Soon after starting on the path, we began to hear the sonorous low gears of trucks. They had never sounded so welcome. After three hours, we came out on the Kisangani road. We bathed in the Epini River, washed our clothes, laid them out on gray slabs beside the water, and rested. In the course of our trek, I had lost about fifteen pounds.

We didn't have to wait long in Epini, a roadside settlement about the size of Opuku. A pygmy there who spoke French—the first I had met—brought me the honey of stingless melaponines. It was very liquid and had a slightly medicinal aftertaste. As we were drinking it a little Citroyenne van approached from the west. I jumped up and flagged it down. A soldier and three women in the rear compartment made room for us, and a few hours later we were in Epulu. Baudouin and Gamaembi got out and carefully shook the red dust from their clothes. Gamaembi had changed into long pants and a T-shirt with the picture of a rock star on it. Baudouin had rolled down his pants and put on a T-shirt from Healy's Deli, Katonah, New York, which I had given him. But Epulu hardly seemed worth dressing up for. Half a dozen beer joints with half a dozen mud-caked trucks parked in front of them, a couple of stores, and that was it, at least in the center of town. We entered a room where some truckers and local women were drinking beer and laughing together. This was BaBira country, and Baudouin and Gamaembi were as much strangers in it as I was. I ordered a round of Primus and they drank from their glasses slowly and shyly. It was not often that they got to drink beer. One bottle would have cost them four days in a shamba. We ate some stew and checked into two of the concrete huts in back—remnants from when Epulu had had a tourist trade. Inside each was a bed with sheets, a kerosene lantern, and a bucket of water.

Late in the afternoon we walked down to the Epulu, a big river full of rapids and tall, dark boulders. Several plovers and sandpipers, down from Europe for the winter, were pacing the bank, and on one of the boulders an African darter was holding its wings out to dry in typical anhinga fashion. Baudouin was blown away. He had never seen such

169

a big river. Beside it stood the ruin of a large hotel destroyed during the Rebellion and an overland touring truck surrounded by colourful nylon tents. A group of pygmies had come to the truck with *bangi* and strings of little fish to sell the passengers, a dozen young Europeans who had set out from Copenhagen four months earlier. The Danes and the French were not speaking.

Across the road was a park which at one time contained examples of most of the animals in the Ituri Forest. But the Simbas had massacred all the animals and there was little to see, only two okapis—extraordinary creatures—and a couple of forest antelope. The keeper pointed out a blue duiker that had a large enclosure to itself. Its colour was that of a shadow, its height not much more than one foot. I would never have noticed it.

An American couple, John and Terese Hart, had just settled in at the Station de Capture des Okapis, as the park was called. They had served in Zaire with the Peace Corps, and now they had returned for doctorate work. John was going to study the blue duiker. He was a Midwestern version of Richard, full of ideas and completely caught up in his subject. We sat on the porch of a spacious fieldstone house which for some reason the Simbas had passed over; the Zairian government had given it to the Harts for two years. With a series of cascades plunging under a steel bridge before the house, it was one of the nicest spots I could remember setting eyes on. John told me that although a pygmy could net a hundred kilos of meat a week and commercial demand for meat was growing, the only animal as yet in any real danger was the elephant. The diversity of primates was still 'unreal,' and even the okapi seemed safe, as long as the forest was left intact. 'But Zaire is sitting on big environmental problems,' he said 'There is real concern that before it emerges a number of irreplaceable resources, especially undiscovered drug plants, will be lost. The multinationals have big plans here. We've heard that they have bought up cutting rights to vast parts of the *cuvette*; and rain forest, you know, is like an island. As it shrinks, the extinction rate will accelerate.'

That night the pygmies of Epulu had a dance. 'They're gearing up for a big wedding in a couple of weeks,' John said as we walked by flashlight with Terese and their four-year-old daughter to a camp several hundred yards from the road.

When we got there everyone was doing a baboon dance on all fours. A very short young woman with tremendous breasts was dancing euphorically in the firelight. Bells were strapped to the tops of her calves. You could tell she was the bride-to-be. The women sang the songs of the *elima*, the girls' coming-of-age festival. I thought how little changed these pygmies were by their long contact with Europeans. 'The tribes have begun to enter the world of change we have brought, but the BaMbuti have kept their nomadic spirit,' John said. 'You give them a shirt and they will wear it for three days, then they will give it away. I think the key to understanding them is probably their music. You can do years of time-allocation studies and still not know them. It's only in our society, strung out on our resources and hung up on efficiency, that the notion of optimization has become important.' As I took that down, a pygmy man, fascinated by my jottings, held a lantern over my notebook.

In the morning I went to the forest with Terese and Kenge, the father of the bride-to-be and the most famous pygmy in the West. Kenge and the anthropologist Colin Turnbull had been in a sense each other's protégés twenty years earlier. There is a memorable passage in Turnbull's book *The Forest People* in which Kenge, whom Turnbull has taken to see the savanna for the first time, asks about some buffalo he has spotted grazing several miles away: 'What are those insects?' Turnbull had concluded that Kenge's field of vision had always been so limited that he had never learned to allow for distance. Now Kenge was a dignified man in his forties, with a mustache and gray at the temples; and a new generation of *muzungus* had come to learn about his people. Terese was a botanist, and Kenge was telling her the names and uses of plants. As we walked through the village I saw that several of the women who had been with the truckers the day before had men. Their men evidently didn't mind their being with other men as long as they brought the money home.

Kenge showed us the fruit whose inky juice was used for body paint, and the stump of a tree which had been cut for a dugout canoe. Terese pointed out a wasp-pollinated fig tree and four relatives of the *mangungu*, all growing in apparently the same conditions. She examined the extrafloral nectaries on a sapling in the pea family, which Kenge said was used for hut frames and pipe bowls. Deeper in, the forest became an almost pure stand of tall trees the same

171

species as the sapling—*Gilbertiodendron dewevrei*—and an important source of timber. Their eight-inch pods and broad brown leathery leaves littered the ground. Terese was thinking of doing her thesis on them. Kenge showed us a lily which, cut up and thrown in the river, would bring rain in time of drought, and he took us to a mass grave for some men who had died in an accident when the steel bridge was being built across the river during the forties. Condemned prisoners were used for the dangerous work. Terese said that many trees in the forest flowered and set fruit continuously, not just once a year.

I spent the afternoon writing a report for Richard, and at four o'clock we piled into the Harts' Toyota jeep—John, Baudouin, Gamaembi, myself, one of the pregnant young wives of the *chef de station*, and a couple of pygmies—and set out for Mambasa. From each rise we could see *Cynometria alexandrii* in snowy bloom all over the forest. After an hour we came to a big truck stuck to its axles in a muddy depression, with dozens of other trucks backed up in either direction, and everybody helping to dig it out. It looked as if we were going to be there for a while, but John thought he could get past, and putting the jeep in four-wheel drive, he ran it up on the lip of the road, and we made it. It was a road of national importance—part of the Transafrican Highway—and sometimes we got up to thirty on it.

We reached Mambasa after dark. It was between Epulu and Isiro in size and importance. A substantial part of the population was Moslem. Arab slavers in the last century had planted the seed of their faith. The *chef*'s wife, close to the end of her term, got out at the dispensary. I parted with Baudouin and Gamaembi in the main square, where the beloved Father Longo had been killed with a spear during the Rebellion. 'One Ascension Day,' Turnbull writes in *The Lonely African*,

as Father Longo was saying the Mass, a host of pagan pygmies came in from the forest, bearing gifts of forest flowers and leaves and fruits, and danced into the church to make their offering. Then they stood at the back of the church, chattering happily, until the Mass was over, when they danced their heathen way back to their heathen forest, full of love and gratitude to Father Longo for the love and kindness he had showed them over the years.

172

I gave Baudouin and Gamaembi my letter to Richard, his sleeping bag and ground cloth, and some plastic bags Nadine had wanted back. They would be home in four days. When I got home, months later, there was a letter full of news from Gamaembi.

After we parted, they had spent the next night with his *grandfrère* Apimo, Gamaembi wrote, and Apimo had asked them all about the trip, and whether they had not been afraid to be with a *muzungu* for twelve days. Gamaembi had told him everything—where we had slept each night, what we had eaten, how I had written everything down and had taken pictures of everybody. 'Eh. I still remember the American song you taught us,' the letter continued (a sassy ragtime version of 'Five Foot Two, Eyes of Blue'). 'And you'll never guess what happened three weeks after I got home. I took another wife. The girl is from the *groupement* of Andape, forty-three kilometres from Opoku, and she belongs to the little *fungu* of Anduchu. It was a great wedding, I understand. I wasn't there myself.' The groom's presence is not required at a BaLese wedding, and Gamaembi was, I have since learned, prospecting for gold along the Nepoko River, north of Opoku. 'My brothers carried in a substitute for me on their shoulders. The bride-price negotiations went on for two days. In the end, I had to give her family eight hundred zaires and a goat. So there went the money for my store.' The letter ended with a request for a digital wristwatch and a pair of Adidas running shoes, size 8. 'Please send them. It will bring me glory when my brothers see that I really have a friend in America.'

John and I continued to the Combonian mission just out of town. He wanted to talk to Father Carlo about a mechanical problem with the Toyota. Father Carlo, a man of about forty-five with an appealing bearded face, greeted us with the news that our President had been shot earlier in the day. As we sat by the radio, waiting for the next broadcast, Father Carlo stroked the dense fur of an animal on his lap about the size of a cat. Its hands had a thumb and three fingers; the forefinger was undeveloped. Its feet were similar, with a big toe and three little ones, but there was a claw in the first position, which John thought might have been for grooming. He said the animal was a prosimian, more closely related to lemurs than to monkeys and called a *potto*. It lived in trees and spent the day curled in sleep,

173

becoming active after dark. He showed me the bony processes coming off its upper vertebrae, which it erected on the back of its neck to protect itself from the bite of palm civets. It was a very solid creature. I got the impression it could have fallen from a tall tree without being hurt. We stayed up late talking. 'These people don't see the necessity for progress,' John observed. 'Their lives are directed by the presence of the forest. The climate is conducive to postponement.' It seemed easier, in the long run, to explain the pre-industrial world than the extraordinary spurts of cultural evolution which had taken place in Europe since the Renaissance. Father Carlo had hundreds of books in his room, and he seemed deeply satisfied with life in the jungle. As he showed us where we could sleep, I asked if it was hard to live without a woman. He smiled slowly and said, 'Some people smoke and it gives them a headache.'

In the morning I got a lift with him as far as a school that he was building. I hadn't walked a mile when a truck taking palm oil to Bunia stopped for me. The road followed the route that Henry Morton Stanley had forged across the Congo nearly a century earlier. We were in the vicinity of Starvation Camp, where his Emin Pasha Relief Expedition, out of food, decimated by diseases, and under attack by 'malicious dwarves,' nearly met its end. Further east, we passed the site of Fort Bodo, which Stanley had built to cover his rear guard. He thought Bodo meant 'peace.' It actually meant 'white.' He was too busy fighting the local people to establish much rapport with them. 'The tribes of the forest are the most vicious and degraded of the human race on the face of the earth,' he wrote. At the beginning of the century Alexander von Humboldt had said much the same thing about the Indians in Amazonia. That idea persisted until this century, when anthropologists started to live with 'savages' and to report that they were people.

At noon I got off at a place called Lolwa, which Bob had said not to miss. 'Lolwa: the Protestant mission is a very friendly place,' Jeff Crowthers writes in his fact-filled guide, *Africa on the Cheap.* 'Described by one visitor as "just like home!" Be prepared to see the light.'

I walked down from the road into a beautiful garden with tall spruces and trim cypress hedges, expanses of lawn and all kinds of flowers, even a tennis court behind the charming cottage on whose door I knocked. A kindly old

174

white woman opened it and said in English, 'Come in. You're just in time for lunch.' She took me into her guest room, where there were two beds with immaculate white spreads under canopies of mosquito netting. I poured water from a pitcher into a basin on a stand, washed my face and hands, gave myself the once-over in a flower-backed hand mirror, and went into the dining room. The woman was named Ella Spees. She introduced me to her husband Bill and a plain, cheerful American woman who was 'doing the Lord's work in the high country,' she explained, and who had come for a visit. She rang a bell, and a black man in a white jacket—one of the villagers—brought in a leg of lamb with mint jelly, peas, and roast potatoes. I said I had heard last night on the BBC that the President had been shot in the lung but was out of danger. 'We're rooting for him out here,' Bill said.'He's an upright, moral man. Carter was a man of faith, too, but he wasn't decisive enough about homosexuality or communism or getting us free from the Arabs, and he made all that fuss about the environment.' Bill kept informed with *Time*, *Newsweek*, the *Reader's Digest*, and a shortwave radio.

Ella told me they belonged to a group called the Plymouth Brethren, who had thirteen hundred missions in sixty 'fields' throughout the Third World and Europe. I asked if the Brethren were like Baptists. 'We're even more like Billy Graham,' she said. 'We're evangelical and fundamental, and we emphasize the scriptures. It's all there in the Bible.'

'The words themselves are God-breathed,' Bill explained. After forty-three years together he and Ella had grown to think and even to look alike.

'My father and mother and two brothers came here in nineteen twenty-nine,' Ella told me. 'They're all gone to the Lord. It took four months from Alameda, California. We took a boat to Mombasa, Kenya, then a train to Nairobi. I was sixteen and I loved every minute of it.

'My dad was a Scot. He was one of the foremen that cut the Panama Canal. A Negro doctor from Barbados led him to the Lord, and he started to preach after hours. One day he fell off a boat. He couldn't swim. Sharks were circling. A Panamanian Negro rescued him. The U.S. government gave the man a gold watch. So Dad always felt he had a debt to pay to the Negro people.'

'When we got here it was thick forest. We started burning

175

and clearing. The BaBira and the pygmies still carried shields. They still raided each other's villages. The BaLese wore heavy iron rings on their arms and legs. I don't know how they could walk.'

I asked what the BaLeses' houses were like. By 1929 the BaLese had given up their communal longhouses and adopted mud-plastered single-family huts, and the Efe were living in little leaf domes, as they always had.

Bill and Ella had gone to the same Sunday school in Alameda, and he had been corresponding with her brother. They fell in love in 1938, while she was on furlough, and got married. He came back with her. He was a tennis champion and gave it up to 'take the Gospel to the ends of the earth.' Ella reminisced about how they set out from Nairobi in a panel-bodied Model A. 'It took a solid week, same as today. We had a flat just outside the city. Bill had never changed a tire.' But he learned quickly. He became a mechanic, a carpenter, a welder, a plumber, a bricklayer. He taught himself the basics of each trade, as you have to when you are on your own. He built a beautiful church with real seats, a rarity in the Congo. He built the cottage and made all the furniture in it from scratch, and in 1949 he installed solar panels so he and Ella could have hot running water.

For ten years the Speeses went out every month for a week and tried to evangelize pygmies. 'We took our children on these safaris,' he told me. 'They never got sick, and some of their happiest memories are of playing with pygmy children. But when you camp out with pygmies, you find that under their happy-go-lucky exterior they are terrified of evil spirits and of death. At night they would pick up burning logs we had laid in a circle around us to keep away army ants, and throw them at spirits in the forest. I asked what the spirits looked like. They said little lights.'

The Speeses got nowhere with the pygmies. 'We were very burdened about them,' Bill went on. 'Then suddenly, a few years ago, they started to take an intense interest in the Gospel. Now we have thirteen literate preachers among their people, and after all these years we've had the joy of seeing three little pygmy churches spring into being. Even if we had to leave, it would carry on. The other day Ella showed a cut-out figure of Satan to a pygmy woman, and the woman pulled down her lower eyelid at it, which meant I'm not afraid of you, buster. We're getting a lot of converts. In central Africa it's very fruitful. The trouble is it's hard getting recruits to come out here, and the ones who do come only stay for a year or two. You don't get people who are willing to stick it out for a lifetime any more. This continent is in turmoil. It has a bad image. But in spite of all the troubles the opportunities and openings in the Gospel are greater than ever.'

The Speeses were in Kampala, Uganda, on business when the Rebellion spread east from Mombasa. 'It was an anti-Christian, anti-white thing—a reversion to the primitive,' Bill said. 'The Simbas were anointed by a woman who draped her huge breasts over the back of their necks as they knelt before her. They were high on *bangi* and believed they were invulnerable. Over three months they killed eighty thousand people in Haut-Zaire. Father Longo, a very useful man, was martyred at the crossroads in Mambasa. The Belgian Tibermont, who had a sawmill right down the road, they trussed up like a chicken, shot, and threw into the Epulu. He had a good business in mahogany and teak. Boebelmanns managed to escape by hiding in the trunk of his car for two days, but he lost the plant collection he had been making for twenty years. The Belgians' policy was paternalistic. They figured that if you did a lot in a material way the natives would keep shut about clamoring for independence. From 1940 the rules about an official hitting a man got stricter.'

After lunch the Speeses took a nap. I sat in the parlor and read Paul Schebeste's classic ethnography, *Les Pygmées du Congo Belge*. There was a photograph in the dining room of Schebeste and the Speeses standing in a forest clearing with some pygmies.

When the heat of the day had passed Ella brought me a glass of raspberry Kool-Aid, and said she was going to the chapel to run the four o'clock prayer meeting, and if I was coming up to be sure to lock the door. I heard Bill out back talking to a group of villagers in Swahili. He explained that he was 'paying off the servants so they won't pester my wife while I'm gone.' In a few days he was leaving for Alameda to take care of some family business. As Bill showed me around the mission, we could hear people in the chapel practicing two-part harmonies for the Swahili hymns they were going to sing that Sunday. Bill had his dog Shep, a big German shepherd, on a leash. He said there were ten to twenty thousand BaBira in and around Lolwa, and about five thousand pygmies. Three hundred children were in the grade school, and seventy in the high school. 'The *authenticité* and Zairianization decrees made it impossible for us to do our work between 1972 and 1976,' he told me. 'They took over our school, but they got it in such a mess they had to give it back.'

We looked into the reading room, where a teenager was buried in the pages of a *National Geographic*. Most of the books and magazines were religious and in Swahili. Bill showed me the orphanage and the Bible school where 'Ella takes raw pygmies and after twenty months has them reading. And this is Ella's old folks' home. Very fruitful work. This is home until they die. If there is someone in the village she won't take them because there are so many needy cases. She feeds them according to their strength. If they're strong enough to work in the garden, they do, because it's important psychologically. They age quickly. Some of them are only fifty. They seem to do well and then boom.'

We went into the dispensary and met one of the male nurses, who said the main health problem at Lolwa, as at Opoku, was the bacillus that was going around and giving people dysentery. Everybody had worms; there was a good deal of bilharzia and filariasis, and some malaria. 'It will be a great day when they come up with a vaccine,' Bill said. 'Yaws used to be bad with the pygmies, before penicillin brought it under control. I used to give a hundred shots a week.' A medical team from the mission went on the road and treated seven hundred lepers, and a midwife delivered fifteen to twenty babies a month. The midwife talked to Bill about a woman whose labour was going badly, and they decided she should be driven to the hospital where Nadine's finger was treated.

What an admirable life, I was thinking, when we met a toddler on the path. The little boy had barely started walking. He couldn't have been more than two. Shep jumped up on him and knocked him down. The dog would have done worse if Bill had not reined him in and said, 'Take it easy there, Shep.' Shrieking with terror as the dog loomed over him, the boy finally got up and tottered down the path into the arms of his mother, who picked him up and walked quickly away. Bill made no attempt to comfort the boy and did not apologize to his mother. Something Joaçim had said about missionaries came to mind. He didn't think they had much love for people.

That night we had 'griddle cakes' for supper. 'Just like home.' Ella laughed. Afterwards I sang them some gospel songs I knew. Ella said I reminded her of their son, whom the Lord had called to conduct a literature campaign in Lyons, France. 'And what about you, Alex?' Bill asked. 'Have you found the Lord?' I avoided the question with something like Well, not officially. 'It's so easy to clinch it,' he pressed, and I could tell they would have welcomed me into the fold then and there if I had been willing.

Ella asked if I wanted to take a hot bath. I said that would be wonderful. Bill took me to the bathroom. 'Make sure you keep the drain plugged, so the snake doesn't come out,' he said.

'What snake?' I asked.

'A cobra,' he said. 'It rears up its hood and everything.'

It was a real American bathroom, with a red rubber hot water bottle hanging on the door, and on the windowsill three familiar bottles full of red, lemon, and gold fluid and labelled Lavoris, Vitalis, and Listerine. I sat up late in bed, reading the Speeses' most treasured possession, a first edition of Stanley's two-volume *In Darkest Africa*. 'We lost all our wedding presents, but the English books lived through the Rebellion,' Ella had told me. 'They were all over the floor. It took us almost two months before we could get back in the bedroom.' Bill had great respect for Stanley. 'Everything in Stanley is right on,' he said—'his maps, his tables of languages. He had an iron constitution, a strong will, the ability to lead people, and he found the Lord through Livingstone.' Stanley's hair had turned white when he returned to England with the thousand-page manuscript he had written on Zanzibar in sixty days after the expedition was over. It had proved little. The Emin Pasha, 'a bit of a kook,' as Bill put it, had not really wanted to be rescued when they finally reached him. Stanley had more or less had to kidnap him. But the prose was triumphantly, indomitably Victorian. Only Theodore Roosevelt's *Through the Brazilian Wilderness* could hold a candle to it for pluck and gusto. On page seventy-five of the second volume I found an example of the rhetorical device by which you say you are not going to describe something, then go on to

179

describe it. Praetermittio, I think it is called. This had to be one of the great praetermittios in English:

Now let us look at this great forest, not for a scientific analysis of its woods and productions, but to get a real idea of what it is like. It covers such a vast area, it is so varied yet so uniform in its features, that it would require many books to treat it properly. Nay, if we regard it too closely, a legion of specialists would be needed. We have no time to examine the buds and the flowers or the fruit, and the many marvels of vegetation, or to regard the fine differences between bark and leaf in the various towering trees around us, or to compare the different exudations in the viscous or vitrified gums, which drip in milky tears or amber globules, or opaline pastils, or to observe the industrious ants which ascend or descend up and down the tree shafts, whose deep wrinkles of bark are as valleys and ridges to the insect armies, or to wait for the furious struggle which will surely ensue between them and yonder army of red ants. Nor at this time do we care to probe into that mighty mass of dead tree, brown and porous as a sponge, for already it is a mere semblance of a prostrate log. Within it is alive with minute tribes. It would charm an entomologist. Put your ear to it, and you hear a distant murmurous hum. It is the stir and movement of insect life in many forms, matchless in size, glorious in color, radiant in livery, rejoicing in their occupations, exultant in their fierce but brief life, most insatiate of their kind, ravaging, foraging, fighting, destroying, building, and swarming everywhere and exploring everything. Lean but your hand on a tree, measure but your length on the ground, seat yourself on a fallen branch, and you will then understand what venom, fury, voracity, and activity breathe around you. Open your notebook, the page attracts a dozen butterflies, a honey-bee hovers over your hand; other forms of bees dash for your eyes; a wasp buzzes in your ear, a huge hornet menaces your face, an army of pismires come marching to your feet. Some are already crawling up and will be presently digging their scissor-like mandibles in your neck. Woe! Woe!

And yet it is all beautiful—but there must be no sitting or lying on this seething earth. It is not like your pine groves and your dainty woods in England. It is a tropical world, and to enjoy it you must keep slowly moving.

I was awakened at dawn by a procession of people screaming and wailing, drowning out the bird din, as they streamed by my window. An old man in the village had died, Bill explained. He had got drunk on banana whisky, gone into a coma a few days ago, and never come to. The mourners were crying, 'My father, my father.' Bill said the whisky was on the borderline with methyl alcohol and could blind you.

Bill and I had made a date to play tennis that afternoon, but after breakfast I felt anxious to move on and asked for a rain check. Bob had played him and almost won. 'He plays very decently,' Bill had told me. The matches drew a large crowd. Bill had trained several ballboys.

As I sat beside the road, people from the village kept passing on their way to the house of the man who had died. One of the mourners stopped to talk with me. The old man had been a retired government official, an important man in the community, and he had died of 'hypertension,' the mourner told me. There would be a three-day funeral for him. 'But it won't be an entirely sad occasion, because death is part of life. We will dance to show his family how we loved him. We will sing, but we will not beat the drum. After two years of mourning there will be a big celebration to drive his soul from the village.' I asked if the canes some of the old men were using as they passed us had any symbolic importance. The mourner said no, the men had weak knees from malaria. A policeman walked by carrying a shotgun in case trouble broke out when the party who had brought about the death was identified.

After the last mourners had passed, two women shook hands and curtsied as they met on the road (something Ella had probably taught them), then two boys and a girl came down the tree-bordered alley to the school. They had been kicked out of class for fooling around. The boys threw stones at a large blue-headed lizard clinging face-down up in a tree. The girl, who was about thirteen, tall and slender, with an oval face and a red dress on, sat on a large boulder above me. 'What continent have you come from?' she asked. When she heard it was North America she asked if I had anything in English to spare. I gave her a pamphlet that Bill had pressed on me. It was by a Chicago businessman who had found Jesus and was titled *Show Me the Reason*.

Soon I was heading east on a truck. We passed the monadnock which Stanley had named Mount Pisgah, because from its summit he had seen the end of the jungle, and the golden hills of the savanna, the 'land of milk and honey,' beyond. We came to the swift gray Ituri River. A few years

181

earlier Bill had lain prone on the bridge and with a high-powered rifle blasted to smithereens a huge crocodile that had attacked some swimming children. The bridge was narrow, and from the other side you came on it without warning, out of a blind curve. A truck had stopped in the middle of the bridge. The driver was a Somali who had left Nairobi a week earlier with four hundred sacks of dried fish he hoped to sell in Kisangani. He had just barely avoided driving into the river and was standing on the bridge shaken and watching the current carry three sacks that had fallen off the truck.

Suddenly the forest stopped. There was no transitional forest as there is in Amazonia. The trees ended in a wall, and then there was grassland. Huts began to appear more often. Their roofs were no longer thatched *mangungu* but grass. The hillsides of Komanda were terraced with huts. The people were Nilotic, better off that the forest Bantu, and mostly Moslem. From Komanda I could continue east to Bunia and up into the Sudan, or I could go south into Kivu, into the western arm of the Great Rift Valley, which is filled with lakes and great herds of ungulates. I sat out a cloudburst in a shack where tea and meals were served, and decided to see Kivu. Soon I was sharing the back of a truck with several men, women, children, pigs, smoked antelope carcasses, reeking sacks of dried fish, barrels of palm oil, and cases of empty Primus bottles. One of my companions was a border guard named Jean-Pierre. He had been a 'dynamic youth,' he told me, and been sent to Marseilles on a scholarship, but an involvement with a fourteen-year-old girl and subsequent deportation had ruined his chances of becoming a member of the country's 'modern elite.' The road went back into the forest. We scattered three Anubis baboons ambling on it, and after fifteen miles it returned to the savanna. Jean-Pierre and I hitched together to Beni. When we got there, after a succession of rides, it was dark. He went off to see one of his wives. I checked into the Hotel Beni. The shack where I had supper was run by a former provincial governor from nearby Uganda. Uganda was in chaos. There had been several governments since the overthrow of Idi Amin, and none of them had taken. At least six different guerrilla groups hostile to the latest one and to each other were abroad in the country, and thousands of refugees were coming over the border to Beni. Kivu is much richer and more developed than Haut-Zaire. The main street of Beni, Avenue Mobutu, was more built up than anything I had seen in the forest.

In the morning I got a ride in a Land-Rover with three wives of coffee planters. The road was smooth. As they chatted in Greek we climbed quickly into bright hill country with tremendous views. The forest flooded the flat lowlands to the west like an ocean. To the east, incongruously framed by roadside banana leaves and partly blocked by a large cloud, were the snow peaks of the Ruwenzori massif, the legendary Mountains of the Moon, whose ice is said to be among the world's hardest because of the great difference in day and night temperatures.

The women let me out in the middle of Butembo. At six thousand feet the air was dry and clean. It was high enough to grow wheat and potatoes, and tall pines stood on the hills. The sunlight was very strong not only because of the elevation but because the Equator passed a couple of miles out of town. I ran into a young man who had been on one of yesterday's trucks. He had just unloaded some gold. 'It is easy to carry, and the profit is great,' he told me. I had a late breakfast at the Hotel Oasis, a rambling, run-down brick-stucco-bamboo complex with twenty-seven rooms on various levels and no end of courtyards and outbuildings. The dining room was full of nostalgic oils of rural Europe. I sat for an hour talking with the owner, a genial Belgian named André Van Nevel, and his mulatto daughter Anita. His common-law Zairoise wife was half owner of the hotel, so they had not been dispossessed by the Zairianization decree. Van Nevel had spent all but the first twenty of his sixty-four years in and around Butembo, importing medicine and mining wolfram and caciterite before building the hotel in 1945. 'See that balcony?' He pointed through the window. 'One paratrooper went up the stairs and disarmed the forty-four Simbas who were holding it with four machine guns.' The Rebellion reached its southern limit at Butembo. Seventeen paratroopers had mowed down hundreds of drugged, deluded young rebels and looters. The survivors had taken off their newly acquired shoes so they could run faster, Van Nevel told me sadly.

I bought a hat in the market from one of the dozens of women sitting in colourful *pagnes* under black parasols. Two boys carried my bag to the end of town, down the mile-long store-line main street, and all they wanted in return was my address to write me. Tea and *arabica* coffee were the big businesses.

A few men were already sitting on a hillside waiting for *une occasion*. I removed a splinter from the big toe of a young schoolteacher who told me that he had only one wife. 'The Bible says man was made to have one wife,' he explained. 'As a schoolteacher, I must set a good example. But also I can't afford another one.' After a while a truck pulled over for us. The road rose tortuously into sheer hills covered with lush montane forest. Some of the slopes had been planted with eucalyptus, and every few miles the staggered huts of a village would come into view. After about an hour, as we labored up a gully, a key way on the rear axle snapped. The left wheel had to be removed to get at the problem. We got out and stretched. Tree ferns and ground ferns with five-foot fronds had sprouted on the nearly vertical walls of the gully. Two men drove up in a new Fiat station wagon. I asked if I could go with them. The driver was Ugandan. He had been a chauffeur in Kampala. The passenger, his new boss, was a customs official on his way to Matadi, near the mouth of the Zaire. His brother had died a month ago, but he had only just got the news. 'That's the trouble with this job,' he said. 'It's far from the family and everything.' He also complained about the pay, three hundred and fifty zaires a month. I asked how he had been able to buy a new car. He said that his brother had helped him, but later he admitted that his brother's salary had been even less than his. I didn't pursue the subject, as it occurred to me that he probably got the car in return for letting things in and out of the country. I asked about the ivory trade. His station was in Virunga Park, formerly Albert Park, which the Belgians had created to protect the extraordinary fauna of Kivu. He said that two years ago, when he had first come to the station, there had been plenty of elephants in the park, but this year he had hardly seen any. He thought local people were in on the poaching.

After a while he took the wheel, but he kept shifting much too soon. The Ugandan was too polite, scared, or indifferent to bring it to his attention, but I hated to see him ruin his new car, so I did. Then I said I would show him about shifting if he wanted me to, and he moved over. It was nice to be behind a wheel, taking switchbacks in the darkness. We didn't see a truck or even a lighted window until we reached Kanyabayung hours later. It was a big village, with hundreds of tile-roofed whitewashed houses packed together on a hillside, and as I discovered in the morning, a series of shacks with food and drink served by men in Moslem skull caps, and a flophouse for truckers. Virunga Park, which began in a few miles, was closed at night, so we checked into the flophouse. I was so tired I hardly even felt the bedbugs. In the morning through a wall I heard the customs official arguing with a woman.

We came down from the hills below Kanyabayung with a blinding sunrise in our eyes. Suddenly a vast plain opened below us, with a river gleaming on it and jagged mountains—some of them active volcanoes—on the other side. The road steepened. We passed a defassa water buck standing in tall grass and chewing warily, and joined a slow file of canvas-backed trucks crossing the valley floor. I asked if we could pull over to photograph a small herd of elephants near the road. The largest one came at us with its ears flared out in threat. Its tusks were long and curved, like the ones I had seen on the runway at Isiro.

A little further on we met four park guards. They were armed and on foot. There were no vehicles for them in the park's budget, so it was almost impossible for them to do their job. They no longer got a bonus for each poacher they caught, as they had in more prosperous times (I read a few weeks later in an unusually frank article in *Elima*, one of the state-owned newspapers in Kinshasa), their pay often arrived months late, and it was not surprising that some of them were unable to resist getting into poaching themselves. There was a small monument in the park to the guards who had stayed honest and been shot in the line of duty .

These guards were watching a school of hippo wallowing in a branch of the river. I got out of the car and walked toward the hippos, ignoring the shouts of the guards. Even if I had understood what they were saying, that no one in the park was allowed out of his car, I would not have wanted to be kept back from the first hippos I had met in the wild. There was hardly any space between the twenty colossal bodies. A certain amount of jostling was going on. Now and then one would grunt or snort or raise its head from the water, open its mouth slowly, and bare the tushes with

185

which it was capable of killing a rival. One saw me, and a nervous shudder, building quickly into anger, passed from body to body. I squeezed off a few pictures and wasted no time getting back to the road, where the customs official was persuading the guards not to arrest me. Virunga's twenty-two thousand hippos are the largest concentration on earth.

In the middle of the plain there was group of buildings and a checkpoint where vehicles were searched for guns and ivory as tall, scruffy marabou storks walked around importantly and baboons sat on their haunches and begged at windows. I parted company with the customs official, who had a plane to catch at Goma, and walked up to the buildings. The place was called Rwindi. It had a hotel where every effort was made to meet *muzungu* requirements. I ate my heaviest breakfast since the Inter: ham, eggs, cheese, a quarter of a papaya, toast with marmalade, café au lait, orange juice. There were more white-jacketed waiters than tourists, not an unusual situation for Third World dining rooms.

After a while a party of six, in high spirits, came in and sat down. They seemed *sympathique*. I went over and explained that I was on foot and had been told that if I wanted to see the park, I would have to go with someone who had a car. Exchanging looks, they decided by silent vote that I could join their safari. A large Belgian woman at the end of the table, whose name was Nicole Merlo, seemed to be in charge. She had grown up in Kivu and still lived there. 'Twenty years ago this place worked,' she said a little bitterly. 'Now it is *un peu laissé*. But I couldn't live anywhere else.' She and her husband raised Swiss cows and made cheese. They had not been expropriated because Nicole had gone right to Mobutu with their case, and the Big Man had made an exception. She was a formidable woman, no one to cross. The other five were cousins or old friends of hers. Claude, a veterinarian, came from the same town in Normandy as the young doctor Charles and his father did. Celeste was a nurse at a hospital in Burundi. The two elderly women were from Belgium. The party had two cars: Nicole's Land-Rover and Celeste's blue Renault. An old guard with a rifle came along. Nicole addressed him as *bwana*. It was the only item I heard that word in Zaire. He did not call her *mem-sahib*. I asked him whether the tusks I had seen in Isiro could have come from the park. He said that a few days before three vans from Isiro had been stopped at Rwindi and found to be loaded with ivory.

Claude knew his horned ruminants; he had hunted them. He pointed out topi, bongo, kob, and impala as they stood and watched us singly, in groups of three or four, or in large herds. 'Leaps of thirty feet in length or ten feet in height are within their powers,' Dorst wrote of the impala. But we did not see them in the air. We drove up to a male lion panting under a bush. He gave a sudden thunderous roar, then got to his feet, circled the bush slowly with tail held high, and crawled on his belly further under the bush, where we could see the gray-golden sheen on his rib cage rising and falling and one of his eyes struggling to stay open. The eye seemed all iris with no detectable vertical slit in the opalescent geometry of its cells. We saw a jackal trotting in the distance and the tails of warthogs swishing in circles as they grazed under an acacia. With their flat, rakish crowns and spotty distribution, the acacias looked like trees in an architect's mock-up.

We went out on some sand flats and drove among stands of cactuslike euphorbia and met a herd of buffalo at a water hole. As they turned to curl a lip and stare balefully at us, the bases of their horns flowed down on their heads like hair parted in the middle. We passed a large, sun-bleached hippo skull. Claude said the hippos were dying of an intestinal gangrene, a *charbon bactérien*. At noon we reached the shore of a huge body of water, formerly Lake Edward, now Lake Idi Amin Dada. Amin and Mobutu had been good friends and had renamed the two lakes along their common border for each other. Lake Mobutu Sese Seko, formerly Lake Albert, is up near Bunia and separated from Lake Idi Amin Dada by the Ruwenzori massif. Now, with Amin out of the picture, the lower lake was going to have to be renamed again. Some were already lobbying for Lake Vitshumbi, after a fishing village where we stopped for lunch. The village consisted of several rows of mud huts and a couple of dilapidated colonial buildings. An old tame elephant hung around it—everybody ignored him—and hundreds of marabou storks were there for the fish heads. The shallow, murky gray-green lake was full of the Nile perch *Tilapia*, a chunky, pink-scaled omnivore that gets to be a foot or two. We looked into a shed where some women with cleavers were swamped with perch the men had brought in that morning on the floors of long dugouts. We ate some, smoked on a wood fire and seasoned with hot piripiri pepper. They were superb. Antic marabous fought over the leftovers, catching tossed morsels in their bills and clicking appreciately as they maneuvered them into their gullets. As they stood on roofs like gargoyles, heads tucked, one foot raised, a red hump on their back and a mangy air sack at their throat, or did a gangly ballet for us down on the flat, they were *êtres moches*, Claude decided, sorry creatures, walking caricatures.

It was a nearly perfect day. We saw all the animals I had hoped to except rhino, giraffes, and zebras, which are not found in the park. In the middle of the afternoon we stood on a bluff of the Rutshuru River, which had carved the valley. The bluff looked over a sweeping bend lined with *Phoenix* palms. A dozen hippos in various states of emergence, some showing only pink-rimmed eyes, cocked ears, or backs as smooth and dark as boulders, let the current take them and caromed listlessly off each other. 'Tough life,' Claude said. An African fish eagle—snow-white from the shoulders up—sat in a tree watching dozens of white-backed vultures gathered over a carcass on the bank. The birds were so thick we could not see what they were eating. Rain had started to sift down from a mountainous anvil-headed cumulus; and the smoky striations beneath it, still distant but coming slowly our way, claimed the river bend by bend. I felt an exhilaration I had only known a few times: standing at the rim of the Grand Canyon, snorkelling my first coral reef, witnessing the birth of our children.

We spent the night at a White Friars mission, where two of the twelve orphans Nicole had adopted were at school. They went with us in the morning to Rutshuru Falls, an even sheet of water plunging into a lush green glade. Nicole and her friends left me at the base of a volcano named Nyiragongo. I asked the man who came out the guards' hut how long it would take to reach the top. He said about five hours, and sent a boy into the village. The boy came back with a man who said he would show me the way. My guide wore a tweed jacket and introduced himself as Drivamunda Sinamenye Wabizigye, ex-Emanuel. We started climbing through dense acanthus forest, The leaves were spiked, like the leaves of horse nettle. After an hour we had risen into an elfin cloud forest. A large lapis-lazuli butterfly, the blue

Salamis, was floating among the small, warped trees. We could see the beginning of Lake Kivu, the next lake to the south in the series. A good-sized city, Goma, spread along its shore. Across the valley, in Rwanda, were lots of little round hills which looked like overturned bowls and were terraced with beans and potatoes. The black lava soil around Lake Kivu is prodigiously fertile. I had seen twenty-foot manioc along the road, twice the normal height. Drivamunda told me that Nyiragongo had erupted on the tenth of July 1977, killing two hundred people in thirty minutes as it poured lava across the valley. 'At ten o'clock that morning my wife brought me a plate of sweet potatoes and beans,' he recalled. 'Suddenly the ground started to shake. My plate fell to the floor. I went outside. Nyiragongo was smoking like mad, and the trees on its slopes were breaking before a wave of fire. I put my child on my shoulders and we ran all the way to Rwanda without looking back. After thirty minutes we reached a place it normally took an hour to get to. Then we looked back, I had lost my house and my possesions, but at least I still had a family. Every tenth of January since that day there is a festival. We eat and drink as much as we can, because who knows what God has in mind.' He believed that those who had died must have been condemned.

As we rested, a cold mist set in. Drivamunda predicted that it would rain for the rest of the day, and said there was no use going further. He had been climbing the volcano two or three times a week for fifteen years now and knew its weather. 'There is nothing up there but a great hole,' he said. 'It takes four hours to walk around.' He said it would be very cold at the top, which is over ten thousand feet. I asked about the vegetation. He said there were only a few low plants, which he called *les immortels*, in the crater. He did not mention the bamboo forest, the dogwood forest, the heath forest, or the prairies studded with giant surreal lobelias and senecios, through which one passed on the way up. If I had known about them (I didn't until I returned to Kinshasa), I would have wanted to continue.

On the way down we cut over to one of the dry rivers of lava. The lava was black and red, light and porous, three or four yards thick and full of crevasses, so brittle we broke through it with each step. Drivamunda showed me a cavity shaped like a huge skull. 'Here an elephant was buried as it ran,' he explained. 'Two weeks after the eruption we came here to dig out the tusks. The lava was hard but still warm. The tusks had been cooked so hot they crumbled in our hands.' There was a lot of fresh elephant dung around the hole. The writer Peter Mathiessen, who was shown the grave a year after the eruption (there was dung around it then), wondered if some elephants had been communing with their dead fellows. Drivamunda carried two flares in his pocket in case we ran into any.

We sat down and, pooling our food—my tin of sardines, his stalk of sugar cane—had a picnic. Then it started to rain. We ran down the lava to the guards' hut, past a mound where the old guards' hut had been smothered, past the rusty frame of an overturned tourist bus. As soon as it cleared, I stood along the road and before long I was sitting in the back of a van with boxes of fresh cauliflower and strawberries, watching the immense flat-topped silhouette of Nyiragongo, the Hunchback recede behind me. I arrived at the Hotel des Grands Lacs in Goma before dark. It was Saturday night, and the night club was already full of women dancing together, waiting for the guests to come down.

In the morning, as I walked along the lake, everybody was carrying palm wisps. It was Palm Sunday. The lake was lined with elaborate European villas. The ancien régime had lived well here. I could have been in Montreux, Switzerland, except that every so often a dugout would pass and snap me back into the tropics. Lake Kivu is much longer than Lake Mobutu Sese Seko or Lake Idi Amin Dada, but it has no fish because of the methane gas that bubbles into it. I wondered who was living in the villas now. In many of the driveways there were two Mercedes.

In the afternoon I went to the airport and booked a flight that was leaving in a few hours to Kisangani. As I sat in the waiting room, a French hippie latched on to me. He was a strange, pale, half-crazy young man with a black velours jacket, veins pulsing at his temple, and mustaches covering his mouth, and he had been bumming around Africa for five months, getting in trouble everywhere he went. Trouble seemed to hover over him like a swarm of black flies. In nervous bursts of hiptalk, words I hadn't heard in a while like 'dig' and 'groovy,' he raved on about his lingering hepatitis, his hassles with the police, his acid trip with a Peace Corps volunteer, his plan to hitch to Peking in the fall, how expensive the taxi to the airport had been, how well you could live in Zaire if you had money, how sick he had got on banana wine. It was almost as if he were talking to himself. After a while two soldiers came to him and said there was something wrong with his passport and led him away shrieking in protest. That was the last I saw of him.

When the plane came in I walked out on the runway and talked with the pilot. It would be a few more hours before we took off. 'They're never on time, but they don't have heart trouble, either,' the pilot, a Cuban living in Miami, said laughing. Hawkers came around with strawberries, onions, potatoes—things you couldn't get in the *cuvette*. A shrivelled old woman close to death was taken aboard by four men. A few baskets of live chickens were loaded on. The plane was a brand new 707, too big and expensive to pay for itself with internal flights, the pilot told me. After the Cuban revolution he had joined a group of exiles who 'kept fighting for things we believed in.' Under contract with the United Nations, he had helped liberate Kisangani during the Rebellion. 'Zaire has come a long way since then,' he said. 'It is a country of tremendous vitality and disarming friendliness, whose resources have barely been touched. It may be broke at the moment, but there is every reason to be hopeful. It belongs to the young, and they are handling technology with increasing confidence. A growing number of pilots with Air Zaire are Zairois.' We talked about Mobutu, whom he had flown several times. 'He had the ego of all these men,' the Cuban said, 'but a *caudillo*, a strong man, is logical here. It has to be centralized now. The country isn't ready for a Lincoln. One day, like Haile Selassie, he will no longer be useful. But if you get rid him, you create a political vacuum, and what will happen?' The great south flank of Nyiragongo loomed over our conversation. One tongue of lava had stopped just short of the airport's large fuel depot. If it had blown up, it would have taken half of Goma with it.

The actual flight to Kisangani took less than an hour, but it was not until eleven that, in a thick fog, I entered the city. All the moisture the sun had burned off that day was settling out again. Kisangani had grown up in the middle of steaming jungle during the previous century, much as Manaus had in the Brazilian Amazon, except that its founders had been interested in slaves and ivory instead of rubber, and Manaus had gone on to become more of a metropolis. Kisangani was more like a second-magnitude Amazonian city—Santarém, maybe, or Iquitos. Except for the Zaire Palace Hotel, another of Mobutu's modern towers, where I checked in, and a couple of high-rise apartment buildings, most of the downtown was still two stories.

I wasn't sleepy, so I went for a walk with the young man who had taken me to my room; now that the plane had come in, he was free to go home. His name was Kembo, and he said he was so fed up with his salary, two hundred fifty zaires a month, that he was thinking of giving up city life and planting a *shamba* somewhere. He took me to the square where, during the Rebellion, executions had taken place before the statue of Patrice Lumumba. Here, according to a book called *Out of the Jaws of the Lion*, about the American missionaries who were held hostage by the Simbas, the mayor of Kisangani was publicly eviscerated, and his entrails were eaten by a laughing officer of the Armée Populaire de la Révolution. 'I was just a boy then, but I remembered seeing the bodies in the streets and dogs eating them, and people dying of starvation,' Kembo recalled. 'There was no salt in the city.' Some of the rubble had still not been cleared. Kembo showed me a building that had been strafed with bullets.

A few wide tree-lined avenues crossed each other in the center of town, then the layout became more and more haphazard. The main street twisted and changed blocks unaccountably as it ran out to the *zones*, where most of the city's two hundred thousand inhabitants lived an urban version of village subsistence. It was lined with flat-roofed two-story buildings. Stores with metal signs in front of them occupied the ground floor, and the owners lived above. Old men in rags—night guards—slept in the doorways of the stores. Some of them had made a little fire at the point of three logs as if they were still in their village. The stores had evolved considerably since V. S. Naipaul did his research for *A Bend in the River* here more than five years earlier. Goods were no longer on the floors but on shelves. Some of the stores had televisions and pocket calculators, Yamaha motorcycles and zodiac rafts, in their windows. A popular item in the city was a cloth bag with wood handles and the names of fashionable Paris stores ticked on it ad infinitum. It was just the right size for the women to take to market.

The steaming darkness was full of life. Bullfrogs croaked in slimy ditches. An invisible swarm of birds cackled and squeaked in a tree in front of the Central Prison. Groups of young women made their way to the night clubs. Many of these *femmes livres*, as Kembo called them, had been in marriages arranged when they were little, which had not worked. Some had been sterilized by venereal disease. 'They are all looking for a husband,' Kembo told me, 'but that does not often happen, because there are more women here than men.' As we passed, one of the women, with smoking eyes and flashing teeth, said something in Swahili to Kembo. 'She said, "Give me that *muzungu*," ' he translated.

Kembo took me to New Pop City, the city's most 'select' club. Two couples were expertly boogying in a flickering strobe light to vintage rock 'n' roll. Everyone else was nailed to their seats, not sure how to take the music. Then a Zairian rumba came on, and the seats emptied. Everyone came out on the floor and danced slow and loose, shaking their shoulders deliciously.

I slept late, and in the morning was awakened by a military band playing in the square below my window. The occasion was a reunion between the regional and subregional governors. The music began as a conventional march, then the band picked out an insignificant transitional snatch and started to play it over and over, becoming intoxicated with the syncopal possibilities of its five notes. I went out on the street and was immediately besieged by the halt and lame who worked the hotel entrance. Men with no legs poled up on boards with wheels. The ones who had hands held them out. All sorts of literature had been laid on the sidewalk, everything from Stendhal to French detective novels, pamphlets on nutrition, and Biblical comic books. I bought the previous evening's *Elima*. The lead story was headlined 'L'*Animation Rurale, Une Impérieuse Nécessité*.' Across the street a boy with a little stand on the curb sold chocolate-flavored Bazooka bubble gum, Nelson razor blades, West Point and Geisha pilchards (actually anchovies from the Peruvian trench, caught and canned by Japanese trawlers), White Crane coils of mosquito-repellent incense, from the People's Republic of China, and Alaska condensed milk, a product of Holland. The humidity was like a brick wall. I was dripping before I got to the end of the block. Most of the passersby carried parasols. I walked down to the docks and asked at the office of ONATRA, the state-run transport company, about the next riverboat to Kinshasa. The agent said the *courier* was due Saturday and would leave the same day. I reserved a first-class cabin on it.

The *courier* did not appear until the following Tuesday, so I had eight days in Kisangani. I could have flown to Kinshasa immediately, but I wanted to go down the river. John Hart had given me the name of the old Arab who had sold him his jeep, so I looked the man up that morning. He ran a sawmill. Massive red trunks of *Gilbertiodendron*, the tree Terese had been interested in, were piled in the yard. They were for local consumption, the man told me. He also shipped a *bois de luxe* called Formosia to Europe. He was in his late sixties. 'My father was an Arab, my mother was *métisse-Arabe*, so I am a *quatron*,' he told me. 'There aren't many of us left here. The Greeks, the Lebanese, the Pakistanis, the Indians—most of them left when they got their stores back empty. I was originally a coffee grower in Ubundi, ex-Ponthierville. The Simbas kept me prisoner for twenty-two months in the forest. They said I was in the opposite party, but I am not even remotely political. I don't know how I survived. Many of the rebels themselves died of hunger. I was skin and bones, eating forest fruits, waiting to die. Some of us were eaten. It still exists discreetly, you know.'

'What?' I asked.

'Cannibalism. From time to time people in the forest disappear. A year and a half ago a German was found half eaten. His house had been set on fire to destroy the evidence.

'In nineteen sixty-seven I was forced to exchange all my money—twenty million, five hundred thousand francs— for five thousand zaires. It wasn't even enough to buy a truck. I tried growing coffee, I tried to do *commerce*. It was impossible. So now I am just a foreman in a sawmill.'

I asked if by chance he could change a few traveller's checks for me. I had almost gone through my brick of zaires. He said no but gave me the name of a Greek woman. I went to her *taverna*. She said she did not buy dollars, but she gave me lunch—pork roast, ice cream. Like the Arab she was nervous that something would happen again. 'I've had to pack up and leave and come back and start over so many times, it would be nice at my age if life could be a little sweet,' she said, tossing a morsel to her pet crowned crane, a tall, stately bird with a black tiaras. 'My husband is sixty-five. Who knows how long he has to live. Five years. Ten years. Twenty years ago we had three villas in Butembo and the best hotel in Kisangani. Now we have a cheap hotel for campers and hippies. When the currency was changed two years ago all the money we had in the bank was frozen. They say they will give it back in ten years.'

The woman said to try the Procure, the regional headquarters of the Catholic missionaries. As I walked there a boy ran up and offered me a carved stick, the ceremonial cane of a *chef coutoumier* of the BaSonge, one of the southern tribes, I later learned. It was a fine piece of work, with a man beating a drum below the circular handle and under him a woman with high, jutting breasts and hands at her side, like a Greek Kore. The wood was black, heavy, and hard as rock. I bought the cane for two dollars.

There were paintings for sale on the sidewalk in front of the Procure, a red brick compound down near the docks. Among the usual jungle primitives—snakes wrapped around trees and flicking their tongues, women peering provocatively through foliage—were a few gory primitives of the Rebellion and one of some Belgians administering a lashing to some prisoners while others in jail stripes escape into the jungle.

I walked to the end of a cloister. A young priest looked up from a desk as I stood in his doorway. He offered me six and two-tenths zaires to the dollar, not a very generous rate. Next to his office was a door with a sign on it: IVORY BOUGHT AND SOLD. 3—6 PM. I asked to look inside. There were all sorts of carved ivory figures, including a row of Virgin Marys with hoods shielding their modestly down-turned faces and hands clasped together in prayer. They really bothered me. What a thing to kill an elephant for, I thought. What a sacrilege. There were also some eggs and ashtrays of malachite, a semi-precious form of copper ore, green with black swirls. My grandmother had had a lot of malachite in her house. It had been popular in Old Russia. I bought a few eggs for our living-room cabinet.

A few days later I found a prosperous *commerçant*, a Dutch mulatto, who gave me nine zaires to the dollar. 'The trouble with Zaire is that it's badly run,' he told me as we drove through the city in his Mercedes. 'We need people in the government who have confidence in the country and will work for it, not just fill their pockets and run. As it is now, Rwanda is a great exporter of *arabica*, but the Rwandans don't even grow it. It comes in from Kivu illegally. Last year three hundred tons of ivory shipped out of Zaire by *grandes personnes* were seized in Antwerp. Most of the ivory from Haut-Zaire is bought under the table by Senegalese. They come to Kisangani just for this. We exist to enrich our neighbors,' he said disgustedly.

He left me at the local campus of the university. The buildings must have seemed dynamically modern at the beginning, but two decades of weathering and social unrest had taken their toll. I climbed an embankment to one of the dormitories. The poured concrete was cracked and coated with black fungus. Students were washing their clothes, cooking on hotplates, napping on bunks. A shirtless freshman was playing a guitar that lacked two strings. He said he would graduate with a degree in biology in five years. He led me through some grass that was over our heads to a small building called CREDE, the Centre for Interdisciplinary Research. Its director, Benoit De Vernhagen, who was in Belgium at the time, had produced a scholarly history of the Rebellion, which I looked through that afternoon. It was forested with footnotes. Obscure documents were reproduced in full, but you never learned why there had been a rebellion in the first place. Some who knew De Vernhagen and had read *A Bend in the River* thought he must have been Naipaul's model for Raymond, the President's old *professeur*, the once-eminent Africanist who has fallen from grace. I talked with the acting director, an articulate *citoyenne* with a degree in psychology. 'I think the future development of our country will be in the villages, because it is no longer possible to take initiative in the cities,' she told me. I asked if anyone had studied the ivory trade. 'No,' she said. 'It would be compromising, because people in high places are at the bottom of it.'

'What if something happens to Mobutu?' I asked. 'Will the country fall apart? Will there be another bloodbath?'

'That is what the West thinks,' she retorted. 'But the regional structures will hold. The country is now at the stage of regional self-awareness.'

'But won't there be a purge of the corrupt entourage from Equateur?'

'That is only natural,' she said.

I had moved by then to the Hotel des Chutes. My room had a ten-foot ceiling and looked on the river. I could go to the window and watch long dugouts with outboard motors side-wind across the current as they took people to the other side. The trip back was very quick.

I could lean over the courtyard. There was a garden with papaya and banana trees. If I could not sleep, hiding from mosquitoes under a sweat-dampened sheet, I could sit at the entrance with the night guard and watch people pass silently in the moonlight. My neighbour was a student. There was a shortage of housing at the campus. He spent his time listening to a big radio cassette player and studying French sex magazines.

One morning a little snake slithered out on the terrace where I was having breakfast. The waiter beheaded it with a machete, although it was a harmless one. Another morning there was a knock at my door and a young Australian came in. Hitching from Uganda, he had passed through Lolwa a few days before. Bill Spees had invited him to play tennis and had beaten him soundly. He had heard in town about a muzungu with a guitar , and figured I must have been the one the Speeses had told them about. He had come to Africa eighteen months ago for a three-month tour. He had caught the microbe, the bug that makes some people stay, as I had heard an old Belgian in Kinshasa call it.

I presented my card at the City Hall, which was a mistake. A little man with an MPR button in his label, who said he was a radio announcer, asked what I wanted to see in Kisangani. I said I was thinking of going up to Wagenya Falls and watching the fishermen. He said I would need a special permit because the falls were important to the national security; there was a hydroelectric plant up there. We spent the morning going from department to department trying to get the permit, but no one knew anything about it. I finally solved the problem by offering to forget about going to the falls. The radio announcer showed me out to the street, apologizing for being of so little help. We shook hands.

In the afternoon I walked up to the falls after all. You could hear their faint roar from the Hotel des Chutes. They

197

were the last of a series of rapids which began a hundred twenty miles upriver, at Ubundi. The biggest of them, Stanley Falls, was thirty miles above Kisangani. A boisterous motorcade of taxis passed me on the road. People were sitting on the windows, blowing whistles, and singing jubilantly. One of them had become a father. The river was low at this time of year. Dozens of pilings connected by vine cables stood in the rapids. Twice a day the men walked out on the cables and pulled up the traps—ten-foot-long baskets that were left in the water from eight in the morning until three in the afternoon, lowered again at five o'clock, and left overnight. A variety of fish got stuck in them, like two-foot catfish. 'The best-tasting is the *capitaine*,' one of the fishermen told me. 'It has no teeth and a head like a gorilla.' The man's name was Losandu. I hired him and his brother Losambu to take me back to town in their long dugout. They paddled from a standing position, bending at the waist each time they jabbed the water with a short, strong stroke. The shafts of their paddles were ten feet long. The canoe could hold thirty people and was made from a *bulu* tree. Squares of tin had been nailed over the cracks. Along the bank children were casting little nylon nets or angling with worms and seeds. Two girls were standing thigh-deep in a quiet eddy below the falls and making music on the water with their cupped hands. I asked Losandu how it had been possible to stick the pilings in the rapids.'There are holes in the rock which our ancestors found, and which we still use,' he explained.

One morning I went to see the *ivoiristes* at work along the road to Tchopo. Tchopo is a *zone* of Kisangani and also a tributary of the Zaire. Most of the city is on an island at the Tchopo's mouth; *kisanga* means 'island' in Swahili. The *ivoiristes* sat in stalls chiselling and filing sections of tusk into busts of women and turning chess pieces on lathes. The finished carvings were sandpapered and buffed with a fluid poured on leathery *mambombo* leaves. After much sniffing and questioning I realized that the fluid was Brasso. One of the *ivoiristes* kept it in a little bottle labelled tincture of belladonna. He said he was allowed to have up to twenty-two pounds of ivory. Most of his raw material came by truck from small villages in Haut-Zaire. The journey was risky; if you met a soldier who had put a pole across the road and you did not have money to pay him, you could lose everything. But once the ivory reached Kisangani it was sold quite openly. 'In a village of twenty men,' the *ivoiriste* told me, 'three will know how to kill elephant—with spears, pit traps, or a trip wire that releases a spear from above. The hunters get fetishes from their witch doctor—little bottles of *mélange* to rub on their bodies so the elephants won't hear them. Sometimes I buy ivory from a *commissaire de zone* who has confiscated it from a poacher or bought it unofficially. I do not ask questions. When there is no ivory I work in ebony.'

I visited Kembo several times at his house in the *zone* of Kadongo. The street he lived on was full of children. The houses on it had no water, plumbing, or electricity; but with tin roofs, cinderblock walls, and floors of wood or concrete, they were more substantial than village huts. Kembo belonged to a tribe called the BaBoa and came from Buta, a good-sized town a hundred and sixty miles to the north. About three hundred BaBoa lived in the *zone*. They stuck together. If there was a death, the whole colony would come to the family's house and dance all night. If one of them was in trouble with creditors, his *frères* would bail him out. If one of them got rich, he was expected to share his good fortune. Throughout the country there is a hidden tribal system, which has nothing to do with the government or the official economy, for seeing that people in need are taken care of. Centralized welfare or social security would never work as well.

Kembo introduced me to his grandmother, who said '*Bonjour, papa,*' and hurried along, stooping a little and averting her eyes. 'That is the customary sign of respect,' he explained. Much of the inner part of her earlobes had been cut away, leaving only the borders—a form of scarification peculiar to the tribe. Kembo said the younger BaBoa did not do it any more. 'It used to be that a girl in our tribe was betrothed at two or three. Now if a woman doesn't want a man, she doesn't have to marry him. Before, dowries were given in spears and hoes. Now they are given in money. There is less ceremony in the younger generation. People used to stay in mourning for two or three years. Now they wear black for ten months.

'I have just come out of mourning for my mother,' he said, and showed me a photograph of her. She had died at the age of forty-three. 'About a year ago she started to bleed. The hospital here is no good so I took her to the American one in Nyankunde [where Nadine went]. They treated her and she was well for two months. Then she started to bleed again. We went back to Nyankunde. They said as soon as her blood is forty per cent we will operate. But it never reached forty per cent. I was giving her weekly transfusions—we were the same type—and getting others to donate. One morning as I sat with her she suddenly bolted stiff and almost overturned the bed. I had to hold her down. I asked what is it but she would not speak to me. The nurse came and said hurry to the market and get some bananas. I prepared them with fish. The nurse said no, that is not what I said. Only bananas. She ate one little banana, then she bolted again, then she was still. I felt her pulse get weaker and finally stop. Then I thought, How am I going to take care of my *petits frères* and *soeurs* without her? I wanted to die, too. I went crazy. The nurse had to keep me from killing myself. I sat on the steps holding myself, wondering, Is this a dream? Then I realized: It was death.'

Not far from the Zaire Palace were two tennis courts. In the late afternoon a group of young *évolués*, most of whom had learned the game in Europe, came there to play. One of the regulars was a portly thirty-nine-year-old exporter of rubber and medicinal plants named Posho Koko. He reminded me of Joaçim. He had the same regal erectness, the same quick, cagey mind. But he had been to college in Belgrade and had seen a bit of the world. I visited him at his warehouse on Saturday morning. 'My grandfather was the chief of Yalokombe, a village not far from here,' he told me as he sat at his desk in a large, dark room with bulging burlap bags piled against the walls and sunlight falling through ventilation chinks onto them. 'He was scared of the Belgians. My father was a general *commerçant*. When I was fifteen I decided to become one of the dynamic young Zairois who could relate well to Europeans. Until nineteen sixty-two I worked in the Belgian consulate here. Then I was a stenographer-typist for Gizenga [leader of the MNC, a political party based in Kisangani, and a loser in the early struggle for power]. When a provisional government formed here, I was attached to the Ministry of Finance. But in nineteen sixty-three Mobutu annulled the provisional government. He wanted a federation centered in Kinshasa. I was *cassé*, forbidden to play politics, so I turned to sports. I became the most famous soccer player, the heavyweight boxing champion, the tennis star of Kisangani. Then I joined Petrofina, the Belgian oil company, as a secretary. In six months I rose to *chef de service*. The Rebellion came. All the Europeans in the city were imprisoned. I was left in charge of Petrofina. I brought food to the Hotel des Chutes for my boss, for the American consul, for the Belgian president of the Chamber of Commerce. I was safe because I controlled the gasoline. The Simbas needed me, so they did not touch me. But they told me, If your boss escapes you will die in his place. They were here to kill. It was not a movement of liberation. It was a vengeance against the bourgeoisie, anyone who was well off.

'When the city was liberated I was caught on the other side of the river. There was no way to cross. The Simbas said, Where are your friends now? They strung me up, aimed, and fired. I fell to the ground, wetting my pants. They missed. They stood me up again. Two of the Simbas— they were just kids—said, Wait, isn't he the famous soccer player? So they untied me and let me run into the forest. I stayed in hiding for two weeks.

'When I returned to the city my house was destroyed. The looting by South African mercenaries had been worse than that of the Simbas. But they didn't find the six million francs I had taken from Petrofina's safe and stuffed in a mattress. I turned them over. I was a hero. Petrofina made me the regional director. I held that post until nineteen seventy-eight. But one day, in a time of hardship, I helped a Belgian priest with some gas. He sent me two cows. I was accused of *faire des troques* and fired.

'So I started this business. After two years it is doing well. Twenty miles from here I have four hundred fifty acres of rubber trees and three hundred fifty of coffee. In Bukavu I have a cinchona plantation. [Cinchona bark is the source of quinine.] I've just invested in a pig, poultry, and goat farm. My agents go to villages all over the forest buying medicinal plants.' He opened a drawer and threw some plastic bags on his desk. One was filled with cola nuts, the stimulant in Pepsi and Coca-Cola. Another contained roots of a shrub in the ginger family, which were good for lumbago. The Calabar beans had a drug in them, physostigmine, which ophthalmologists use to contract pupils. The *Strophanthus* seeds, besides being the pygmies' arrow poison, were used like foxglove as a cardiac stimulant. The leaves of *Rauwolfia vomitoria* contained the alkaloid reserpine, which is used to sedate people with hypertension or chronic mental illness. Posho Koko had got into the medicinal plant business at a good time. Hardly anyone in Zaire was doing it. He also handled eight kinds of beetles. He opened a cigar box full of dried *Goliathus orientalis*. They had menacing antlers, mauve sheath-wings, zebra-striped dorsal plates, and were three or four inches long. He said they were important for scientific research. A man in Zurich was paying thirty dollars for every *Goliathus* Posho Koko could send him.

I was awakened at seven the next morning by hundreds of ecstatic voices singing the Alleluia chorus in the church at the Procure, a few hundred yards downriver. It was Easter Sunday. By the time I got there the choir and the congregation had joined in a Swahili hymn to drums, tambourines, and wood knockers. It was a large church, lit with hanging clusters of vertical fluorescent tubes. Between hymns a resplendently robed *muzungu* priest conducted the service in a businesslike monotone, while maybe a thousand Zairois listened raptly. The women were spangled with antennae. One man, in shorts with high socks, had an elongated skull, shaved bare on top. He was a Mangbetu from up around Isiro. The Mangbetu were an ancient tribe. They bound their infants' heads in vines so the skull would grow tall and pointed. The wall behind the altar was covered with ceramic murals of John the Baptist surrounded by sheep, and of Adam and Eve in grass skirts and leopard-skin hats, holding hands. Over a statue of Christ, leaning out from a cross and spreading his arms in welcome, was a legend in Swahili: *Mimi Ndimi Ufufu Na Uzima*, which meant 'I am the Resurrection and the Life.' He and the other figures were black, of course.

I went to the office of ONATRA to get my ticket stamped ahead of time. The actual departure was a mob scene, I had heard. To leave the city you needed a stamp from the port authority, from the police, and from customs. A fellow passenger took me to the three officials, explaining that I should give them each a *matabish* to speed the process. We breezed past the first two. They stuck my ten-zaire note quickly in their breast pockets and without even looking up validated my ticket. When I handed the money to the customs man, he, too, pocketed it, but then, looking fiercely at me, he said, 'What do you mean, trying to bribe me?' He put an official form into his typewriter. 'What is that for?' I asked. He said, 'I am having you arrested.' 'Wait a minute,' I stammered. 'I thought a little beer money was always appreciated.' He lit into the fellow passenger for 'giving a foreigner the wrong impression of how we do things,' and took his identification card. The man had to pay eighty zaires to get it back, and to clear up the trouble I was in, I had to rebribe the customs man with ten more zaires through his assistant, who also required ten zaires as the middleman. Obviously, I couldn't give it to him directly. The passenger, who had only been trying to help, was very upset. Eighty zaires was a lot of money to him. He said the whole thing would never have happened if a soldier had not been in the room when I gave the first bribe. The customs man had to seem above that sort of thing.

The courier arrived late on the morning of the twenty-first. Hundreds of mamas were already crowding the dock to get first crack at what the passengers had brought from the capital and along the river. Others had set out basins of fruit or were roasting sticks of goat meat. An impromptu market had sprung up, as it always did when the courier came. I made my way through the smoke and the smells and the colors to a chain-link fence, showed my ticket to a soldier, and was let through the gate. The boat had three decks surrounded by railing. In 1948, when it was brought up in sections from South Africa, it had been the top of the line in riverboats. But everything on it which was not absolutely neccessary had broken long ago. Under the windows of the wheelhouse, at the bow, was a plaque that said TSATSHI, after a famous colonel killed in Kisangani during the Rebellion. No one knew what the boat had been called before. Lashed to the Tsatshi were two barges, the Myanza and the Mongo, two stories each, and a flat, nameless barge onto which some military trucks were being driven. The first-class cabins were on the Tsatshi. Second and third class were on the barges. Second class did not seem like much of a deal. Everybody on the Mongo and the Myanza got the same food—a bowl of manioc gruel called fou-fou, ladled out twice a day—and slept in the same crowded four-bunk cabins. There were a few mamas who spent their lives on the barges and had little stores in their

203

cabins. They would buy white beans trucked from Bunia to Kisangani and sell them in Kinshasa for double, and on the way back they would bring bolts of the colorful wax-printed cloth from Holland which the women of Haut-Zaire made into *pagnes*.

The steward was in town buying provisions, I was told, and only he could open the heavy padlock to my cabin. During the wait I made friends with my neighbour Dennis, a 'barracuda' in the French special forces. He had been in Zaire for two years, training its army in the art of modern warfare. He was part of the aid that France, wanting to keep a fatherly hand in the affairs of Francophile Africa, had been pouring into the country. As he leaned on the railing in a jaunty red beret, combat boots, and spotted fatigues and took slow drags on a Gitanes, he told me about some pygmies who had been drafted as scouts during the recent trouble in Katanga. They had proved to be very brave, some of the best fighting men the army had ever seen. But one day, sick of taking orders, they had up and killed their commanding officer.

We got under way. The hospital, the campus, the elaborate villas of the colonial era, many of which were deserted, passed quickly as we ran with the current. The river here was the width (a few hundred yards) and café-au-lait color of the Rio Branco, a subtributary of the Amazon, but the trees along it were not as awesomely tall or closely packed. Soon the sun sank into the water behind us. The low clouds caught fire, then slowly turned rose, and as the rose faded from them, the sky between went green—a colour I have only seen in tropical sunsets. Before long fireflies were sparking in the wind. A powerful spotlight above the wheelhouse began to roam the banks, freezing mud hut walls and racks of foliage in its glare. Once, for an instant, it found a whole village dancing and cheering on a bluff. Then it moved on and left them in darkness again. Downriver, a bonfire from the next settlement cast a long diamond on the water.

The steward came and opened the cabins. I went into mine and peeled off my second drenched T-shirt of the day. The furniture was basic: a metal locker and two metal beds. The brown linoleum floor was coming up in places. The bathroom had a toilet without a seat, a rust-streaked sink and bathtub, and a door to a cabin on the other side. In other words, I had to share it. I sat in the tub and threw the dirty water that sputtered from the faucet on myself. It was the only way to cool off.

When I came out on deck, Dennis, who seemed less intimidating and even a little smaller now that he had changed into blue jeans, gave me a glass of Ricard, a clear anisette aperitif that became cloudy when he added cold water from his canteen. We spread out my map of central Africa. After Kisangani the river, which had just crossed the Equator and was running north, headed west in a gradual arc that crested a little after Bumba, at two degrees of north latitude; then it dipped back down to the Equator. Joseph Conrad described the Congo's course as a 'snake uncoiled, with its head in the sea, its body at rest coming over a vast country, and its tail lost in the depths of the land.' Because it crossed the Equator twice, the level of its lower reaches was constant; somewhere in the basin it was always raining. Its unsuspected change of direction had thrown off early explorers. Livingstone, watching it run north, had thought it was the Nile. Mungo Park, watching it run south, had thought it was the Niger. Stanley had settled the question by following it to the sea, which took from 1874 to 1877. The middle part, from Kisangani to Kinshasa, was fully navigable and just about a thousand miles long. Below Kinshasa there were rapids again—one of the reasons why most of the valley is still intact. One seventh of the world's hydroelectric potential is said to be in the rapids of the Zaire.

The cook's boy came beating the bottom of a pot with a spoon. Dinner was served. Dennis and I went upstairs and sat at one of the six tables in the dining room. The others were taken by Zairois who nodded politely to us and ate in silence. I recognized one of them as a young gold smuggler who had been staying at the Hotel des Chutes. The cook passed out a miscellaneous collection of chipped and cracked china and dished out some rice and boiled beef. That was the menu for the whole trip. 'Rice-beef, beef-rice,' Dennis groaned on the third day, but almost nobody in Zaire got to eat beef. The potatoes that appeared on the evening of the fourth day were such a rarity in the *cuvette* that some of the other passengers, afraid to try something new, left them on their plates. The cook kept coming over and asking if everything was all right. I kept telling him it was.

Every ten or fifteen minutes, as we neared a village, dugouts would glide out of the darkness loaded with fish, game, fruit, and handicrafts the villagers had made. Passengers would rush to the railings in an uproar of excitement, and as the canoes approached they would try to throw a piece of their clothing down on the thing they wanted. The paddlers had to bring their canoe alongside very carefully. It could not be pointing downstream. More than one canoe capsized at that critical moment, leaving the paddlers flailing in the wake to recover what they could, swim ashore, and try again next week. Racks of smoked fish and monkey, worth a lot in Kinshasa, began to pile up on deck. With lips burned back on their taut charred skulls, the monkeys seemed to be grinning hideously. Dead but unsmoked monkeys, with their long tails tied to their necks for a handle, were also hoisted aboard. The cook's boy bought a live black mangabey. It was completely black and had a crest on top of its head. One of the passengers picked up a little black-cheeked white-nosed monkey and gave it the run of our deck. It was as cuddly and playful as a kitten. I wondered how it had hit upon orange eyes, a blue face, white cheek whiskers becoming black along the jowls, gray legs, a golden-green back, and a red tail. Once a basket was brought to me, and when the lid was removed a young chimpanzee looked up at me pleadingly. Eels, pigs, mangoes, yard-long plantains, bricks of tchikwanga, a manioc paste wrapped in mangungu leaf, bouncy balls of natural rubber, home-forged knives with wood handles wrapped in wire—you never knew what would turn up in the next canoes. In one I saw a large turtle with a fat unretractable head. In another an antelope lay with its eyes open and tongue out like a dead deer in a Flemish hunting scene.

For twelve zaires I bought a wicker chair from a man who seemed surprised that I didn't try to bring him down, and I took it up to the roof and sat under the stars. Because we were at the Equator, the sky was full of both northern and southern constellations. The Southern Cross was high in it, preceded by the 'false cross' of Carina and Vela—both formations drifting westward as the night went on. The Milky Way arched overhead. To the north were Leo—its sickle-shaped head terminating in bright yellow Regulus—and the Big Dipper, low and upside down and swollen by refraction from the dense air near the horizon. Somewhere up there the Voyager II satellite was hurtling into space. Aboard it was a ninety-minute recorded message from

Earth which (unknown to them, of course) included the yodelling of some BaMbuti pygmies in the Ituri Forest. I brought up the possibility of our being 'not alone' with a young couple who were lying on a straw mat and listening to a tape of music in Lingala. They were going to Mbandaka, four days downriver. The man, who had on a T-shirt with a crudely stitched Statue of Liberty on the front, asked if the extraterrestrials would turn out to be like us. I said maybe they would be much more intelligent and completely different-looking. He asked if I believed in mermaids. He said they were white and beautiful and had removable tails that they took off when they went on land to seduce men. 'I am not sure if they are mortals or spirits,' he said. He said he had seen people go into trances and start talking strange languages, down whole bottles of eau de cologne, and twice with his own eyes he had watched barechested men grow female breasts. The song that was playing on their cassette had a soft refrain in French: *Tu as mouvement.* The woman said it was a beautiful song because the *citoyenne* who sang it was herself paralysed.

In the morning rumors about another *muzungu* began to come from the barges. He had been bitten by a snake. He was dying. His cabin was full of snakes. I made my way to him through the crowded aisles of the *Myanza.* Some of the passengers were playing checkers with bottlecaps or a card game called *pique.* Others had set out little displays of Red Chinese shaving kits, thimbles, fishhooks, flashlight batteries. A naked boy was urinating near an eight-foot crocodile whose jaws were bound with vines. A *mama* beckoned to me and opened a burlap sack that was full of squirming three-inch grubs, the larvae of goliath and palm dynast beetles—like winged termites a prized source of protein. On the upper deck a religious service was in progress. People were dancing and singing while a man pounded a tall, elegantly carved drum.

I found the *muzungu* on the upper deck of the *Mongo.* 'It's a non-stop party,' he said with a grin as several couples down the aisle twisted in slow motion to a rumba tape. He was about thirty, with his black hair in a ponytail that went halfway down his back, and thick-rimmed glasses that made his eyes twice as large. His left arm was in a sling. The hand and fingers and forearm were black and blue and monstrously bloated. 'I was bitten by a small viper, an

Atheris that lives only in Kivu,' he explained. 'I have six of them. I had been handling them for about two weeks, showing them on the streets of Kisangani for fifty makuta [there are one hundred makuta in one zaire]. This one got a little upset and bit me between my first and second fingers. The fangs got hung up and it couldn't let go. Normally they retract right away.'

He was a herpetologist from California. Six years earlier, after a year of graduate school, he had dropped out of San Diego State College to work on a 'lifetime project.' It had taken him to the Philippines and to Nicaragua. For the last three years he had been in Zaire. 'I'm into the taxonomy, phylogeny, and evolution of snakes on a worldwide basis,' he told me. 'About twenty-three hundred species are now recognized. Seventy per cent of them—most of the non-poisonous ones—are lumped into a family called the *Colubridae*. No one has produced a classification scheme that works for all of them. I think the lungs are going to be the key.'

In a strongbox under his bunk he had two cobras, a rhinoceros viper, two burrowing vipers, and the six tree vipers. The rest were harmless, he said: an egg-eater, a juvenile green tree snake, thirty or forty boas, a couple of house snakes and blind worm snakes. In his career with snakes he had been bitten four times by small vipers and twice by cobras, but he did not hold it against them. 'One of them was a six-foot water cobra, but God was with me because it didn't inject any venom. Every snake has conscious control over the amount it injects,' he explained. 'If it thinks you're going to kill it, it will inject two or three times the normal quantity. But if it has been sleeping or is accidentally disturbed, sometimes it will inject no venom at all. I'm convinced that almost everyone who is bitten is the aggressor.'

The more he talked about them the more emotional he became. 'Snakes are so clean,' he said. 'They have no arms or legs, they can't talk, they can't hear, they can barely see, they can never close their eyes (which is how the superstition about their hypnotic powers got going), they don't have bladders, they don't get parental care—and with all these handicaps how is it that every snake from the day he is born knows how to swim, to climb, to crawl on the earth, to catch food, to run from people who want to kill it? How is it that they have successfully invaded every habitat? I think snakes are just the most beautiful creatures God created. Even more beautiful than women. Ballet in motion.'

The next day, when I visited him again, he told me how he had spent seven months in prison on a trumped-up rape charge. 'One night I had a party in Kinshasa. Two sisters— friends of friends—came. I didn't even know them. At five A.M. I told the girls I had to go to sleep. They wanted to keep partying. I threw them out.

'At noon a police inspector came and said I was charged with raping the two girls. I told him it was ridiculous, but he arrested me and took me to Makala, the central prison. My request for bail was refused. Everyone in Zaire with charges against him is incarcerated until his trial. Otherwise they would flee. I got to trial fast—in three months—because I was a foreigner. Some who were as innocent as I was had been waiting for eighteen months. Just before I was tried I was offered extradition, but I hadn't even seen the rain forest and I refused.

'I wasn't allowed to call anyone at the party as a witness. The girls themselves did not appear. There was no jury. The juge-président of the tribunal of the zone of Kalamu just read their deposition and decided that it was true. I couldn't believe the charges. On top of raping them, I was supposed to have injected them with drugs (they must have got the idea from the hypodermic needle I have to preserve my specimens), forced them to smoke marijuana and to drink whiskey (which they did willingly), photographed them in the nude (there wasn't even a camera in the house), and shocked them with an electric device (I had given one of them a massage with a vibrator). The police found a jar of marijuana seeds in the house, so the prosecutor said that I was a 'manufacturer.' He asked me how often I smoked. Every day? Are you an addict? I said, Look, where I come from it's legal. I smoke several times a week when I want to relax or party or when I'm with a girl. I don't drink at all. I'm a vegetarian and a teetotaler. It was such hypocrisy, because when I was in prison I smoked with the guards every night.

'After the judge had retired to deliberate, the court reporter came up to me and said, "He is going to sentence you to ten years and a fine of ten thousand zaires, but if you give him three thousand zaires now he will let you go." But after three months in prison I was broke, and besides, why should I have given him money when I hadn't done anything? I told him I preferred to rot in jail.

'The judge gave me eight months: five for rape, and three for the marijuana. I didn't learn until too late that I had only ten days to file an appeal. The prison was terribly over-crowded, but it had to be one of the most humane prisons in the world. They gave you *fou-fou* once a day, and people came around with food to sell. Kids were all over the place. Some of the women who had been condemned were pregnant and had babies there. Every day there was drumming and dancing. It wasn't really a prison. It was just like being out.

'The director was fantastic. He let me go home and feed my snakes once a week, and any time I wanted to go to the market or the post office I just had to ask for an escort. I brought in my typewriter, my library, and all my lab equipment. I wrote four papers. I learned Lingala. I was much more productive than I had been on the outside. One by one, I smuggled in my vipers and cobras. It was great for them because there were so many rats. I was in a good section, with the foreigners and politicians. One man had counterfeited two million dollars in Brazzaville and brought them in. Two Greeks had printed a hundred thousand pounds of Cook's traveller's checks and tried to buy diamonds with them. A couple of *commissaires de zone*, unlucky ones who had got caught, were in for taking bribes. A famous murderer, for whom the blue-striped prison uniform had been named, was doing life.

'One day I discovered that the key to my house also opened the door to my pavilion at the prison. After that discovery, I went out every night. After seven months, on October fourteenth, nineteen eighty, I was released. It was Mobutu's birthday. He freed all the prisoners with less than two years to go on their sentences.'

The river had spread into an island-studded lake. Classic braided drainage, like the St. Lawrence or the Rio Negro. As he threaded the boat between islands, the helmsman kept changing banks to avoid sandbars. Like a conductor with a difficult symphony to get through, he had a set of charts before him, but the sand kept shifting, he told me, and the depths on the charts had to be verified with an echo sounder. At noon we passed our sister ship, the *Gungu*, with three barges in tow like us. Dozens of passengers on both convoys stood on the roofs and danced and cheered. 'You will reach Kisangani tomorrow,' a man near me shouted. The few huts we saw were on stilts, as they are in the floodplain of the Amazon. The surface of the river was as glassy as black ice. Every so often a dugout would slice across it. Four men, bending at the waist and planting their long lanceolate paddles in unison, could move at a good clip. The canoes were more finished here, though each was still made of a single piece of wood. Their sides had been planed thin and smooth, their bows and sterns came to elegant points. The people on these islands lived almost entirely from the river. Although the soil was rich, they had few *shambas*. They traded fish with the passengers for fruit and vegetables. Without the *courier* they would not have had a balanced diet.

Several miles before Bumba we overtook a migration of butterflies that was scattered sparsely over many acres. I reached out my hand and caught one of the large white insects as it drifted indolently on the wind. It was a female *Cymothoe caenis*, one of the most abundant nymphalids in central and western Africa. The females are highly variable, ranging in wing colour from white to red. The males are darker. Their wings are etched with jagged brown lines. A Belgian collector in Kinshasa told me he had once caught a gynandromorphic *Cymothoe*, with the left-hand wings of a female and the right-hand wings of a male. How far these butterflies were going, where, or why, I could not have begun to say. Maybe they were just dispersing.

Occasionally we would pass small islands of water hyacinth drifting with the current. They had attractive purple spikes and air-filled bladders that kept them afloat until their submerged roots encountered terra firma. Sometimes a quiet shore would have a fringe of hyacinth. Parts of the river were said to be so choked with hyacinth that it was impossible for a boat to get through, but it was not so bad where we went. The aggressive aquatic had been introduced at Kinshasa in 1960 by a missionary from South America, where it is native, and it had been making its way relentlessly up the river. It was already firmly established in Kisangani, and there was already a Swahili name for it, *congobololo*.

That evening, as Dennis and I sat in front of our cabins

211

drinking Ricard, a procession of shrieking and wailing women and girls came up the stairs from the lower deck and went up to the wheelhouse. Their *petite soeur* had fallen overboard. It had happened while they were crossing from the flat barge to the *Mongo*. The girl, who was four years old, had slipped into the space of water between them and had been instantly swept from sight. The delegation pleaded hysterically with the helmsman to stop the boat, but the boat was not supposed to stop for anything, and it was some twenty minutes before he finally took pity and threw the engines into reverse. As word of the accident spread, trading stopped and the canoes that had come alongside pushed off to look for her. It was pitch dark. We were in a channel between two islands with just enough room for the helmsman to turn the convoy around so that it faced upstream. The spotlight began to sweep the water. I shook my head and said to Dennis, 'They will never find her. She probably never came up.' He disagreed. He said that young children thrown into water for the first time usually swim by instinct and have an almost superhuman will to survive. After an hour—most of us had lost hope and a grim silence had fallen over the convoy—one of the canoes came back with the girl alive and unhurt. Her ecstatic *grandes soeurs* clattered down the stairs. As Dennis had predicted, she had swum to a clump of water hyacinth and climbed on. One of the paddlers had heard her calling weakly, 'I am here.' We all felt part of a miracle. Dennis offered a glass of Ricard to one of the soldiers he was training. 'That is Zaire,' the soldier told us proudly. 'Tonight there will be a celebration.' Like most of his platoon, the soldier did not have a complete uniform and wore green tights with black sneakers, a spotted fatigue shirt, and a cartridge belt with a bayonet knife, which gave him a kind of Elizabethan appearance.

The next morning the officials on the boat finally got around to finding out who had bought a ticket and who hadn't, but they were too scared or too lazy to ferret out the stowaways themselves, and got Dennis's soldiers to do it. Dennis was not happy about his men doing ONATRA's work for them, but the soldiers saw it as a way to supplement their meager pay and went to work. Soon lines of sad-looking men tied to each other by their shirttails were being prodded upstairs to the wheelhouse. One, kicking and screaming in protest, was carried up bodily by three soldiers while a fourth lashed him with a belt. About thirty stowaways were found among the three hundred or so passengers. They were given three choices: to pay three times the regular fare, to be put ashore at the next stop, or to offer the soldiers a *matabish* to let them go. Most of them chose the third option.

I combed the banks with my binoculars, but the bird life was disappointing. Every so often I saw a fish eagle in a tree—*le vieux père*, as the steward called one—or a couple of long-tailed cormorants would hurry by, flying side by side low over the water, one of them a little ahead of the other; or a white-winged black tern would be hovering in search of fish, with wings winnowing delicately, like a butterfly poised at a flower. Three black kites hung in the boat's slipstream. Just for something to do Dennis took a twelve-gauge magnum shotgun and blasted away until two of them had crumpled into the water. I was so disgusted I went up on the roof, where rows of smoked fish were baking in the sun and the vice-champion middleweight of the Kake Boxing Club in Kinshasa, a square-jawed man with a T-shirt that had the name Jo Dallas across the back, was giving boxing lessons to half a dozen shirtless young men who had formed a ring around him and his glistening sparring partner. I sat in the shadow of the smokestack and tried to read a paperback, but the water was so bright and the heat so brutal that it was hard to take in a printed page. I found myself reading paragraphs over because I could not remember how they had started.

Toward evening we ran into a squall, which cleared the air for a while, but then a thick, low-lying mist appeared on the water and it became hot and heavy again. The edges of distant cloud packs bloodied as the sun dropped behind them, and the sky became that creamy green again. At about eight o'clock tens of thousands of insects began to fall out of the darkness like whirling flakes of snow. One of them, which had been bombarding a light bulb, landed on the back of my hand. Except for its bulging green eyes it was devoid of pigment, a sheer nylon-stocking colour. It had no mouth or intestines, and no hind wings to speak of. The fore-wings were glossy, transparent triangles densely etched with veins. The tail divided into three filaments. The whole creature was no more than five-eighths of an inch long. I had been in the middle of a similar mass emergence one night in the Rio Negro a few years earlier, and I recognized the insect as an ephemerid, the prolific order to which in North America over a hundred species of mayfly belong. It had probably spent two or three years as an aquatic nymph and undergone some twenty metamorphoses to emerge for a few hours or days at most as this ghostly light-crazed adult. It would live just long enough to mate. The blizzard went on for ten or fifteen minutes and left half an inch of twitching or lifeless bodies on the deck. One of the passengers was an albino, and he came with a broom and swept the ephemerids overboard. He was around twenty, with blotched white skin, frizzy snow-blond hair, and weak gray eyes. I had often seen him pass with a huge fish on one shoulder or carrying a bunch of woven straw drawstring baskets that he had bought on speculation. He made a living doing odd jobs for the crew and retailing goods from the canoes. I asked the cook if albinos were treated any differently. He said most of them married black women and had black children with them; albinism is not usually inherited. Some people considered albinos to be demons and believed that if one was sleeping in the same house with you, you had to wake him up when you were going out, or you would meet him again outside.

Sometime in the night we passed the mouth of the Ubangi, the Zaire's largest tributary, and in the morning coolness we reached Lukolela, where a big logging operation, with enormous stacks of timber, took up acres of the sloping bank. There was more relief ashore now. The forest gave way to hilly savanna with tongues of gallery forest running up gullies. The islands became tall grass marsh with islets of forest. It looked like the sawgrass and hammocks of the Everglades, but still there were no birds. The river became several miles wide and took on a desolate grandeur. At Bolobo the whole population, it seemed, came out in dozens of canoes, whooping like Indians falling on a wagon train. We must have acquired a ton of fruit. After dinner on the last night a man with a Polaroid camera took snapshots at each table and gave them to the passengers, compliments of the chef. The final configuration that pulled into Kinshasa on the morning of the twenty-seventh looked like this:

214

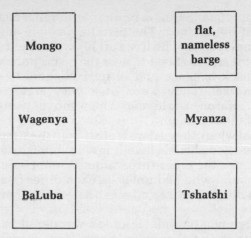

Mongo	flat, nameless barge
Wagenya	Myanza
BaLuba	Tshatshi

We had picked up the *Wagenya* at Lisala and the *BaLuba* at Mbandaka, on the way. There was an even greater madhouse at the dock than there had been at Kisangani. I made my way to the exit through a sea of people. The guard refused to open the gate. He was scared that the *mamas* on the other side would rush in. Suddenly, after about half an hour, he opened it a crack and waved me through.

I stayed at the Memling this time. It was not as modern as the Inter, but it was in the middle of town, and after the accommodations I had been having it seemed almost immorally luxurious. All that day there was a triumphant procession of green pushcarts loaded with the things that had arrived on the *courier*. People danced festively along the route from the port to the central market as the products of the valley went by. One group was doing a dance called the *caneton*, the duckling, while a blind man played a thumb piano. Whenever he sang '*caneton*' the dancers would shout, '*A l'aisement,*' and bending over, they would waddle like ducklings with their tails in the air.

After I had unpacked and cleaned up at the Memling and booked the next flight home I visited a man named Kasongo, whom I had met at the beginning of the trip, He lived in the zone of Kasavubu and was playing checkers, just as he had been when I had left him six weeks earlier. Along with something like eighty per cent of the men in the *cité*, he was out of work. For several years he had loaded freight for Air Zaire, but the pay had barely covered the cost of getting to

215

work. From time to time a brother who ran a factory in the south sent him money. The man he was playing with was also unemployed, and he lived off his wife's *petit commerce*. She took the train to Matadi, near the coast, once a week and brought back bananas and piripiri peppers to sell at the central market. They were 'at a very elevated level of checkers,' Kasongo told me. Their moves were so fast I could not follow them.

The yard where they sat was set off from the street by a rivulet of scum. Ramshackle dwellings inhabited by four related families lined the other three sides. When two members of the compound who had not seen each other in a while ran into each other, they kissed on either cheek then smack on the lips.

The afternoon passed. Chickens wandered in and out of the yard pecking the smooth gray dirt. Hanging clothes fluttered in the sun. Weeds trembled in the shadows. A skink scurried down a wall, leaped to the ground, froze in push-up position, and raised its intricately mottled black-and-yellow head tensely as a fire crackled in the brazier where one of the women was simmering chicken in peanut oil with chopped onion, piripiri, and tomato. A girl was mashing boiled bananas in a mortar with dull thuds of a long stake which she raised and lowered in tune with the mellow rumba that was percolating from a radio. At five o'clock the music was interrupted by a message from the President. He was calling for further sacrifices from the people, blaming the continuing slide of the Zairian economy on the *conjoncture*, the world recession, and urging everyone to keep working even if the pay was low. Kasongo got up and turned off *le farceur*, as he called the President, in the middle of a sentence. 'MPR—you know what it stands for, don't you?' he asked me. I said wasn't it the Mouvement Populaire de la Révolution? '*Pas du tout*,' he said. 'It means *Mourir Pour Rien*. To die for nothing.'

Just before sundown a flock of pure white egrets flew over, necks tucked in, hurrying soundlessly to their roost. When it was too dark to see, the woman at the brazier lit a small kerosene lamp made from an evaporated milk can. I said goodbye to Kasongo and on the way back to the Memling I remembered something that Misi Masamba had told me six weeks earlier when I was driving around with him in his taxi. He had said that there were two kinds of people in the *cité*: those who had

216

possibilités and those who hadn't. Kasongo was probably in the second category, like most of the people there. I stopped at a street corner and waited to cross with a young *citoyenne* and two boys. Suddenly one of the boys tore a gold chain from the woman's neck and, running over to a wall with his partner, vaulted into the shadows of the zoological gardens. It took me a while to register that I just witnessed an assault. I asked the *citoyenne* if she was all right. 'That is how they make their living,' she said, touching her throat with remarkable calmness.

Over the next few days I met quite a few people in and around the government. None was as frank as the man who had visited me at the Inter; none dared give straight answers except for a rehabilitated revolutionary named Kamitatu, who had written a bitterly critical biography of Mobutu while an exile in Paris ten years earlier and was now the Minister of Agriculture. He outlined a plan to get the country's roads back in shape, so that its two million peasant farmers would be encouraged to grow more cash crops in their *shambas*. The plan involved three hundred fifty thousand hoes, which Kamitatu already had, and twelve million zaires, which he was in the process of raising, so that in ten thousand villages a *cantonnier* could be paid to keep up the road. I almost met a member of the hundred-and-fourteen-man Central Committee with which Mobutu had recently upstaged the two-hundred-seventy-three-man National Assembly he had created, in a more democratic frame of mind, four years earlier. (The assembly still met but no longer participated in decisions.) That was as close as I got to the Big Man. Having been burned by so many foreign journalists, he had not given an interview in several years; and since his car was stoned at a soccer match not long before, he had become as leery of public appearances. Crowds no longer cheered at the airport when he returned from abroad. Now he was whisked away by helicopter.

People in Kinshasa were even more nervous than usual because a team from the International Monetary Fund was in town with a new set of austerity measures for the government to meet before the IMF would lend it any more of the billion dollars it had promised. Zaire already owed four and two-tenths billion dollars to foreign creditors and was supposed to be paying them back at the rate of five

217

hundred million dollars a year, but was running behind schedule by about fifty per cent. Even this used about thirty per cent of its gross national product—a deceptive figure, admittedly, since the dollars in which it is expressed are converted from zaires at the official rate, which bears no relation to reality, and the economy that it means to characterize is largely non-monetary and off the books. The only way to shake the debt would have been to declare bankruptcy, but then the flow of foreign capital would have stopped completely, and Zaire was far from ready to make it on its own. That had been tried

I ran into Anna Roosevelt's first cousin Ted Roosevelt at the Inter. As he sat in a well-cut business suit and trim mustache and questioned me excitedly about my trip, I felt the magnanimous enthusiasm of their famous great-grand-father. Once a month, he told me, the Zairian government had been having to negotiate with its creditors for a more re-alistic rescheduling of its debt payments, and he had been coming to Kinshasa as a consultant to help with the presentation. 'This month could be crucial,' he said. 'But that is what I thought two months ago. It has been crucial for the past eighteen months.' His job had kept him so busy that he had not been able to see much of the country beyond the interior of the Finance Ministry. I told him that travel would probably give him a new perspective. Those four and two-tenths billion dollars had not reached most of the country; yet it not only worked, in some ways it was thriving.

'Zaire is one of the richest places for *art nègre*,' Charles Henault said as he took me through the collection at the Musée National des Beaux Arts. 'There are sixty styles in great perfection.' Many of the museum's forty thousand pieces Henault had collected himself, travelling from village to village by Land-Rover, sometimes for months at a stretch, with his Zairois wife, until she died a year ago. Others had been brought to the museum and bartered for on Mondays and Fridays, when the museum was buying art from whoever had it to sell. Now there was no money for ac-quisitions. The museum was on a hill overlooking the river, in a well-guarded compound that included the President's downtown palace. The pieces were in metal cabinets and on open shelves. A wooden woman with a child — the mother of the tribe — had sat on the roof of a chief's hut. A group of *shabi*, protective ghosts, had stood in the middle of a village.

218

A vertical crocodile had guarded a door. Henault showed me a coronation dress of leopard skin embroidered with cowries; sacks full of ancestors' teeth and nails; flasks for gunpowder, for plant enemas, for red paste from seeds of the shrub *Bixa orellana*, which is smeared on the bodies of BaPende women who have just given birth, to help them regain strength; masks for circumcision, hunting funeral rites; huge hollow logs with a slit along their length, for talking over distances; tall congo drums with buffalo, antelope, or goatskin which had to be heated periodically, and some with reptile skin which were not affected by humidity or rain; twenty-pound copper anklets worn by women 'who were quite happy to be so wealthy,' Henault told me. Most of the pieces were from this century but looked older because of their brown patina—soot from village fires—and because they belonged to a long tradition. 'This is what Lévi-Strauss called a cold culture,' Henault said. 'The styles have not changed much in hundreds of years.' There were still some BaKuba villages with nothing foreign in them, he told me, not even metal cook pots. Henault had come to Zaire in 1969 with a Belgian jazz band. He was the drummer. He showed me a stack of bark loin cloths he had picked up a few months before in the Ituri Forest. When he heard that I had just been there, he asked with the sly grin of a pygmy if I had brought him any honey. The cloths had simple, strong patterns of lines drawn on them—about the only art the pygmies got into.

Henault's colleague, Benoit Quersin, had also started with jazz, playing piano and bass. He still played, but he had become more interested in collecting African music and finding the words to explain it. He was the museum's ethnomusicologist, a sprightly man of fifty-four with the energy and hipness of someone much younger. I said I had a tape of Efe yodelling that I wanted to play for him. He said to bring it along to a party he was having on Friday.

On Friday afternoon Benoit's chauffeur Joseph picked me up in front of the Memling. There was a pretty *citoyenne* named Marceline in the back seat. She was going to the party. She said she was exhausted because for the past forty-eight hours there had been a funeral with three bands at her neighbor's house in the *cité*. Strangers had kept knocking on the door and asking to use the bathroom. Marceline was from Equateur. 'I was engaged while still in

219

my mother's belly to a man who was small like Napoleon and had slanted eyes,' she told me. 'Now he is an alcoholic.' She had refused to marry him and had come to Kinshasa, where she met a great-great-grandson of the writer George Sand, who took her to Paris, She opened her handbag and showed me an antique snuff box said to have been a gift to Sand from Frédéric Chopin. A wave of sadness passed quickly over her when she told me that she had lived in Paris for eight years.

The road climbed until we saw Kinshasa sprawled out in the smoky flats below us. Behind walls and luxuriant vegetation we glimpsed big villas. One of the walls was too high to see over and went on for a whole block. Joseph said that Mobutu's main residence was behind it. We passed the campus, which was larger and better maintained than the one in Kisangani, then we hit poverty: heads of dolled-up women painted on a board to advertise a beauty parlor, cane furniture lining the road. Then we came into open hill country that had once been forest but was now dry, hot savanna—a scalped landscape, like Haiti's. The trees had all been cut for charcoal to be burned in braziers in the *cité*.

After almost an hour Joseph turned onto a dirt road, and we rode to the top of Mount Ngafula, where there were some nice houses. Most of them had been built by BaKongo *confrères* of President Kasavubu. The mountain had started to become another Westchester, then Kasavubu was out, and the BaKongo fell with him. Several houses had been started more recently with stolen money. The owners had been arrested. Construction had stopped. The weathered shells, smothered with vegetation, and the land they were on were in limbo. No one dared touch them, because the owner could be pardoned and suddenly return. Some of the villas were weekend retreats for people in the government. 'When they commit a gaffe, they come here and hide,' Marceline told me. One of them had been built for the mistress of a man named Ngunz Karl I Bond, who had been Secretary of State, then sentenced to death for knowing about the last Katanga rebellion before it happened, pardoned, and made Prime Minister. The hopes of the West had been pinned on him. But he had just resigned and fled to Belgium, where he was calling for the overthrow of Mobutu. When a man gave a house to his mistress, Marceline told me, it was called a *deuxième bureau*.

220

Benoit's villa was at the end of the ridge. The previous tenant had been shot dead by bandits. For a year after he moved in, Benoit had kept a pistol in his glove compartment, but the danger had passed. Mount Ngafula was 'no longer chic for bandits', he told me. The villa was a stately, well-ventilated beige colonial that sat on about two sloping acres surrounded by a high concrete wall. A sentinel sat at the gate coaxing tunes from a thumb piano. He, a maid, and a cook were included in the hundred-dollar-a-month rent. 'It is an ecological rather than a class relationship, an association that keeps us safe,' Benoit said of himself and his servants. 'Everyone is the master. You must know who and when.'

We arrived in time to sit on a west-facing balcony and watch the sun set over thirty miles of ridge and valley. A line of mist, showing where the Zaire ran, crossed the view. 'It's extravagant. A little vulgar. *La folie équatoriale*,' Benoit exclaimed as the colors peaked. He had some very sophisticated sound equipment. The Efe would have been speechless if they had heard how they sounded on it. 'Typical camp music,' Benoit said when he heard my tape, and he asked if he could copy it for the museum. I asked if he could explain what was going on. 'That is like asking Reagan to describe his foreign policy.' He laughed. 'It is very complicated. The Bantu are *polyphonique*, too, but their *polyphonie* is vertical.' To show what he meant, he played a tape of fifteen Mongo men and women blending in a powerful a capella chorus. 'You can hear chords,' he said, conducting the rises and falls in pitch with his hands, 'C, F, G. It is compatible with European harmonic thinking. But pygmy *polyphonie* is horizontal. It is completely non-Western, not tonal, but modal. People flip when they hear it. Every second, something new comes in, like a river. And the structure of their music, or lack of it, is a reflection of their values. The Bantu believe in belonging to a clan and staying around the village. Among the pygmies, freedom and individuality are the big things.' Marceline, who had changed from her *pagne* into blue jeans and a T-shirt, was bent over, with hands sweeping the floor to the music. 'What a pity,' she said to me. 'You are always buried in your notebook.'

So Benoit and I stopped working and joined her. The room filled with swaying bodies as other guests arrived. We danced to 'an old blind guy scrunched in his chair' and playing an ivory trumpet, harmonizing with its echoes in the forest. We danced to a six-note *sanza* (the real name for a thumb piano) tuned to F minor and played by a master. Benoit thought the notes that spanned the tonic had been chosen at random—'whatever sounded nice.' We danced to a ballad about Mulele, the leader of the Rebellion, performed by two men who went singing from village to village in Haut-Zaire. 'He was great and strong,' the first man sang in Swahili. 'But he messed up and was killed,' the second sang. 'The phrasing is like Coltrane and Lester Young,' Benoit said. We danced to part of an epic which took several days to perform, about a man who crossed a river on the back of a crocodile and had all sorts of adventures. Sometimes the narrator would break from his dialect into excited French: '*Écoutez?*' We danced to Afriza, a famous rumba band in Kinshasa. Sometimes the music would slow to a slur, as if it had been recorded at seventy-eight rpm and suddenly switched to thirty-three; then it would pick up again. Benoit called this *pleurage*. 'It happens because there was a momentary loss of power during the recording. The voltage in Kinshasa is up and down,' he explained with another hand gesture.

Some of the guests were watching television in Benoit's bedroom. Television is still a rarity in Zaire. A French musical comedy starring Fernandel, made around 1939, was showing for the third or fourth time. Gay Paris, not facing the gathering storm. 'The Zairois love this sort of light prewar comedy,' Benoit told me. One of the *citoyennes* wore glasses without lenses and Bo Derek tresses, which had just hit Kinshasa. Tears of laughter were running down her face. Her Belgian boyfriend was in charge of bridge building in Zaire. He told me that a hundred-ton bridge, given by Great Britain, had been sitting in Kinshasa for two years because he couldn't get trucks to take it to the site. Not all the pieces had arrived, anyway, due to theft en route. 'I dread going to work,' he said. 'It is a nightmare. The people are so excessively badly paid they don't give a damn.' A beautiful *citoyenne* named Moseka, who ran the chicest hair salon in Kinshasa and painted surrealist pictures, was also glued to the TV. 'I took her to a Dali show in Paris,' her French husband told me. 'It was a real drag for me. She stood for an hour in front of each painting.'

INDEX

Jacytara, Lago de, 83, 99
Jacyuaruá, Lago, see Mirror of the Moon, Lake of
Jamaica, 27, 156
Jamundá River, see Nhamundá River
Jamundas (Uaboi chief), 27, 67
Jari River, 12, 75
Jatapu River, 45
Jauja (Inca city), 22
Jesus, Maria Batista de, 85
Jews, Sephardic, 41
Joaçim, 152–4, 179, 200
João (Murituro), 90–2, 100
Jung, Carl, 30

Kamitatu, 217
Kanati, 82–9, 91–2, 94–100
Kanaxeu (Brazil), 82
Kanyabayung (Zaire), 185
Kasavubu, Joseph, 220
Kasongo, 215–17
Katanga, 117, 204, 220
Kauka, see Indio, Antonio
Kaxuiana Indians, 44, 82–5, 91, 100, 101–5
Kembo, 192–3, 199–200
Kenge, 171, 172
Kenya, 125, 135
Keresey, Richard, 76
Kikongo language, 108
KiLese language, 138, 144
Kinshasa (Zaire), 107–16, 117–20, 153, 194, 197, 200, 205, 206, 209, 211, 213, 214, 217, 218, 220, 222
Kisangani (Zaire), 114, 137, 138, 162, 163, 169, 182, 190–208, 211, 215, 220
Kivu (Zaire), 117, 182, 184, 186, 196, 208
Kivu, Lake, 189, 190
Kleinbaum, Abby Wettan, 18, 31
Koko, Posho, 200–2
Komanda (Zaire), 182
!Kung San bushmen, 125

Kuri, 139, 161
Kurumukuri (Brazil), 104

La Condamine, Charles Marie de, 29, 39, 67
Lazaro, Father, 118, 119, 120–1
Lende tribe, 138
Leticia (Colombia), 123
Lévi-Strauss, Claude, 88, 137, 219
Libya, 31
LiNgala language, 108
Lingondo (Zaire), 121
Livingstone, David, 205
Lobato, Teodoro, 69
Lolwa (Zaire), 174, 178, 197
Lonely African, The (Turnbull), 172
Longo, Father, 118, 172, 177
López de Gómara, Francisco, 23, 24
Losambu, 198
Losandu, 198
Loureiro, João, 63, 69, 77, 80, 81, 84–8, 92, 95, 100
Loureiro, Joselia, 63–4
Ludwig, Daniel K., 12
Lukolela (Zaire), 214
lycaenids, 123–5

Machado, Roduval, 69, 70, 71, 75
Machu Picchu, 22
Madeira, 25
Mafada (Brazil), 62
mafuta (palm oil), 129, 144, 155, 156
Mahdi, 126
malaria, 74, 114, 153, 178, 181
Mambasa (Zaire), 162, 167, 172, 178
Mambo River, 160
Mamvu tribe, 129, 136
Manaus (Brazil), 13, 37, 38, 45, 65, 80, 82, 191, 192
Mangbetu tribe, 157, 202
Mangiese (Zaire), 162, 164, 165

A VOYAGER OUT: THE LIFE OF MARY KINGSLEY
by Katherine Frank

'A wonderful story, funny, stirring and touching . . a worthy tribute to a remarkable, an admirable and, though she never knew it, a lovable woman'
Geoffrey Wheatcroft, *The Spectator*

Mary Kingsley accomplished a great deal in her tragically short life. Niece of Charles Kingsley and daughter of an unlikely alliance between an amateur explorer and a bed-ridden cockney domestic, she was born in 1862. Her youth was sacrificed in fulfilling traditional Victorian expectations of a daughter; looking after her invalid mother while her father indulged his pleasure in travelling.

Their deaths allowed her, at the age of 30, a few years of freedom. She was able to fulfill her own desire to travel, and ventured deep into the heart of West Africa, into worlds few white men and no white women had seen before. Her adventures there ranked with those of the most intrepid explorers, always enterprising, enlightening and, at times, highly dangerous. Throughout her travels she still found time to write two volumes of thrilling adventure stories, both of which became bestsellers at the time.

Mary Kingsley is the model for the courageous Victorian female explorer. Her sad but fascinating life has been vividly and sympathetically portrayed in Katherine Frank's highly-acclaimed and remarkable biography.

'Katherine Frank has written a quietly beautiful biography that reveals not only the outer life of an extraordinary traveller but something of her inner life as well'
The New York Times Book Review

'A fresh, sensitive, vivid biography'
Literary Review

'A splendid book'
Guardian

0 552 99314 X

THE PUPPET EMPEROR
by Brian Power

'Power uses the device of the Chinese itinerant story-tellers, blending fact with fiction, to relate the life of China's last Emperor. It is a fascinating tale of a man who started life as the Son of Heaven and ended up in a cadre's uniform pushing paper at the department of historical archives'
Books and Bookmen

He was only three when, in 1908, he was enthroned in Peking at the behest of the sinister tyrannical Empress Dowager shortly before her death. The regency that followed was short-lived; revolution and abdication were overtaken by the Japanese invasion when he was installed as Emperor of Manchuria, presiding over a decadent court with his unhappy Empress an opium addict. Eventually captured by the Russians and imprisoned in Siberia, he finally returned to China and was 'rehabilitated' as a model communist citizen.

'THE PUPPET EMPEROR is a book of striking authority, for Power was born in Tientsin in 1918 and grew up there. His excursion into Old China and his glance at the New are not things to be forgotten in a hurry'
Country Life

'Brian Power mesmerises with this extraordinary tale of corruption and lost innocence, tragedy and mirth'
South China Morning Post

0 552 99293 3

THE FORD OF HEAVEN
by Brian Power

"A white woman is playing Chopin and guests are drinking gin and lime, while outside a coolie sings a song from a Chinese opera. Rival war-lords with their armies steam across the country in trains, the first-class coaches lavishly furnished for their concubines."

This was the China of the '20s, the China into which Brian Power was born. Son of a nervous and melancholy French mother who had wanted to be a nun, and an Irish father, mostly absent, then dead, Brian and his brother were reared largely by their Chinese *amah*. Brian's Chinese was more fluent than his English and he was immersed in the Chinese world of legends, superstitions, and shadowy intrigues.

Never losing the ability to look below the surface of everyday life, he re-creates an extraordinary picture of the mixed European communities exiled in a Chinese city, of Siberian refugees fleeing from the Russian revolution, of the deep-rooted fears of the warlords, Boxer uprisings and the Opium wars.

'This is a unique book'
Irish Times

'This is a world forever gone. Mr Power has recaptured that world with integrity and sensitivity in the child's one dimension.'
Sunday Telegraph

0 552 99247 X

THE HOUSE BY THE DVINA
A RUSSIAN CHILDHOOD
by Eugenie Fraser

'EUGENIE FRASER HAS A WONDEROUS TALE TO
TELL AND SHE TELLS IT VERY WELL. THERE IS
NO OTHER AUTOBIOGRAPHY QUITE LIKE IT'
Molly Tibbs, *The Contemporary Review*

A unique and moving account of life in Russia before,
during and immediately after the Revolution, THE HOUSE
BY THE DVINA is the fascinating story of two families,
separated in culture and geography, but bound together
by a Russian-Scottish marriage. It includes episodes as
romantic and dramatic as any in fiction: the purchase by
the author's greatgrandfather of a peasant girl with whom
he had fallen in love; the desperate journey by sledge in
the depths of winter made by her grandmother to intercede
with Tsar Aleksandr II for her husband; the extraordinary
courtship of her parents; and her Scottish granny being
caught up in the abortive revolution of 1905.

Eugenie Fraser herself was brought up in Russia but was
taken on visits to Scotland. She marvellously evokes the
reactions of a child to two totally different environments,
sets of customs and family backgrounds. The characters
on both sides are beautifully drawn and splendidly
memorable.

With the events of 1914 to 1920 — the war with Germany,
the Revolution, the murder of the Tsar, the withdrawal of
the Allied Intervention in the north — came the disinte-
gration of the country and of family life. The stark realities
of hunger, deprivation and fear are sharply contrasted with
the day-to-day experiences, joys, frustrations and adventures of childhood. The reader shares the family's suspense
and concern about the fates of its members and relives
with Eugenie her final escape to Scotland.

'A WHOLLY DELIGHTFUL ACCOUNT'
Elizabeth Sutherland, *The Scots Magazine*

0 552 12833 3

HIDDEN FRANCE
by Richard Binns

HIDDEN FRANCE is for the independent, discerning traveller who recognises the rewarding benefits that accrue when one gets off the beaten track and well away from package holiday traps. This informative guide book allows the reader to savour the sights, sounds and tastes of rural France; its woods, forests, meadows and pastures; its hills and river valleys; its placid streams and roaring torrents; its ancient villages and medieval buildings, and its vast larder of culinary delights.

Richard Binns has chosen 25 areas in France, each in unspoilt country and nominates four recommended hotels in each area. These are all modest, family-owned establishments, one of which will suit any budget, and offer good, solid value to the visitor.

HIDDEN FRANCE shares with its companion volumes the author's abiding affection for, and comprehensive knowledge of, the France most tourists never find.

0 552 99230 5

FRANCE À LA CARTE
by Richard Binns

FRANCE À LA CARTE is a unique guide compiled by Richard Binns and based on twenty-five years of travelling in France. Together with FRENCH LEAVE 3 this book equips a tourist for the most enjoyable and exciting French holiday they have ever experienced.

The guide uses the different treasures of France under themed headings such as 'Historical Milestones Relived', 'Unknown Rivers', 'Pleasures of Nature' and 'Hidden Corners' to lead the traveller to the many different facets that France possesses.

This book is for every lover of France — the young, the not-so-young, the country-lover and sightseer, the sports enthusiast and the museum browser, the walker and the car driver. FRANCE À LA CARTE offers them all a rich feast of pleasure and discovery.

0 552 99231 3

ADRIFT
by Steven Callahan

'HIGHLY READABLE . . . A TALE OF COURAGE AND DETERMINATION IN THE FACE OF ALMOST INSURMOUNTABLE HARDSHIP'
New York Times

When Steven Callahan's small yacht sank west of the Canaries, he found himself adrift in a five-foot inflatable raft, pounded by storms, scorched by the tropical sun and attacked by sharks.

ADRIFT is the engrossing account of his 6-day ordeal, drifting 1,800 miles across the Atlantic.

'A TALE OF EXTRAORDINARY TENACITY AND COURAGE IN THE FACE OF EXTREME SUFFER-ING. A TECHNICAL SURVIVAL MANUAL AND A SPIRITUAL ODYSSEY ALL ROLLED INTO ONE'
The Mail On Sunday

'THERE HAVE BEEN MANY TALES OF SURVIVAL, BUT *ADRIFT* IS TWENTY THOUSAND LEAGUES ABOVE THE REST'
Kirk's Reviews

0 552 12889 9

A SELECTED LIST OF FINE AUTOBIOGRAPHIES
AND BIOGRAPHIES AVAILABLE FROM CORGI BOOKS

The prices shown below were correct at the time of going to press. However Transworld Publishers reserve the right to show new prices on covers which may differ from those previously advertised in the text or elsewhere.

CORGI BIOGRAPHY SERIES

☐	99065 5	THE PAST IS MYSELF	Christabel Bielenberg	£3.50
☐	99271 2	MY HAPPY DAYS IN HELL	George Faludy	£4.95
☐	99314 X	A VOYAGER OUT	Katherine Frank	£4.95
☐	12833 3	THE HOUSE BY THE DVINA	Eugenie Fraser	£3.95
☐	12863 5	THE LONG JOURNEY HOME	Flora Leipman	£3.95
☐	99247 X	THE FORD OF HEAVEN	Brian Power	£3.50
☐	99293 3	THE PUPPET EMPEROR	Brian Power	£3.95

GENERAL AUTOBIOGRAPHIES & BIOGRAPHIES

☐	12851 1	CHILDRENS HOSPITAL	Peggy Anderson	£3.95
☐	09332 7	GO ASK ALICE	Anonymous	£1.95
☐	13220 9	THE GENTLE ART: A MIDWIFE'S STORY	Penny Armstrong & Sheryl Feldman	£3.95
☐	99054 X	BORSTAL BOY	Brendan Behan	£3.95
☐	12889 9	ADRIFT	Steven Callahan	£2.95
☐	13126 1	CATHERINE COOKSON COUNTRY	Catherine Cookson	£5.95
☐	09373 4	OUR KATE	Catherine Cookson	£2.95
☐	11772 2	'H' THE AUTOBIOGRAPHY OF A CHILD PROSTITUTE AND HEROIN ADDICT	Christiane F.	£2.50
☐	12727 2	MEN	Anna Ford	£2.95
☐	12501 6	BEYOND THE HIGHLAND LINE	Richard Frere	£1.95
☐	13070 2	BORN LUCKY: AN AUTOBIOGRAPHY	John Francome	£2.95
☐	13254 3	ANNE FRANK REMEMBERED	Miep Gies & Alison Leslie Gold	£2.95
☐	13032 X	NO LAUGHING MATTER	Joseph Heller	£2.95
☐	99285 2	GETTING HITLER INTO HEAVEN	John Graven Hughes	£4.95
☐	99098 1	AUTUMN OF FURY	Mohamed Heikal	£3.95
☐	13060 5	KHASHOGGI: THE STORY OF THE WORLD'S RICHEST MAN	Ron Kessler	£3.95
☐	99294 1	TO HELL AND BACK	Nikki Lauda	£2.95
☐	11961 X	SHOUT!	Phillip Norman	£2.50
☐	99158 9	BRENDAN BEHAN	Ulick O'Connor	£2.95
☐	99143 0	CELTIC DAWN	Ulick O'Connor	£4.95
☐	13094 X	WISEGUY	Nicholas Pileggi	£2.95
☐	12577 6	PLACE OF STONES	Ruth Janette Ruck	£2.50
☐	13058 3	THE MARILYN CONSPIRACY	Milo Speriglio	£2.50
☐	12589 X	AND I DON'T WANT TO LIVE THIS LIFE	Deborah Spungen	£3.50
☐	12072 3	KITCHEN IN THE HILLS	Elizabeth West	£2.50
☐	11707 2	GARDEN IN THE HILLS	Elizabeth West	£2.50
☐	10907 X	HOVEL IN THE HILLS	Elizabeth West	£1.95

ORDER FORM

All Corgi/Bantam Books are available at your bookshop or newsagent, or can be ordered direct from the following address:

Corgi/Bantam Books,
Cash Sales Department,
P.O. Box 11, Falmouth, Cornwall TR10 9EN.

Please send a cheque or postal order (no currency) and allow 60p for postage and packing for the first book plus 25p for the second book and 15p for each additional book ordered up to a maximum charge of £1.90 in UK.

B.F.P.O. customers please allow 60p for the first book, 25p for the second book plus 15p per copy for the next 7 books, thereafter 9p per book.

Overseas customers, including Eire, please allow £1.25 for postage and packing for the first book, 75p for the second book, and 28p for each subsequent title ordered.

NAME (Block Letters) ....

ADDRESS..

....